FRANCIS FRITH'S

ANCIENT MONUMENTS & STONE CIRCLES

PHOTOGRAPHIC MEMORIES

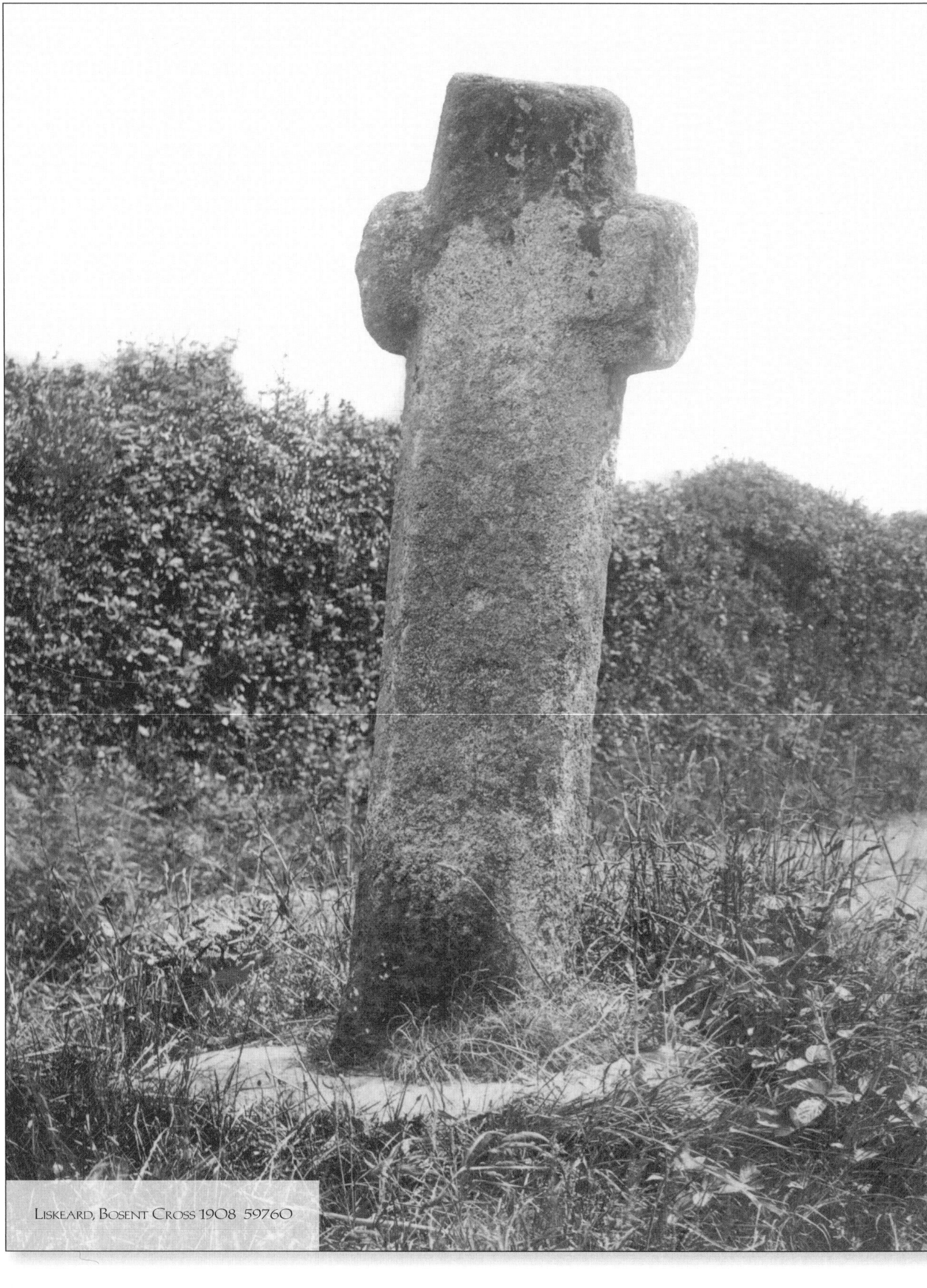

Liskeard, Bosent Cross 1908 59760

ANCIENT MONUMENTS & STONE CIRCLES

PHOTOGRAPHIC MEMORIES

LES MOORES

First published in hardback in 2000 by The Frith Book Company
ISBN 1-85937-143-4

Revised paperback edition published in 2005 by The Francis Frith Collection®
ISBN 1-85937-864-1

British Library Cataloguing in Publication Data

Ancient Monuments and Stone Circles
Photographic Memories
Les Moores
ISBN 1-85937-864-1

The Francis Frith Collection®
Frith's Barn, Teffont,
Salisbury, Wiltshire SP3 5QP
Tel: +44 (0) 1722 716 376
Email: info@francisfrith.co.uk
www.francisfrith.co.uk

Printed and bound in England

Front Cover: **STONEHENGE 1887** 19797t
The colour-tinting in this image is for illustrative purposes only,
and is not intended to be historically accurate

Every attempt has been made to contact copyright holders of illustrative material.
We will be happy to give full acknowledgement in future editions for any items not
credited. Any information should be directed to The Francis Frith Collection.

AS WITH ANY HISTORICAL DATABASE, THE FRANCIS FRITH ARCHIVE IS CONSTANTLY BEING CORRECTED AND IMPROVED, AND THE PUBLISHERS WOULD WELCOME INFORMATION ON OMISSIONS OR INACCURACIES

ANCIENT MONUMENTS & STONE CIRCLES
PHOTOGRAPHIC MEMORIES

CONTENTS

The Making of an Archive

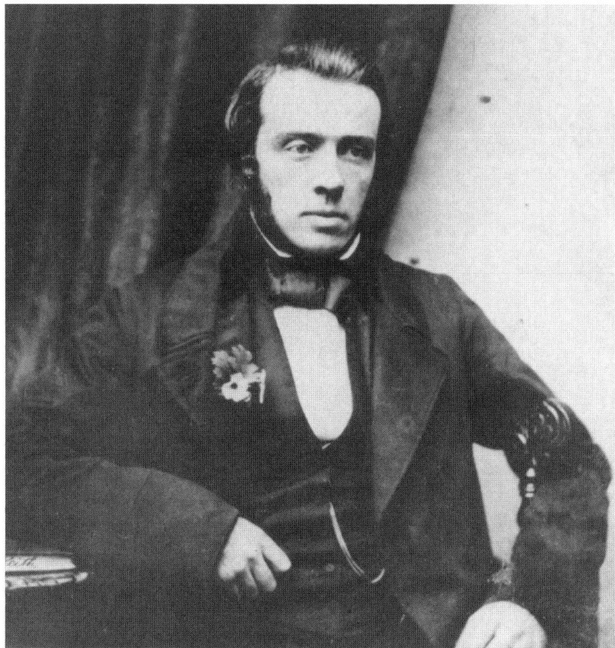

Francis Frith, Victorian founder of the world-famous photographic archive, was a devout Quaker and a highly successful Victorian businessman. By 1860 he was already a multi-millionaire, having established and sold a wholesale grocery business in Liverpool. He had also made a series of pioneering photographic journeys to the Nile region. The images he returned with were the talk of London. An eminent modern historian has likened their impact on the population of the time to that on our own generation of the first photographs taken on the surface of the moon.

Frith had a passion for landscape, and was as equally inspired by the countryside of Britain as he was by the desert regions of the Nile. He resolved to set out on a new career and to use his skills with a camera. He established a business in Reigate as a specialist publisher of topographical photographs.

Frith lived in an era of immense and sometimes violent change. For the poor in the early part of Victoria's reign work was a drudge and the hours long, and ordinary people had precious little free time. Most had not travelled far beyond the boundaries of their own town or village. Mass tourism was in its infancy during the 1860s, but during the next decade the railway network and the establishment of Bank Holidays and half-Saturdays gradually made it possible for the working man and his family to enjoy holidays and to see a little more of the world. With characteristic business acumen, Francis Frith foresaw that these new tourists would enjoy having souvenirs to commemorate their days out. He began selling photo-souvenirs of seaside resorts and beauty spots, which the Victorian public pasted into treasured family albums.

Frith's aim was to photograph every town and village in Britain. For the next thirty years he travelled the country by train and by pony and trap, producing fine photographs of seaside resorts and beauty spots that were keenly bought by millions of Victorians.

The Rise of Frith & Co

Each photograph was taken with tourism in mind, the small team of Frith photographers concentrating on busy shopping streets, beaches, seafronts, picturesque lanes and villages. They also photographed buildings: the Victorian and Edwardian eras were times of huge building activity, and town halls, libraries, post offices, schools and technical colleges were springing up all over the country. They were invariably celebrated by a proud Victorian public, and photo souvenirs – visual records – published by F Frith & Co were sold in their hundreds of thousands. In addition, many new commercial buildings such as hotels, inns and pubs were photographed, often because their owners specifically commissioned Frith postcards or prints of them for re-sale or for publicity purposes.

In order to gain some understanding of the scale of Frith's business one only has to look at the catalogue issued by Frith & Co in 1886: it runs to some 670 pages. By 1890 Frith had created the greatest specialist photographic publishing company in the world, with over 2,000 stockists! The picture on the right shows the Frith & Co display board on the wall of the stockist at Ingleton in the Yorkshire Dales (left of window). Beautifully constructed with a mahogany frame and gilt inserts, it displayed a dozen scenes.

The Making of an Archive

Postcard Bonanza

The ever-popular holiday postcard we know today took many years to appear, and F Frith & Co was in the vanguard of its development. Postcards became a hugely popular means of communication and sold in their millions. Frith's company took full advantage of this boom and soon became the major publisher of photographic view postcards.

Francis Frith died in 1898 at his villa in Cannes, his great project still growing. His sons Eustace and Cyril continued their father's monumental task, expanding the number of views offered to the public and recording more and more places in Britain, as the coasts and countryside were opened up to mass travel. The archive Frith created continued in business for another seventy years. By 1970 it contained over a third of a million pictures of 7,000 cities, towns and villages. The massive photographic record Frith has left to us stands as a living monument to a special and very remarkable man.

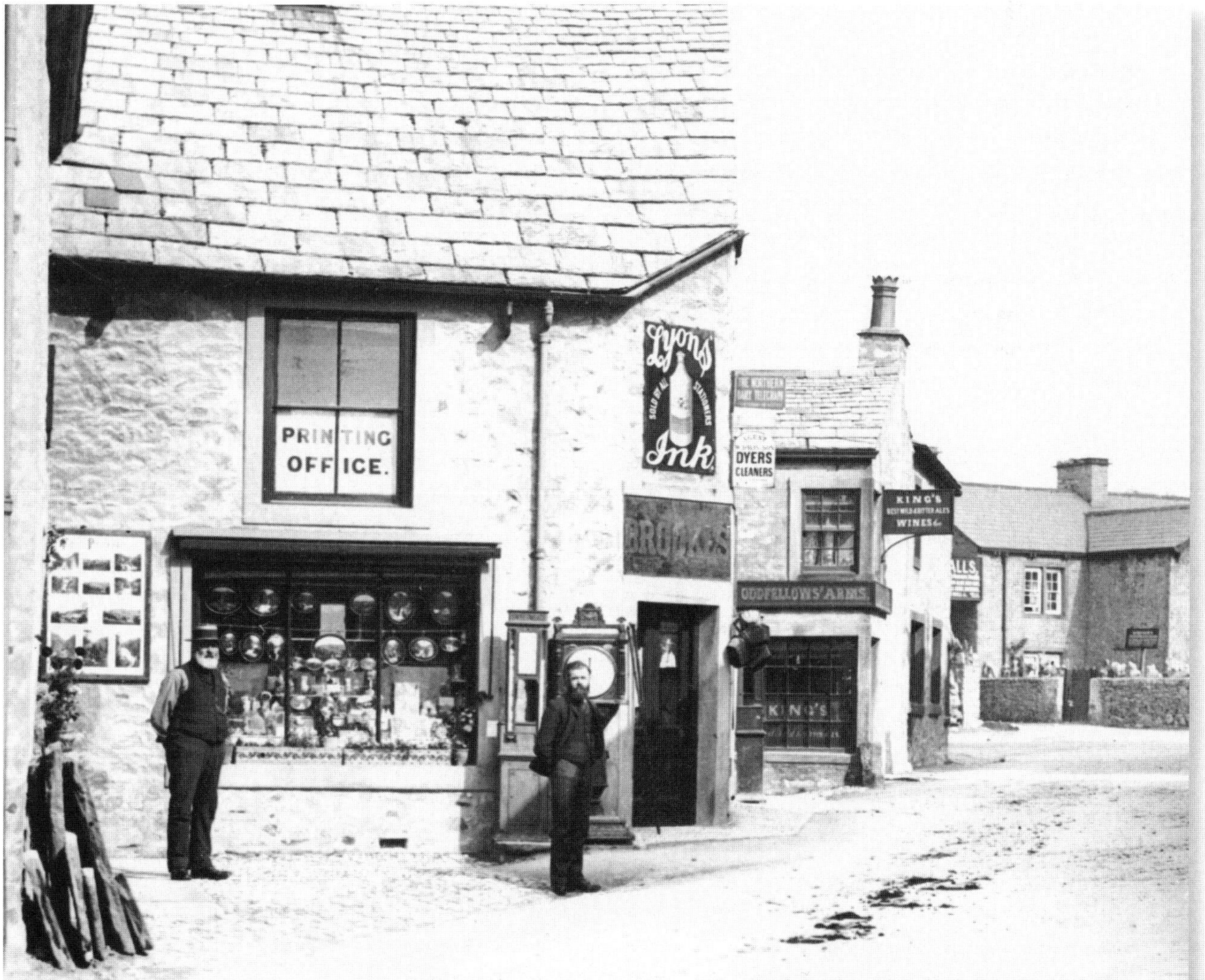

An Introduction

The following snapshots of our past - part of the largest private collection of photographs in Britain - is intended for all those who love the countryside and our rich past. It spans a longer period in the BC eras than in the AD times; that is, from the Neolithic settlers to the Saxon invasions some 4,500 years later, from chambered long barrows to Saxon crosses, from stone implements to the use of metals, from the illiterate to the written word, from symbols on stone to ink on parchments, from tribal society to organised kingships.

The captions and chapter introductions - which sometimes trespass outside the contents of the photographs - are meant to create a broader picture of events than may be gleaned from the picture. They are intended to promote interest with those readers who wish to pursue field archaeology from the comfort of their chairs or those who may wish to don walking boots and seek out these monuments in their natural setting. Approximate geographical locations are therefore included.

Many people have more leisure time today than ever before; as a consequence, they tend to spend more time exploring the countryside outside their own environs. Should reading this book inspire and encourage such activity, should it add to a greater appreciation of our past, then it will, in a small way, have added to our rich cultural legacy.

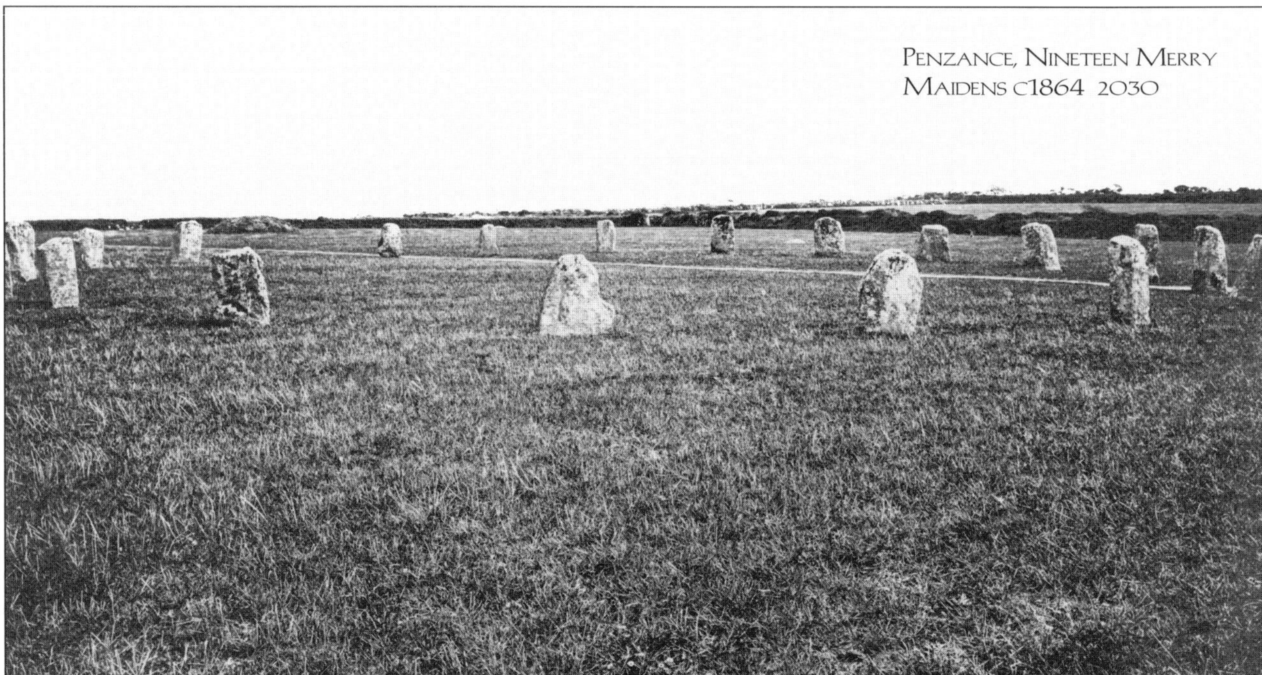

Penzance, Nineteen Merry Maidens c1864 2030

STONE CIRCLES

The period around 4,000BC saw the migration to Britain from the continent of New Stone Age people, and is known as the Neolithic period. It was they who started to clear the afforested landscape and who quickly spread their habitation, customs and ways throughout the British Isles. Fortunately, the chalk ridges in the south of the country formed natural routes for these small nomadic social groups.

A surprising amount of their distinctive pottery still survives - known as Hembury and Windmill Hill wares. It is largely undecorated with simple rims and rounded bottoms, which made the vessels easier to use around the tribal fire. The making of tools became a necessity; the abundance of flint in the south ensured a ready supply of polished flint axes and unbelievably sharp arrowheads. Trade was always important; soon polished stone axes from the Lake District were exchanged for flint artefacts from the south. The Neolithic peoples were, inevitably, hunters, farmers and traders.

The changes in pottery styles allow archaeologists to plot Neolithic development. Gradually, Neolithic pottery became more elaborate with simple decorations indented prior to firing; with modern methods, such pottery sherds can now be dated. In addition, the radiocarbon dating of bones and organic materials, and the refinement in stratification dating, has resulted in a precise chronological table.

What did the first colonisers of the British Isles leave behind as a lasting legacy? Few remains of Neolithic huts survive, but on hilltops scattered throughout the south there are causewayed enclosures known as Causewayed Camps. Their purpose remains a mystery, but they could have been ritual sites, market places or corrals for livestock. It is unlikely that they were built for defensive purposes. The most famous of these is Knap Hill, near Marlborough in Wiltshire, where the long shadows of the setting sun can highlight a series of causewayed banks on its hillside. On a summer evening it is well worth a short walk from the Sanctuary on the A4 near Avebury up to the massive Saxon Wansdyke. It is fascinating to stand here and observe the Knap Hill camp to the south, one of the oldest surviving man-made monuments in Britain.

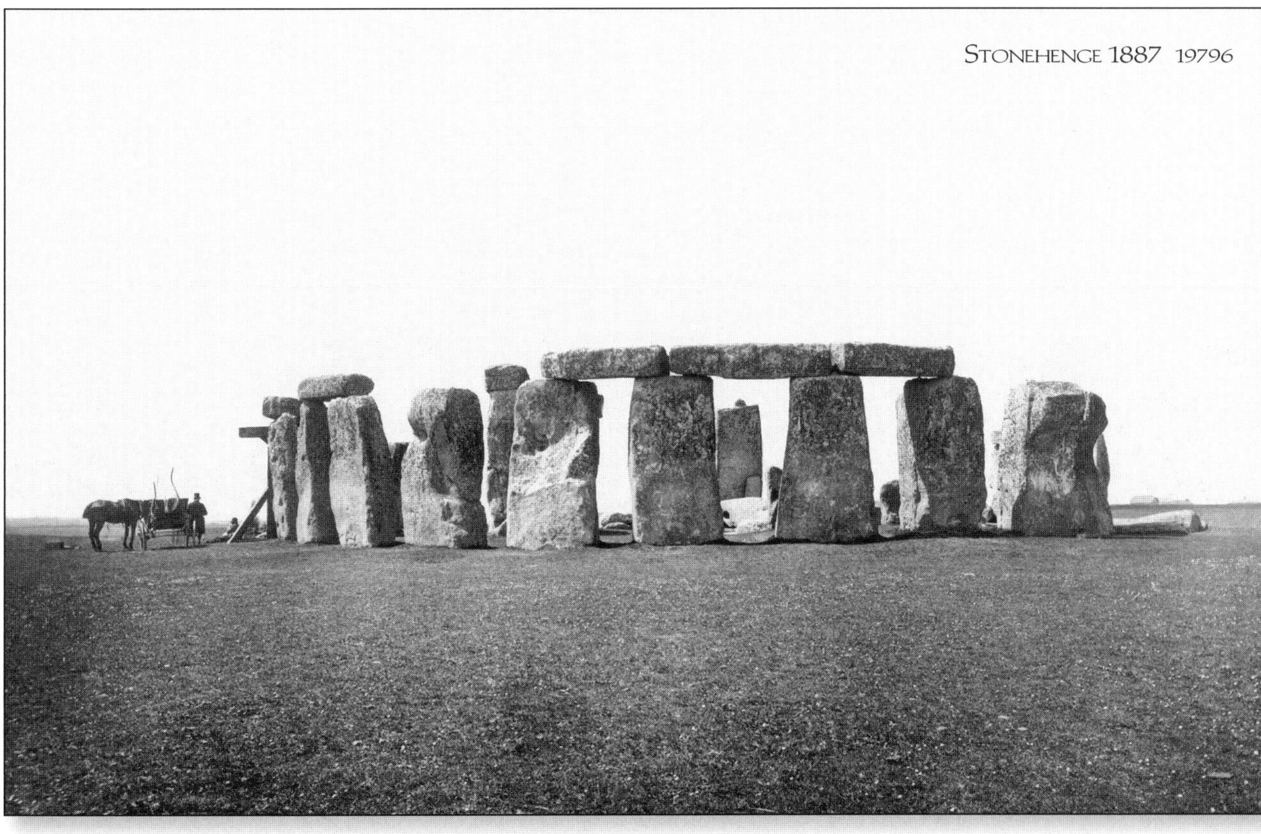
STONEHENCE 1887 19796

Stone Circles

The best Neolithic monuments, however, are the burial chambers, a testimony to the Neolithic peoples' belief in the afterlife. These monuments, known as long barrows, are in fact chambered tombs, and they can be found all over Britain. They are fascinating buildings: some remain intact, while with others only a few raised stones remain to reveal the existence of a single chamber. (See the chapter on burial mounds). The best of these to visit is West Kennet Long Barrow, which is virtually opposite Silbury Hill, near Avebury in Wiltshire. Here the large mound and five chambers can still be explored. The erection of Neolithic burial mounds points to the fact that the Neolithic people were no longer nomadic and had become organised social groups.

Avebury is the largest of all the stone circles in Britain and was built during the Neolithic Age. It stands as a most ambitious and stunning monument, comprising a large circle with ditch and bank, with two smaller stone circles inside - and, uniquely, the village of Avebury is now inside too. The massive stones were bought from Fyfield Down, which is about one mile away beside the famous Ridgeway Path which was used by Neolithic travellers and, indeed, is still in use today. Leading from the Avebury circle were two ceremonial avenues. The Kennet Avenue is the best preserved; it went from Avebury to the Sanctuary, another stone circle about a mile away. Archaeologists tend to believe that this avenue was a ceremonial pathway where decomposed bodies were brought to a priesthood that inhabited Avebury and probably restricted access to it. After a ritual service, the skeletal bones would be placed in one of the chambered long barrows that surround the area.

Around 2,200BC a new wave of migrations occurred of people originating in the Rhine delta. They have become known as the Beaker Folk, and the period 2,200 BC to 500BC is, for the purpose of this exercise, referred to as the Bronze Age. These new people were accomplished farmers and builders, and brought with them the knowledge of metallurgy: they understood that the mixture of tin and copper produces bronze (tin was in abundance in Cornwall). Also, for the first time, gold jewellery appeared with burials found in their distinctive round burial mounds.

Nature, the seasons, fertility and death dominated these people. Perhaps the most outstanding monuments they left were the stone circles that are to be found throughout the whole of the British Isles. The best known of these is Stonehenge. It is still an enigma, though

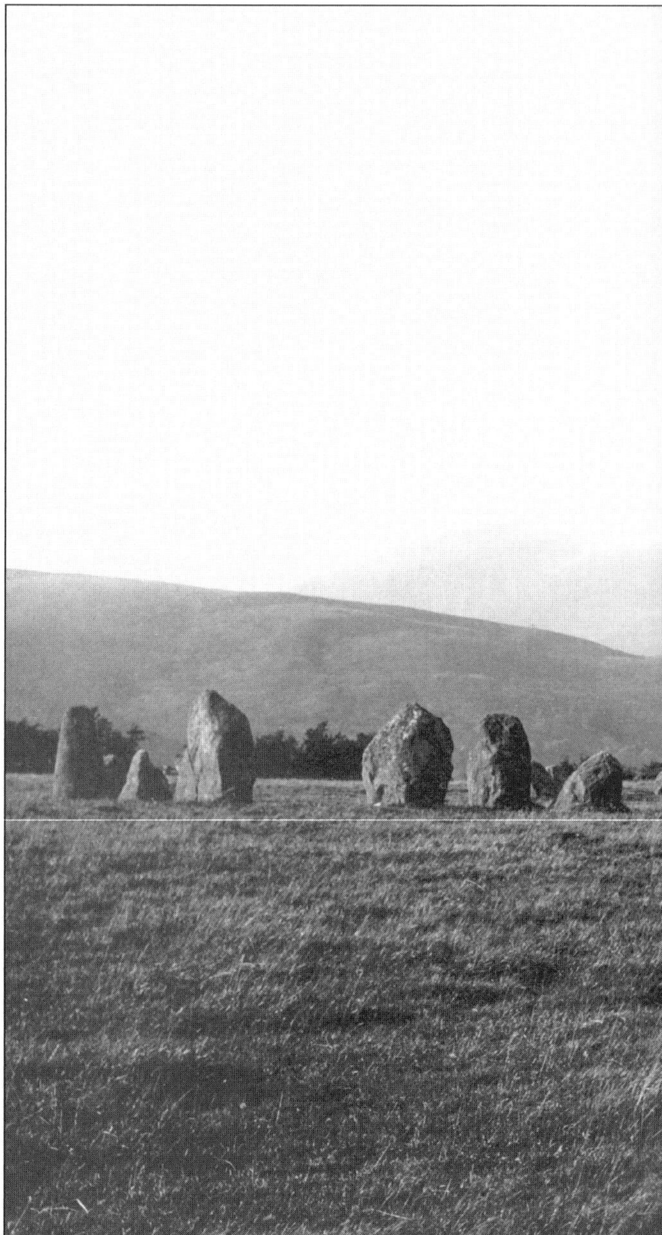

it is hard to discount the theory that it had a strong astronomical purpose. It is also still a puzzling and remarkable monument. Stones were brought from Fyfield Down about 20 miles to the north, the same source as the stones at Avebury. It is highly unusual that the stones were dressed: that is, they were hammered into shape by large football-shaped flint hammers, a technique for which there had been

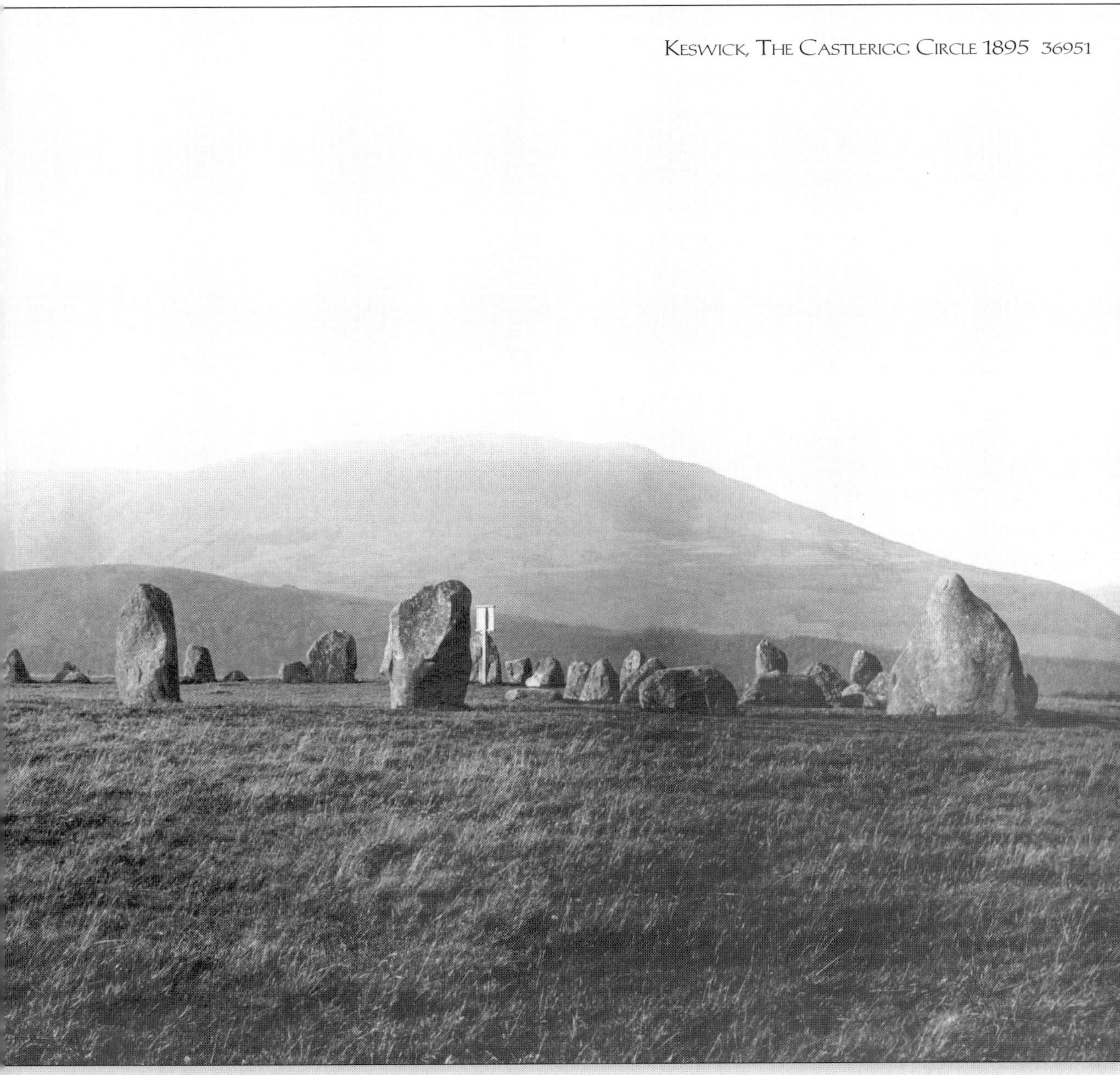

KESWICK, THE CASTLERIGG CIRCLE 1895 36951

no precedent in Britain. Moreover, the first mortise and tenon joints can be seen here - they keep the lintels firmly in place. The precision of the stones, which fit so perfectly together, raises more questions than answers. Where did such knowledge come from?

It is generally accepted that Stonehenge and the smaller stone circles (particularly common in Devon and Cornwall) were temples. Small communities on Bodmin Moor would have their own circle for ritual and funerary purposes. Some appear to be aligned to the movement of certain stars, the sun or the moon, though it can be tempting to take such theories too far. If these circles can be called churches, then Stonehenge would be the cathedral. However, by about 1200BC the cult of building stone circles ended.

Stone Circles

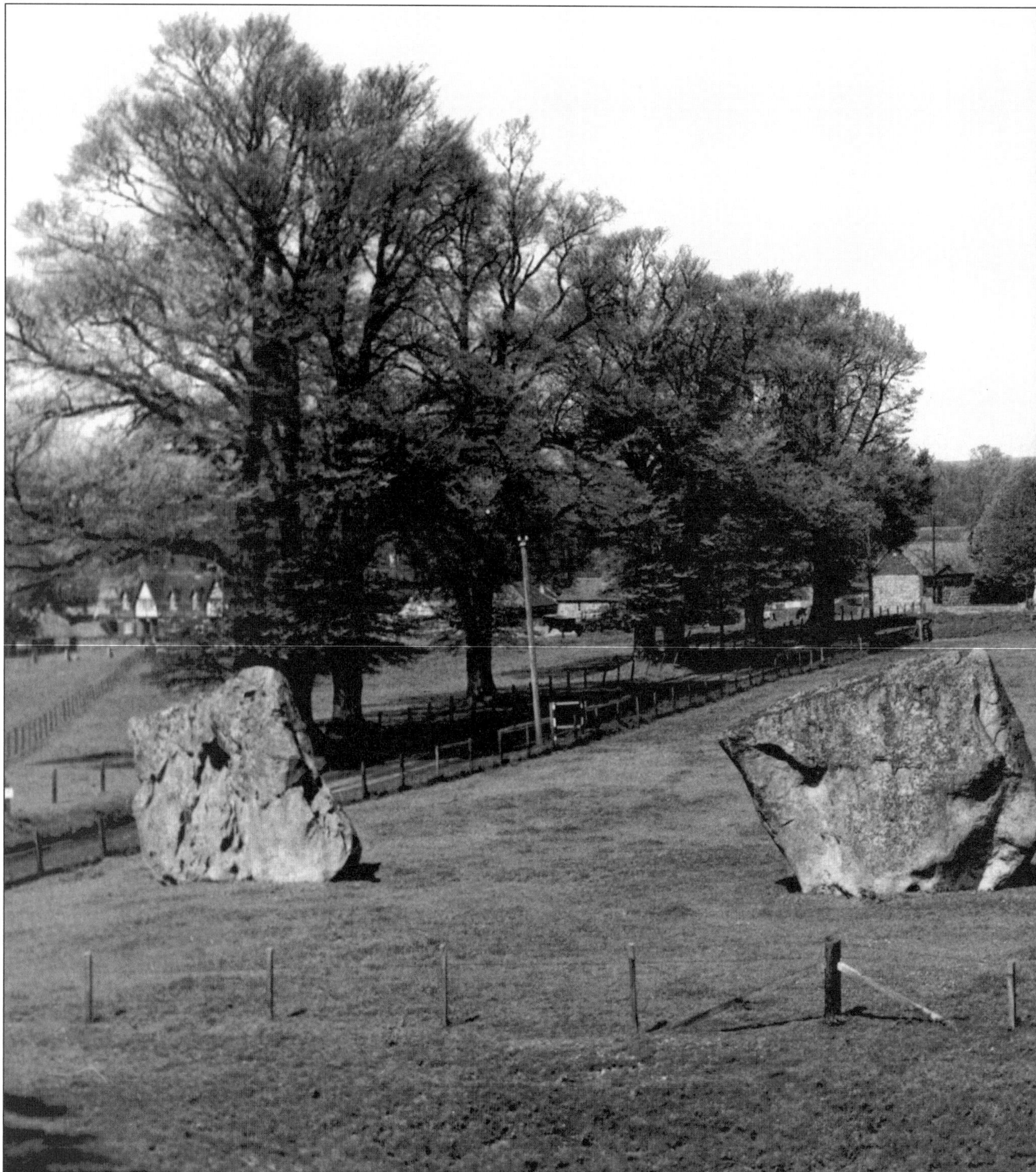

AVEBURY, THE STONES c1955 A80019

The Avebury Stone Circle in Wiltshire is unique: modern village life and ancient stones live side by side in a common and mutual existence where the past is indelibly a living part of the present. The massive circle of stones virtually encompasses the village; here, we can see the Red Lion pub (the white gabled building), the chapel on the right, and domestic thatched housing all inside a stone circle erected some 4,500 years ago.

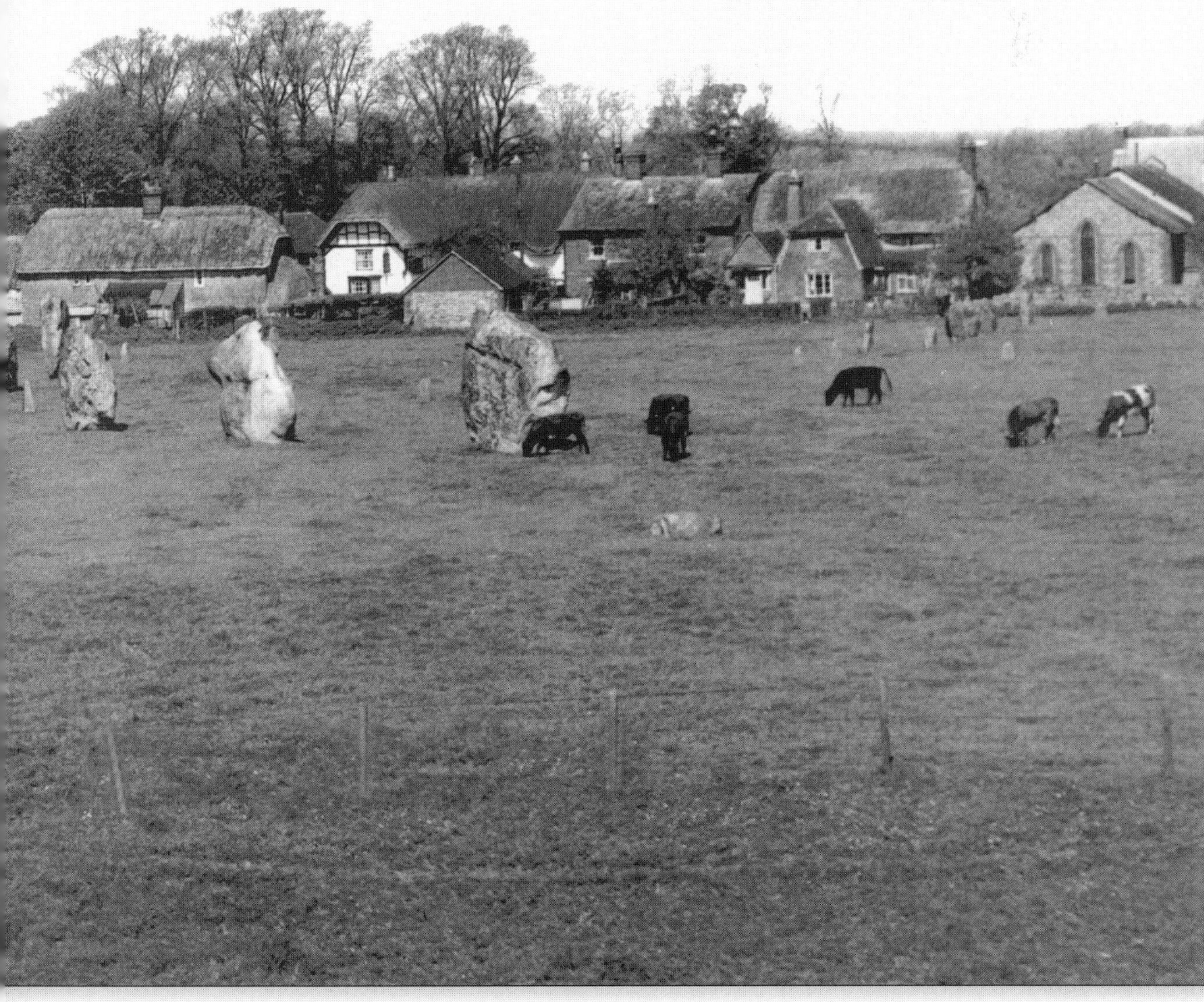

STONE CIRCLES

AVEBURY, THE STONES 1899 44859

The same scene viewed some 60 years earlier than photograph No A80019 (page 12-13) presents a neglected view of the stones. Fortunately, Alexander Keiller (of marmalade fame!) bought the site in 1934 to save it for the nation. The site was extensively 'tidied' and serious archaeological work began. The Avebury we see today owes its survival to these excavations. During the 1940s Avebury was handed over to the National Trust, and it is now a World Heritage site.

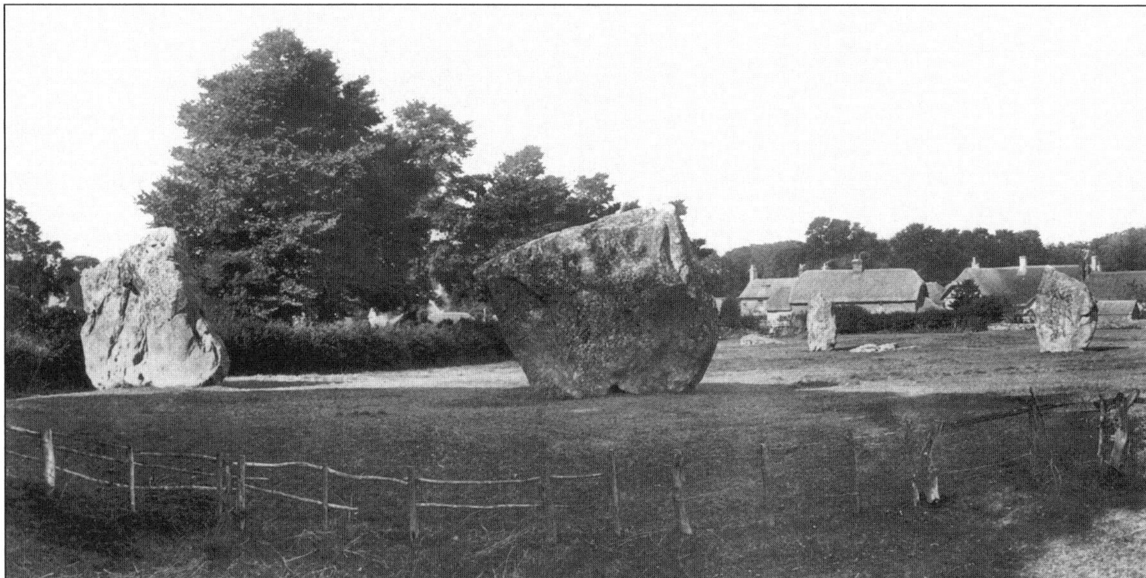

AVEBURY, AVEBURY CIRCLE c1955 A80001

The entire complex comprises an outer circular bank with an inner ditch. Inside was a great stone circle enclosing two smaller circles. The excavated undressed stones can be seen with the tower of the village church just behind the trees.

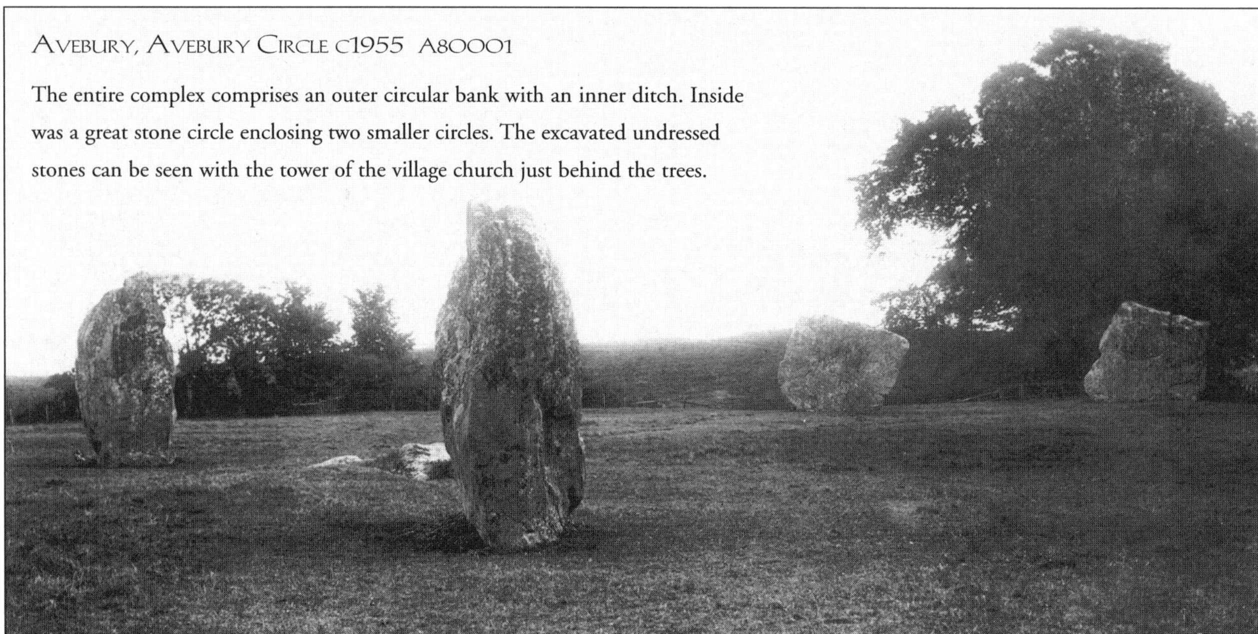

AVEBURY, THE DIAMOND STONE, NORTH ENTRANCE C1955 A80003

The Diamond stone sits alongside the Devizes to Swindon main road that goes through the village. The impressive lozenge-shaped stone came from a surface outcrop of sarsen stones (the word sarsen derives from Saracen, and means stranger) which can be found on the Marlborough Downs about two miles away. The famous Ridgeway long-distance path passes close by, a path that has been used by man for some 6,000 years and is still in use today.

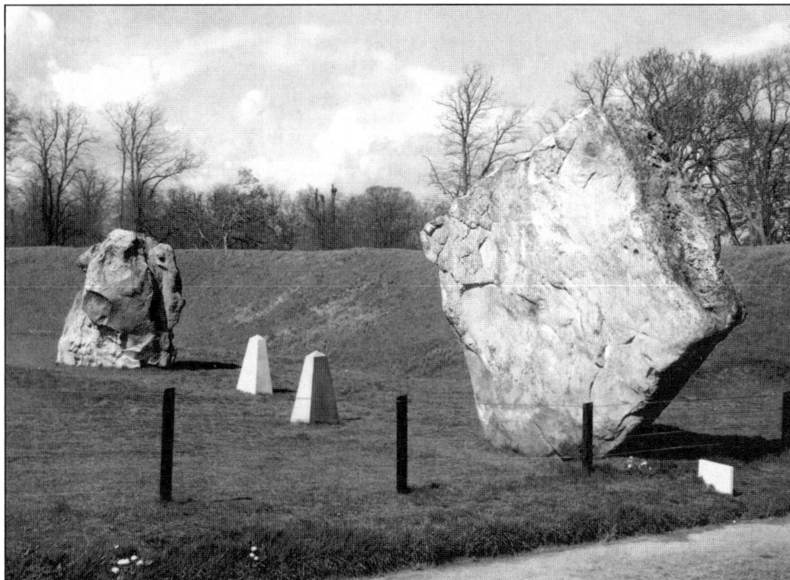

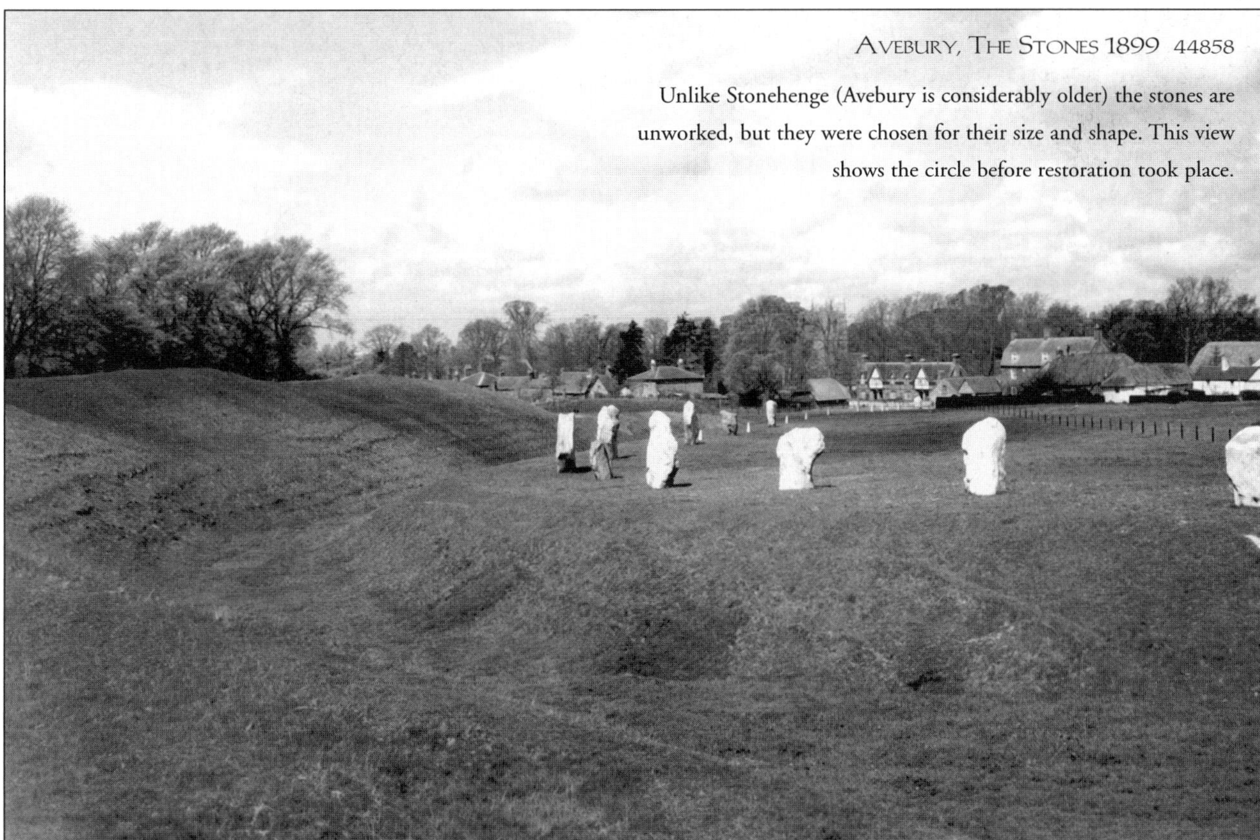

AVEBURY, THE STONES 1899 44858

Unlike Stonehenge (Avebury is considerably older) the stones are unworked, but they were chosen for their size and shape. This view shows the circle before restoration took place.

STONE CIRCLES

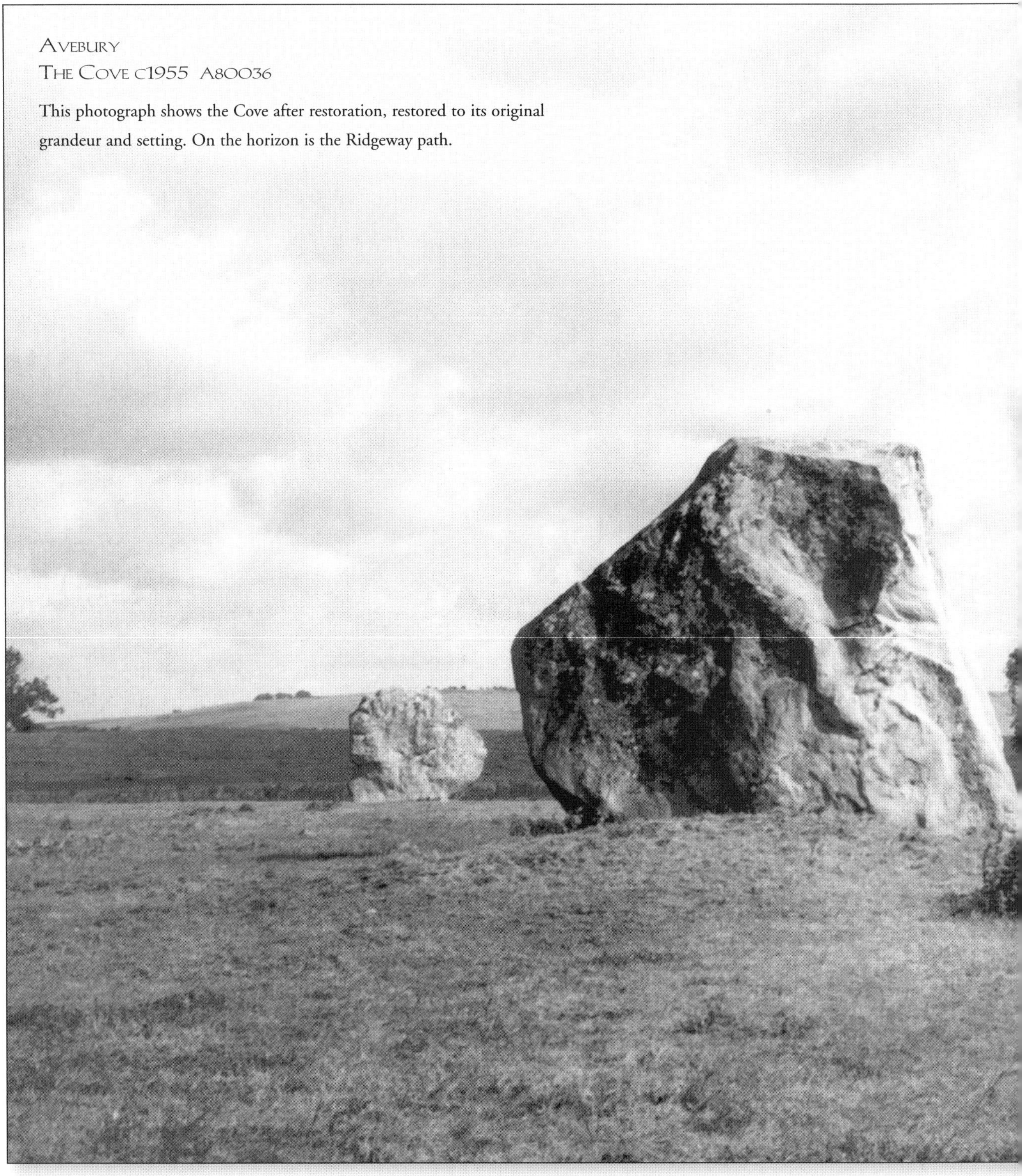

AVEBURY
THE COVE C1955 A80036

This photograph shows the Cove after restoration, restored to its original grandeur and setting. On the horizon is the Ridgeway path.

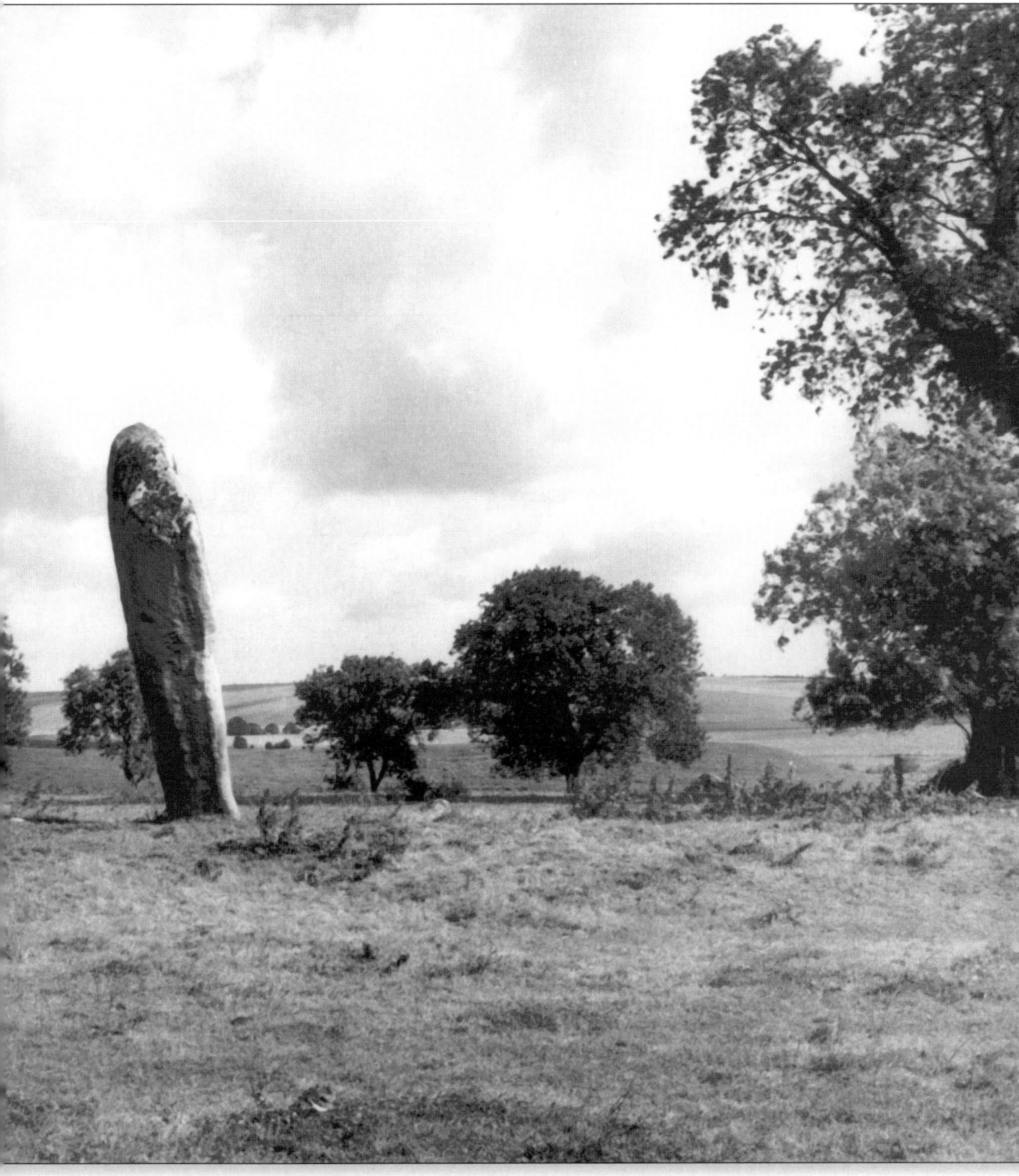

Stone Circles

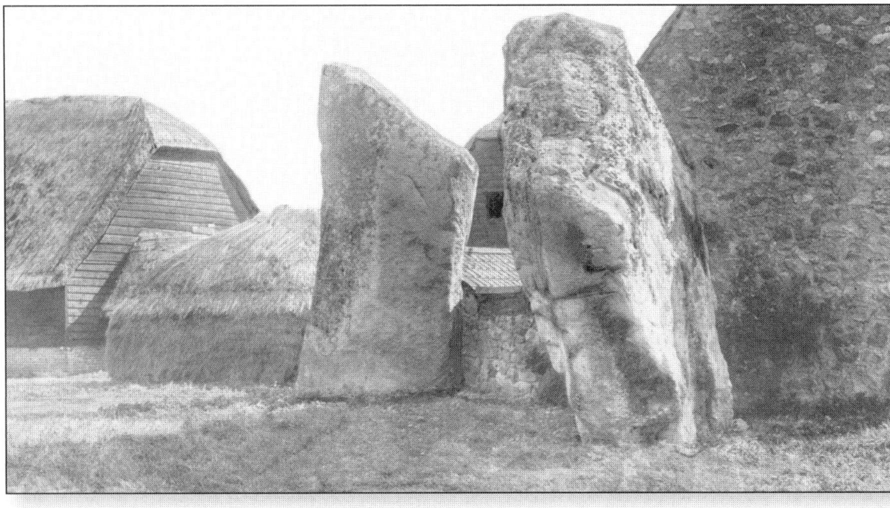

Avebury, The Cove 1899
44860

The barn and outbuilding seen here were demolished in the 1940s as part of the long-overdue restoration programme. Notice the various building materials used, from flint and stone on the right to thatching and wood panelling beneath the half-hip gable of the barn on the left.

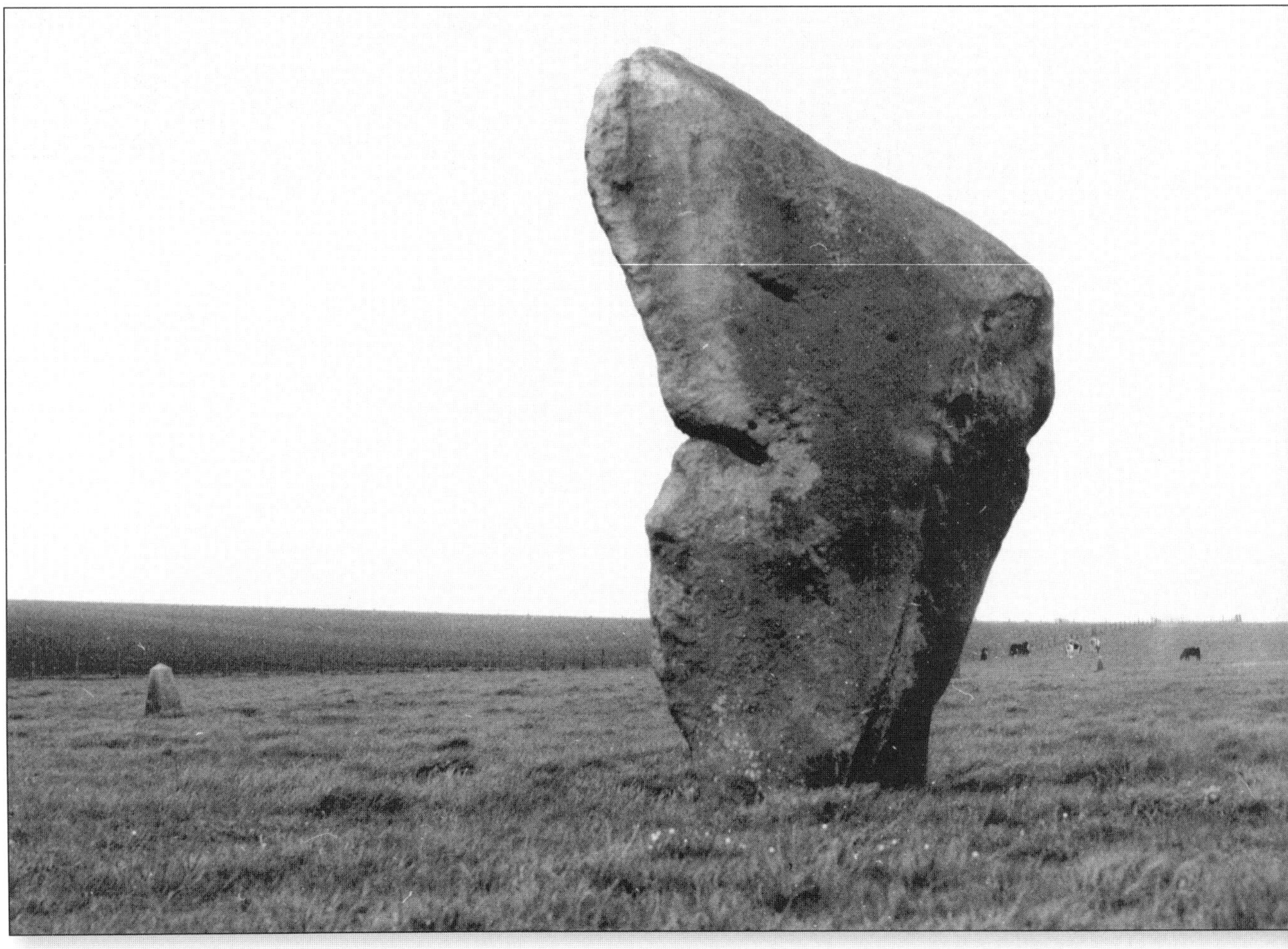

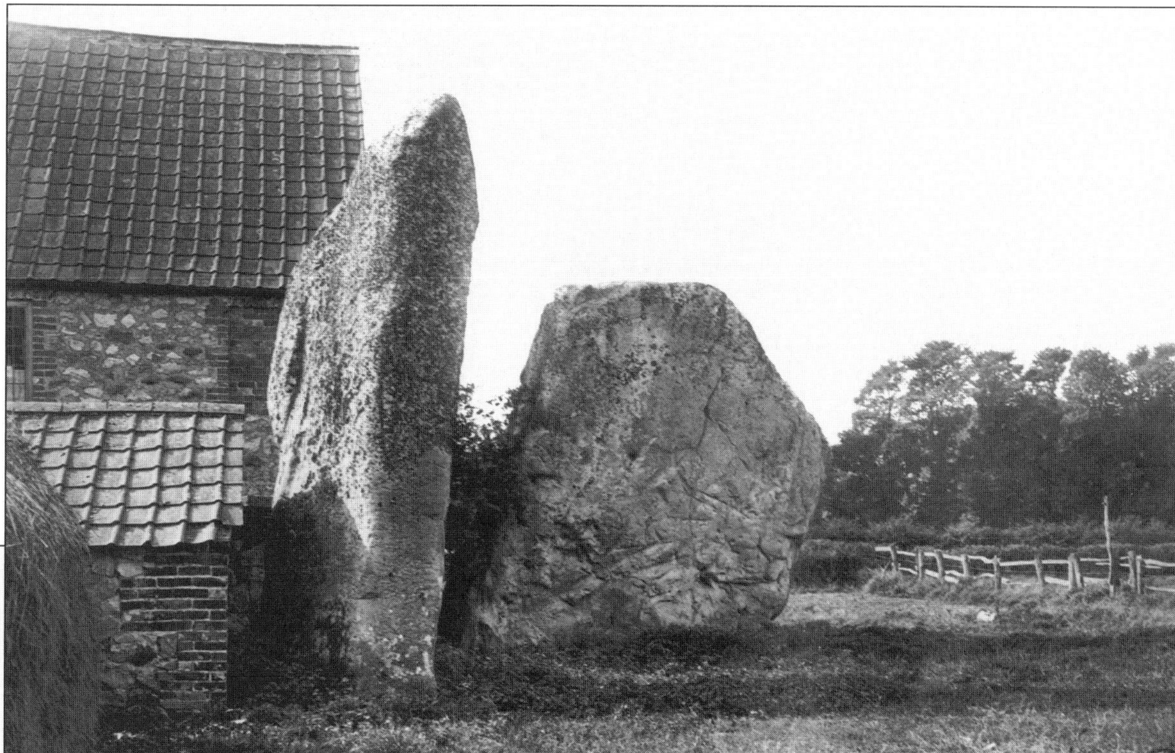

ABOVE: AVEBURY
THE STONES 1899 44861

In the middle of the northern inner circle stands the Cove; it originally consisted of three stones, of which two now remain. It is possible that bodies were left here on funerary platforms - in the watchful presence of priests - to decompose, before a skeletal burial was carried out later in one of the many long barrows that surround the area.

LEFT: AVEBURY, THE AVENUE C1955 A80023

These stones form part of the famous Kennet avenue, a ceremonial avenue that links the southern entrance of Avebury to a smaller stone circle, the Sanctuary, about one mile away. Along this sacred avenue dead bodies were probably carried to the temple of Avebury. Fertility rites dominated Neolithic man; it has been suggested that the shape of the Avenue stones - alternating pillar and lozenge shape - represented male and female fertility.

Stone Circles

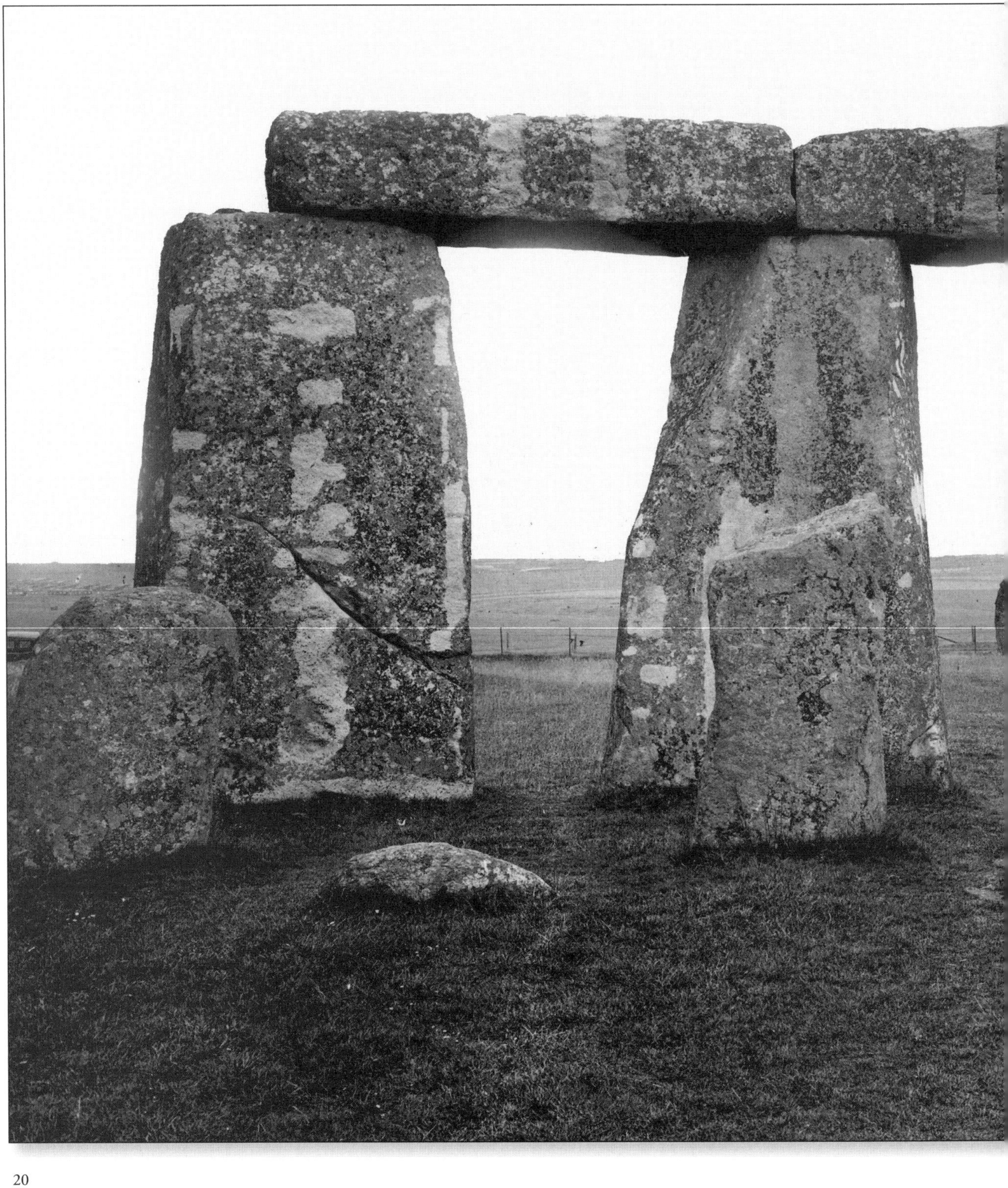

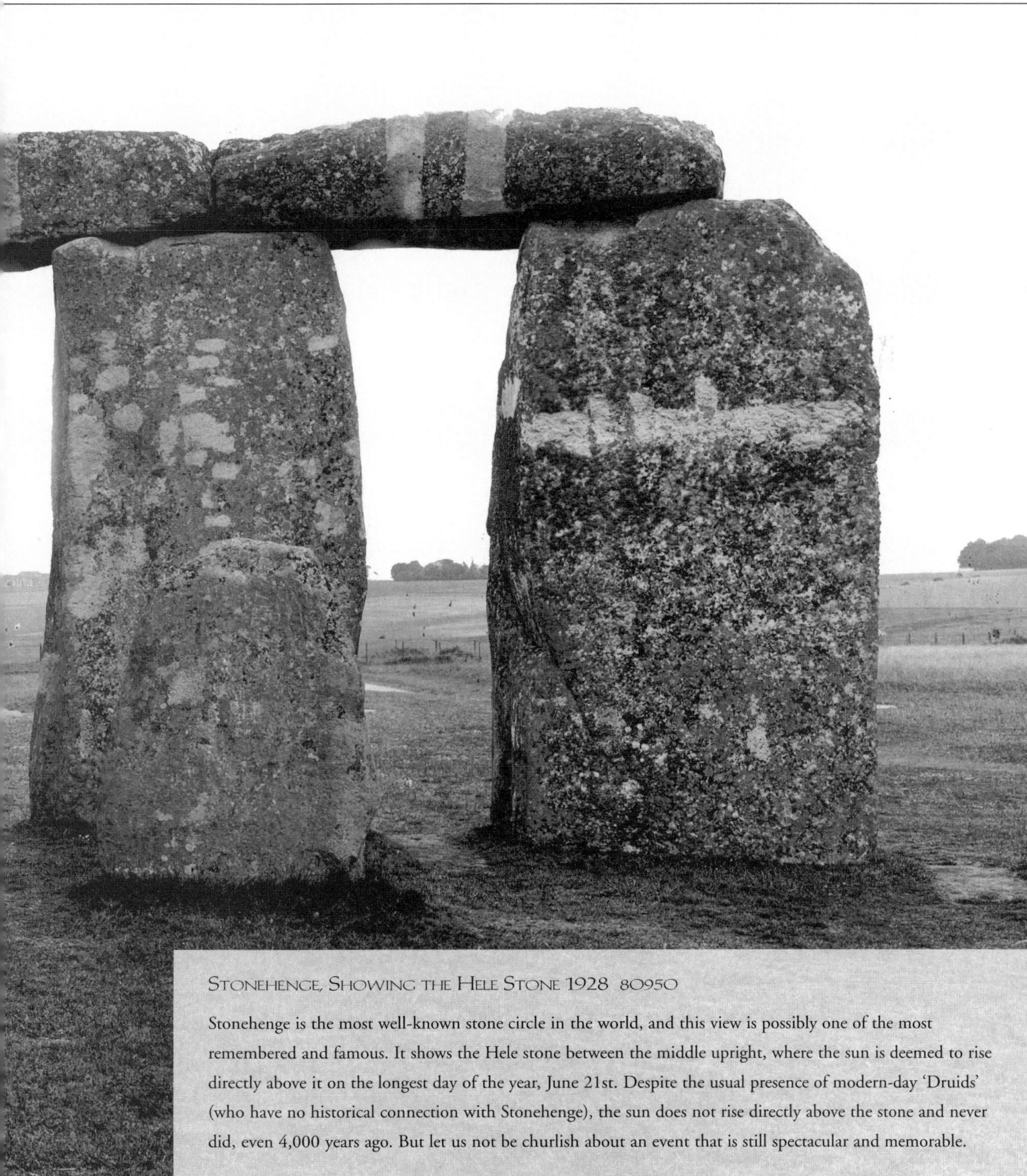

STONEHENGE, SHOWING THE HELE STONE 1928 80950

Stonehenge is the most well-known stone circle in the world, and this view is possibly one of the most remembered and famous. It shows the Hele stone between the middle upright, where the sun is deemed to rise directly above it on the longest day of the year, June 21st. Despite the usual presence of modern-day 'Druids' (who have no historical connection with Stonehenge), the sun does not rise directly above the stone and never did, even 4,000 years ago. But let us not be churlish about an event that is still spectacular and memorable.

STONE CIRCLES

STONEHENGE 1887 19796

As we look southwards from the Hele stone, through the middle arch, we can see the tallest stone of the inner horseshoes of trilithons. The oldest tenon in Britain can be seen, laboriously hammered out with football-shaped flint hammers. The lintel that capped this stone contained the mortise to hold it in place. This was a remarkable achievement for a stone erected some 4,000 years ago; it is one of the mysteries of Stonehenge, since there is no precedent for such a concept.

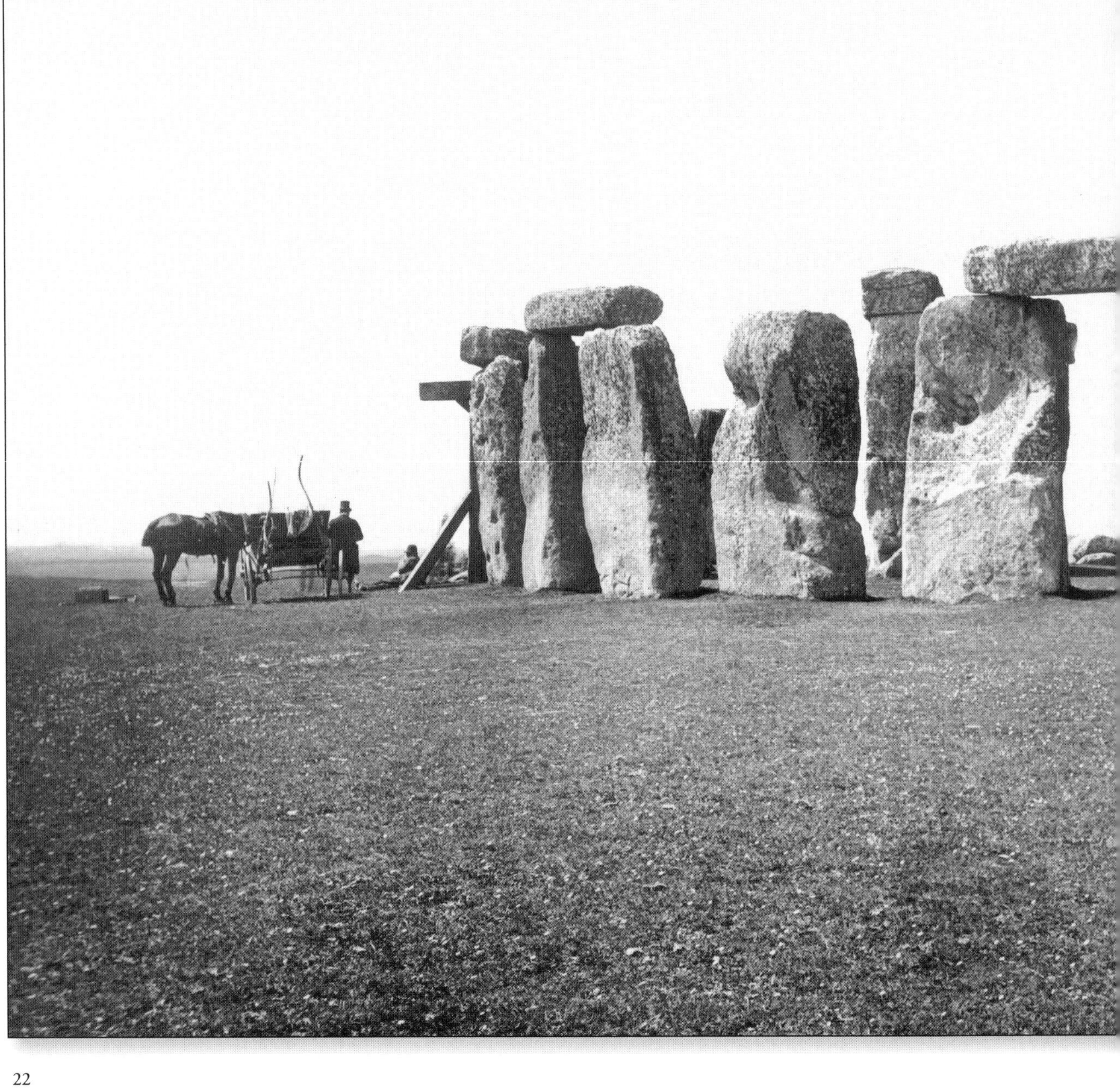

& STONE CIRCLES

STONE CIRCLES

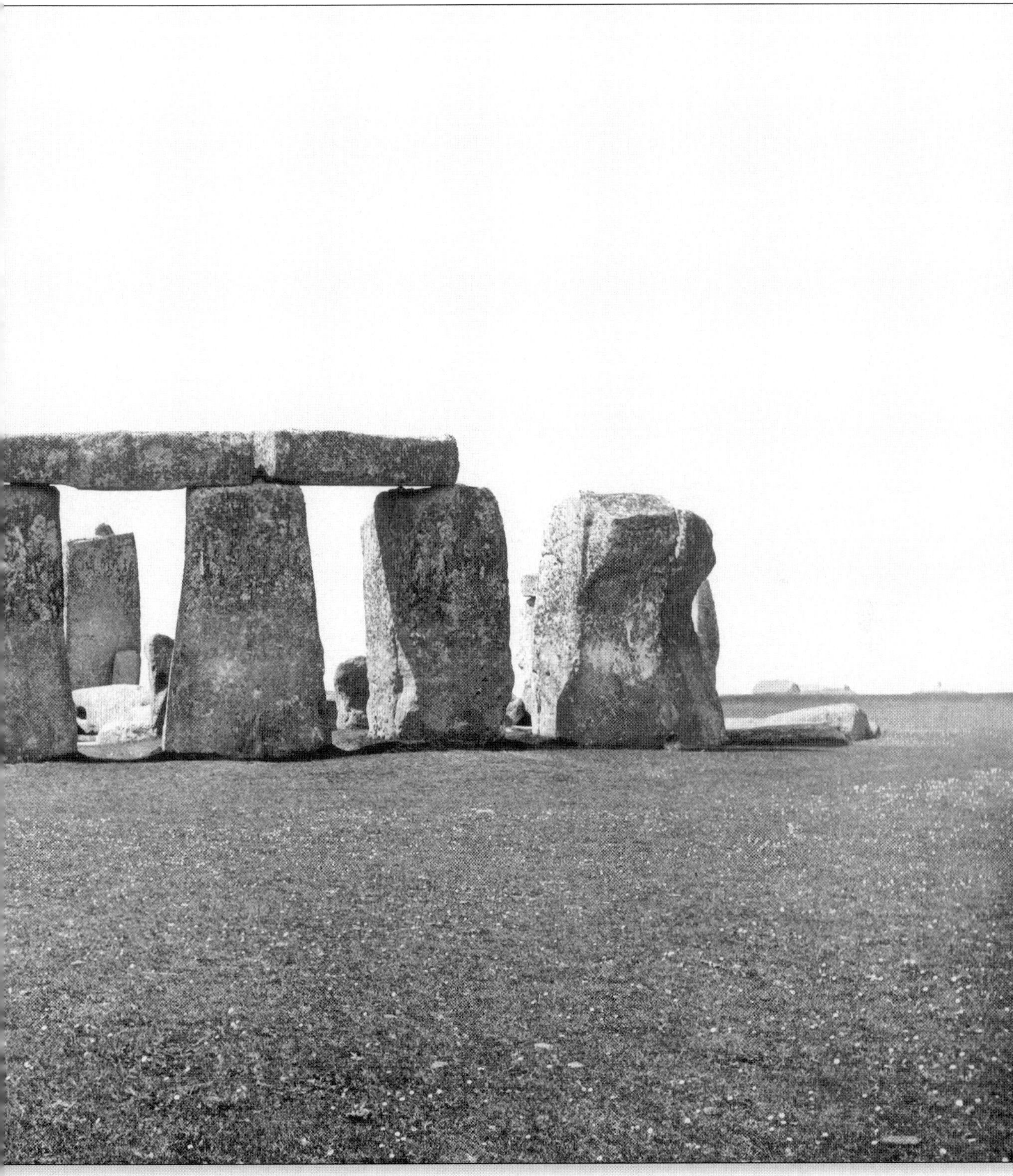

Stone Circles

Left: Stonehenge 1887 19797

The urgent need to restore Stonehenge is demonstrated by this photograph showing Stonehenge in a sorry and cluttered state. The restoration took place in the 1920s: uprights were re-erected - some restored with concrete bases - and lintels capped. Note the wooden supports on the right of the picture and the Victorian carriage.

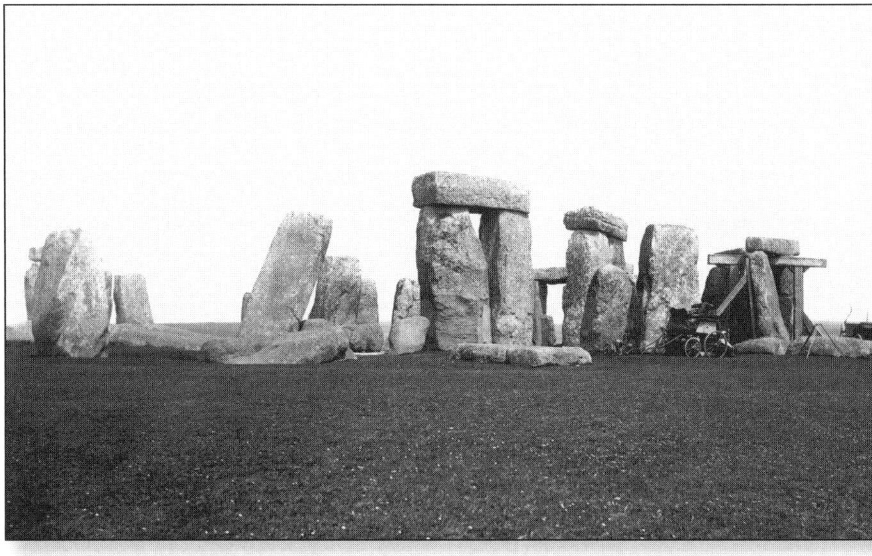

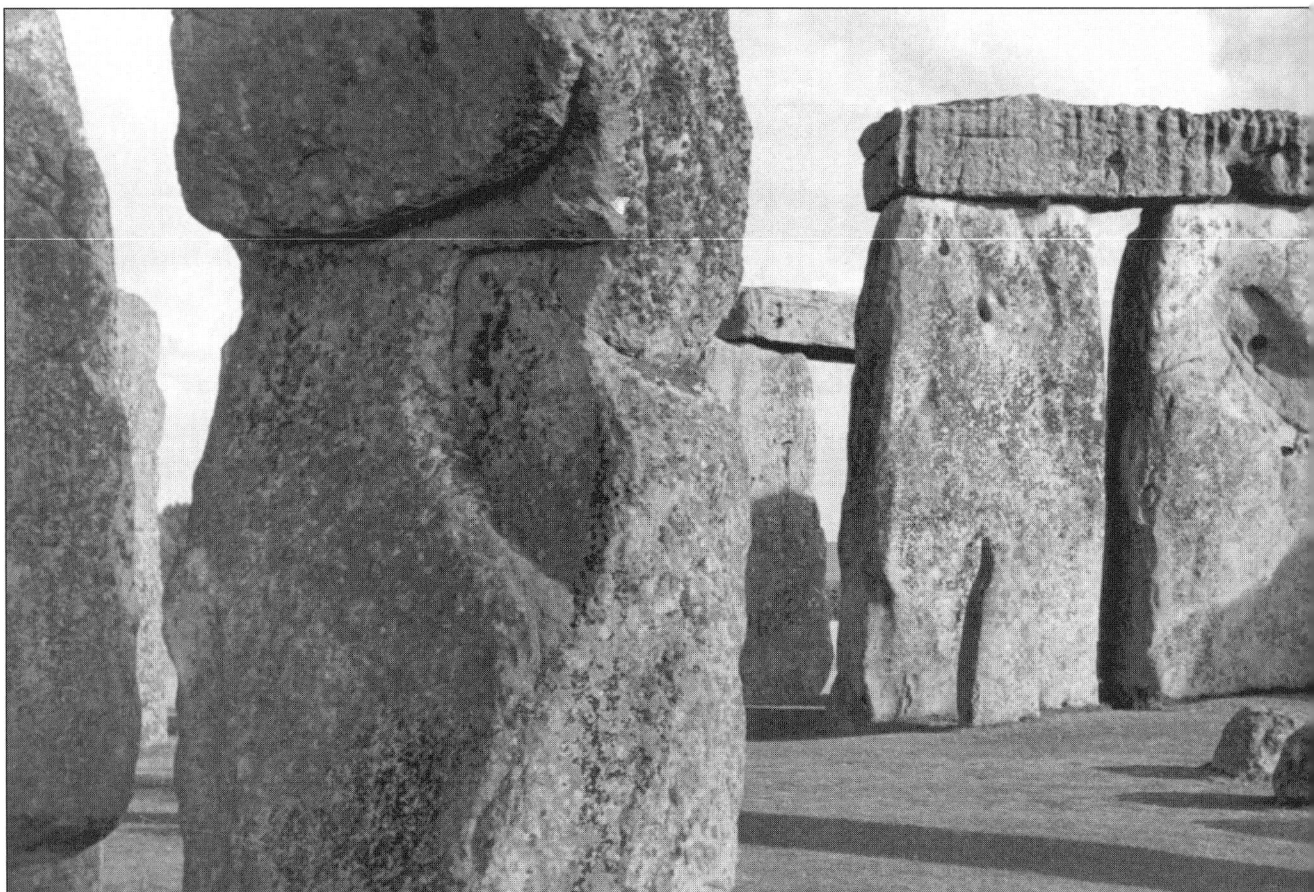

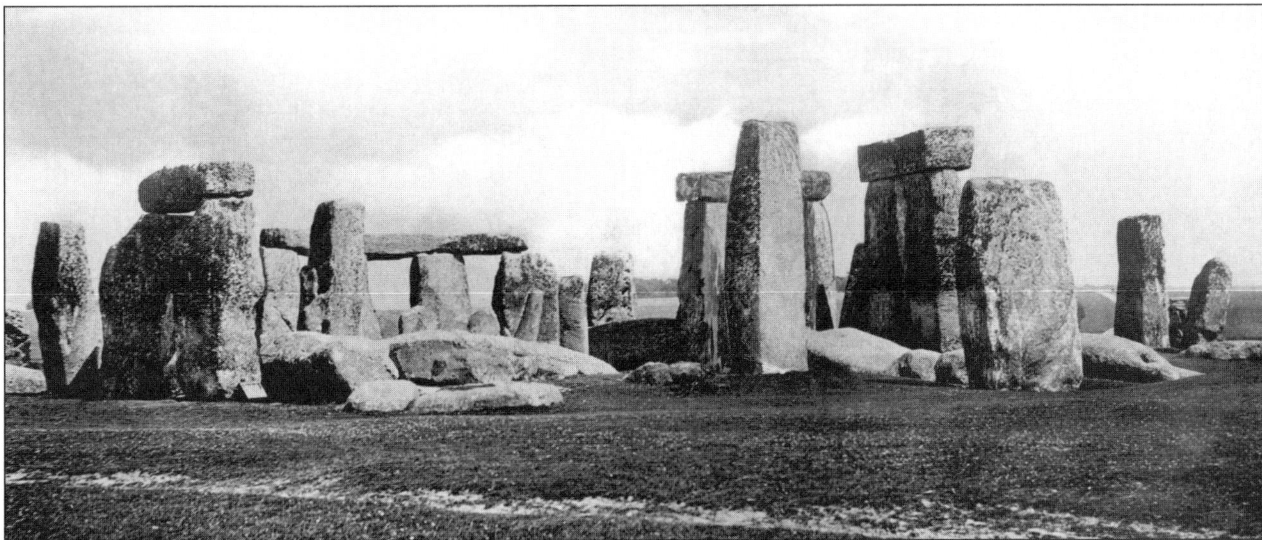

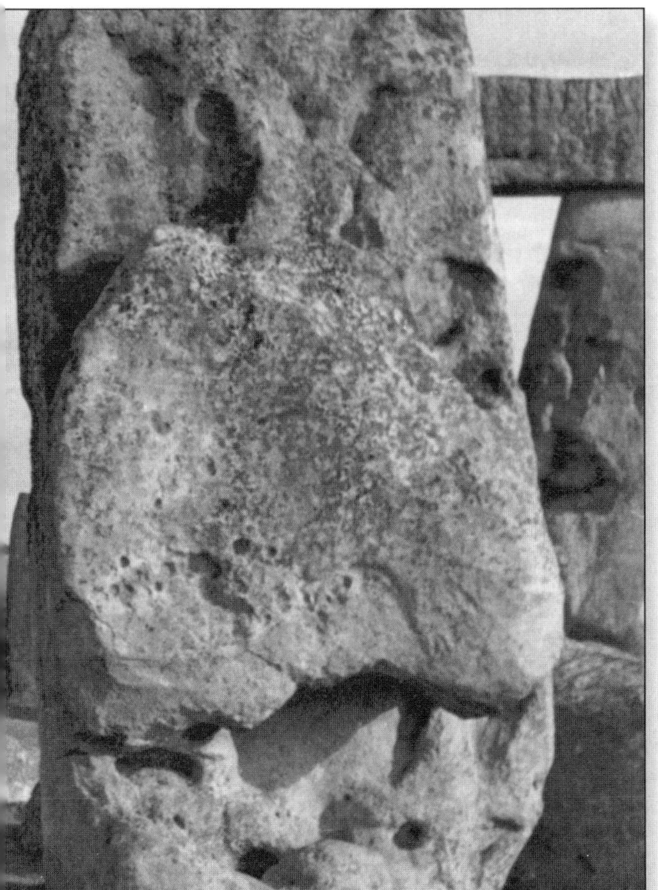

ABOVE: STONEHENGE 1887 19795

Another mystery regarding Stonehenge is that many of the stones have been dressed - again there is no precedent for such work in Britain prior to Stonehenge. The lintels to the right of the picture have been shaped, with mortises beaten into the stone; the upright stone to the centre right has been vertically tapered to avoid optical distortion. The smaller standing stones in the middle of the circle are the famous Blue Stones and come from the Preseli Mountains in west Wales.

LEFT: STONEHENGE C1955 S205083

This photograph demonstrates the rugged beauty of the stones. They weigh up to 40 tons each, and were brought from Fyfield Down, near Marlborough, about 20 miles away, from a surface quarry that can still be visited. (This was the same source as the Avebury stones). The indentations in the stones are fossil remains of palm trees, which grew millions of years ago.

Stone Circles

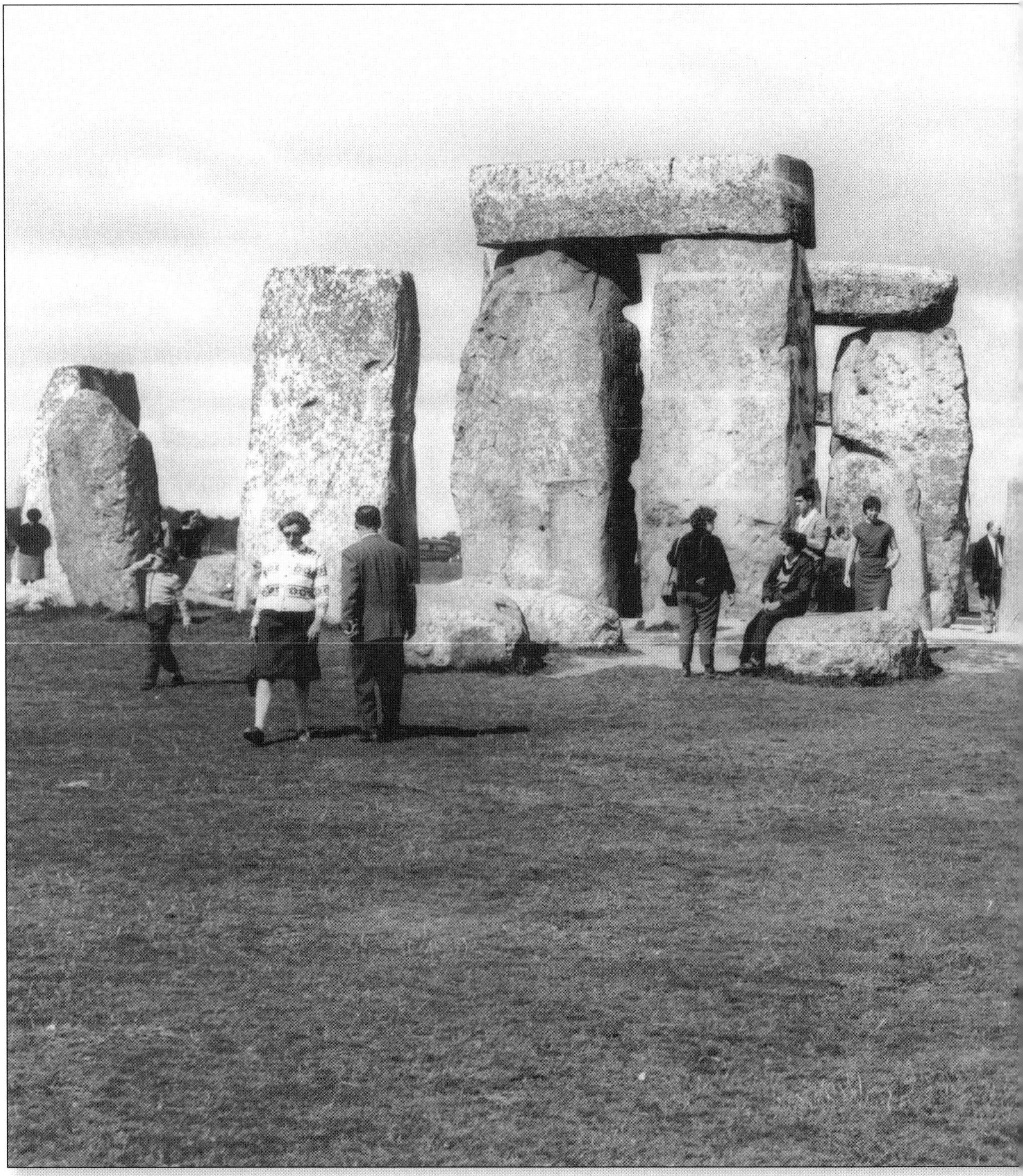

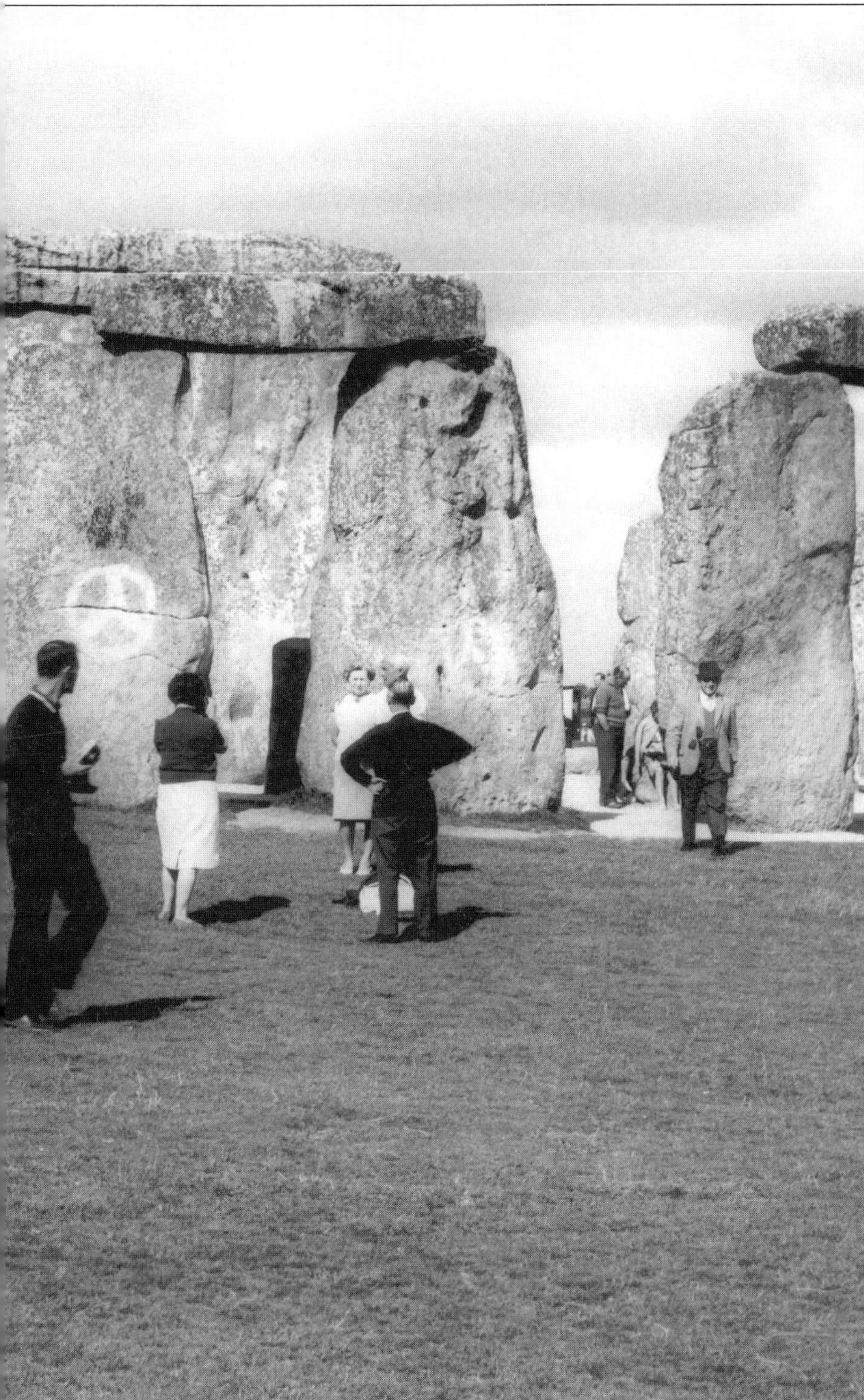

STONEHENGE C1960 S205108

A few years after this photograph was taken the public were denied access to the circle. Visitors' wear and tear was damaging the site. So too were aspects of the 'alternative society', who used Stonehenge for all sorts of spiritual enlightenment or protest, as can be seen by the CND sign daubed on the stone in the centre. Nowadays, the public can view the stones from a perimeter path.

Stone Circles

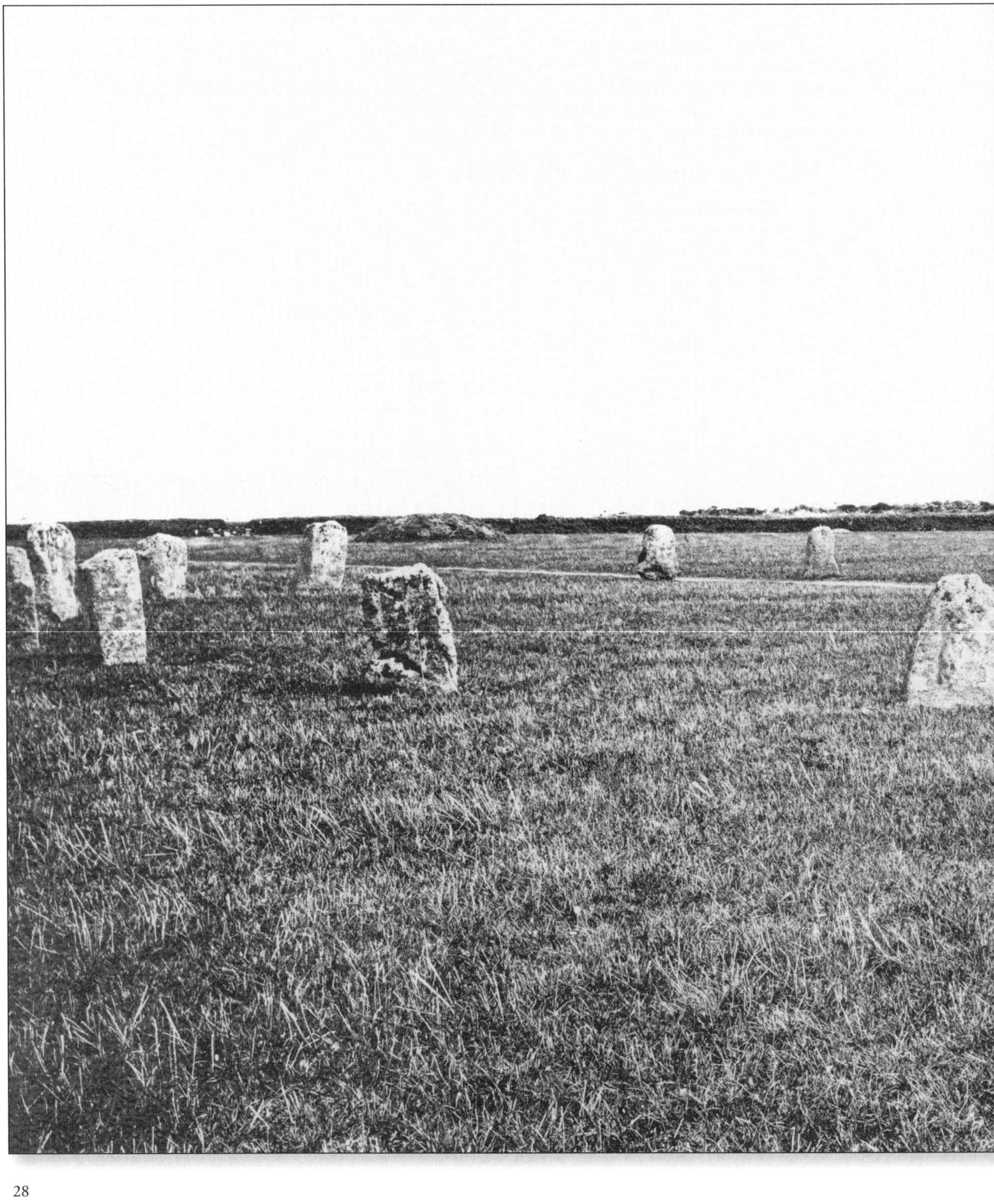

PENZANCE, THE NINETEEN MERRY MAIDENS c1864 2030

Situated near St Buryan, the Merry Maidens Stone Circle is of the Bronze Age; it is one of the most complete stone circles in Cornwall and consists of nineteen stones. The blocks are evenly spaced and are each about four feet high. It is an exact circle, but it appears to have no astronomical significance. The nearby circle of Boscawen-un also has nineteen stones.

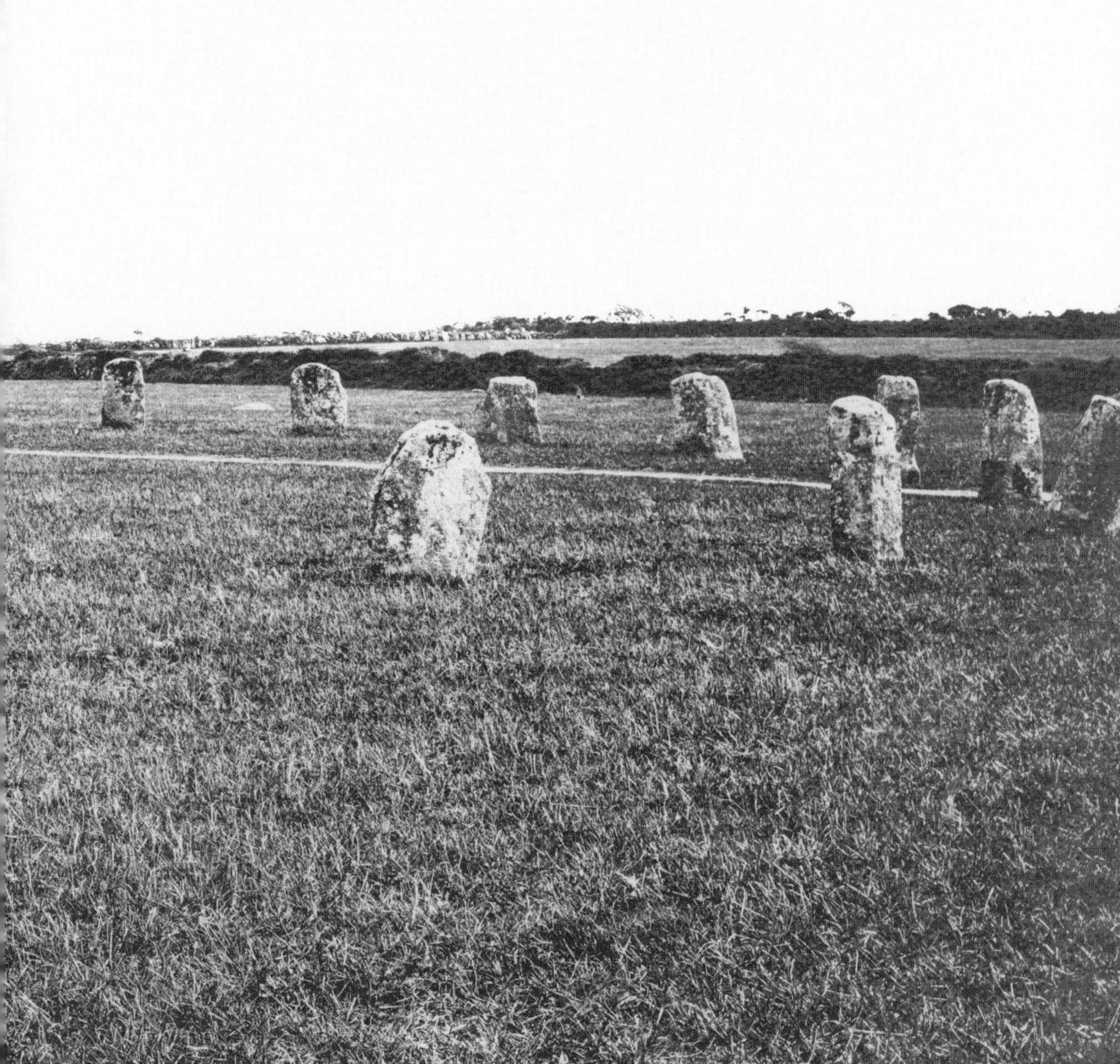

STONE CIRCLES

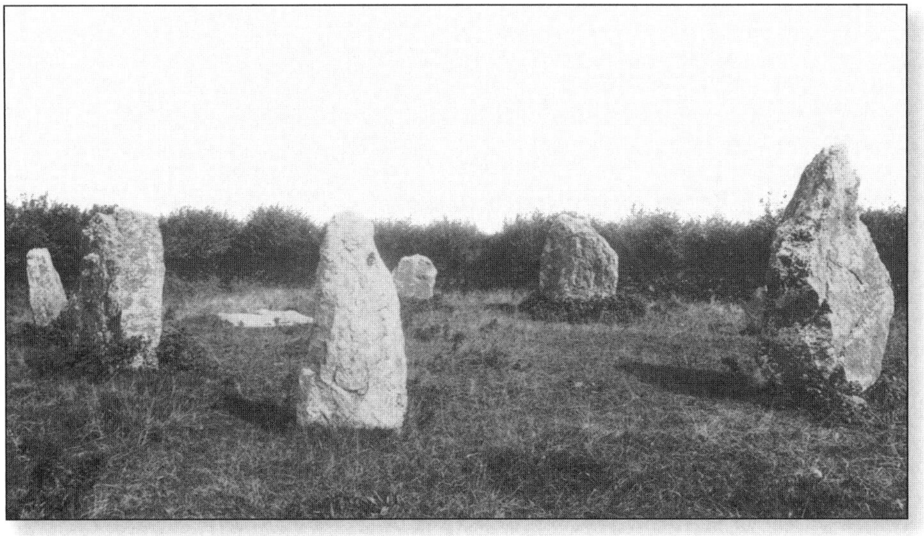

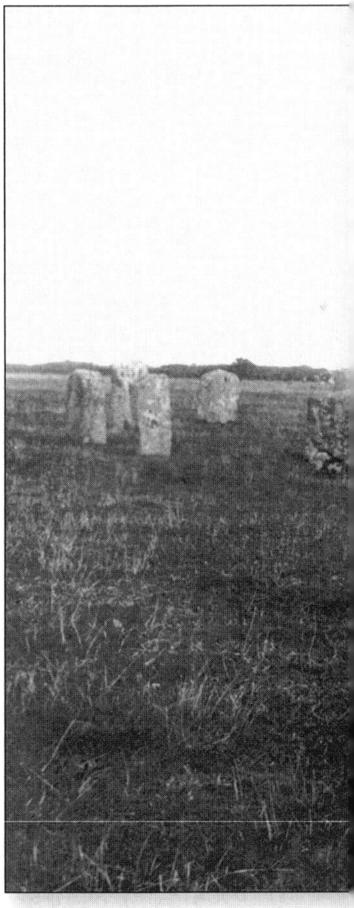

ABOVE: DULOE, THE STONE CIRCLE 1900 45909

This is a small Bronze Age stone circle with only eight stones; it is only distinguished because of the size of the stones - one is nine feet high.

BELOW: CHAGFORD, SCOR HILL, THE SACRED CIRCLE AND KESTOR 1924 76494

In the north-east corner of Dartmoor, in open country, is one of the finest stone rings, Scorhill. It once consisted of 36 stones erected without any shaping. The circle dates from the Bronze Age. In the background is the great boss of Kestor.

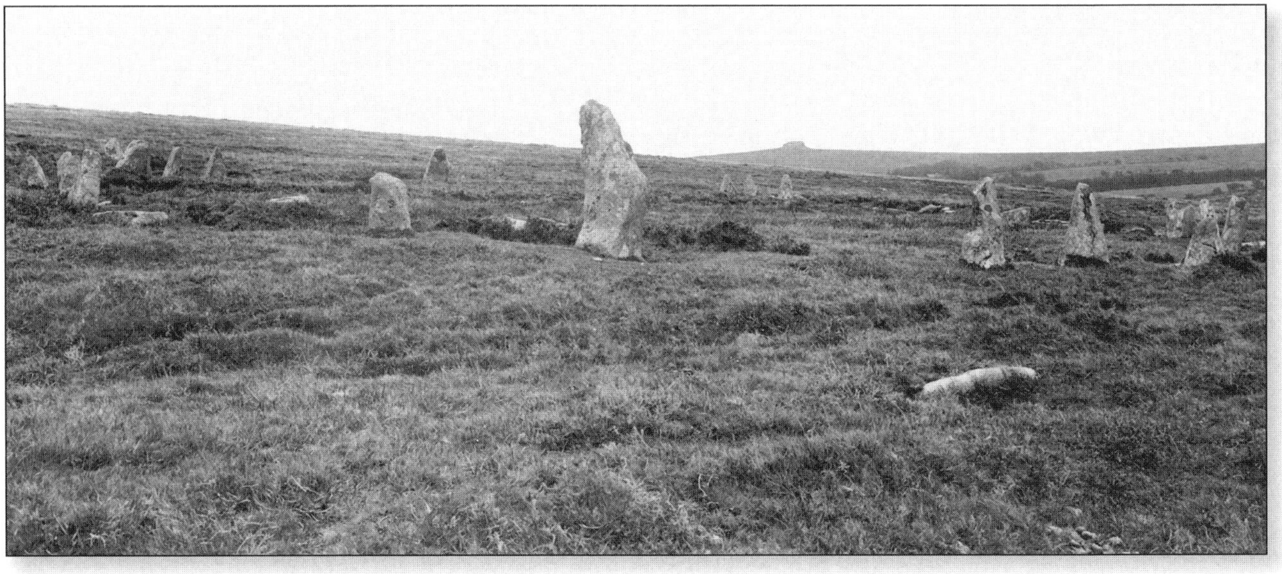

PENZANCE, THE MERRY MAIDENS 1890 22982

This view shows the entrance to the circle on the far side, just to the left. Legend has it that maidens and pipers were turned into stone for dancing on the Sabbath!

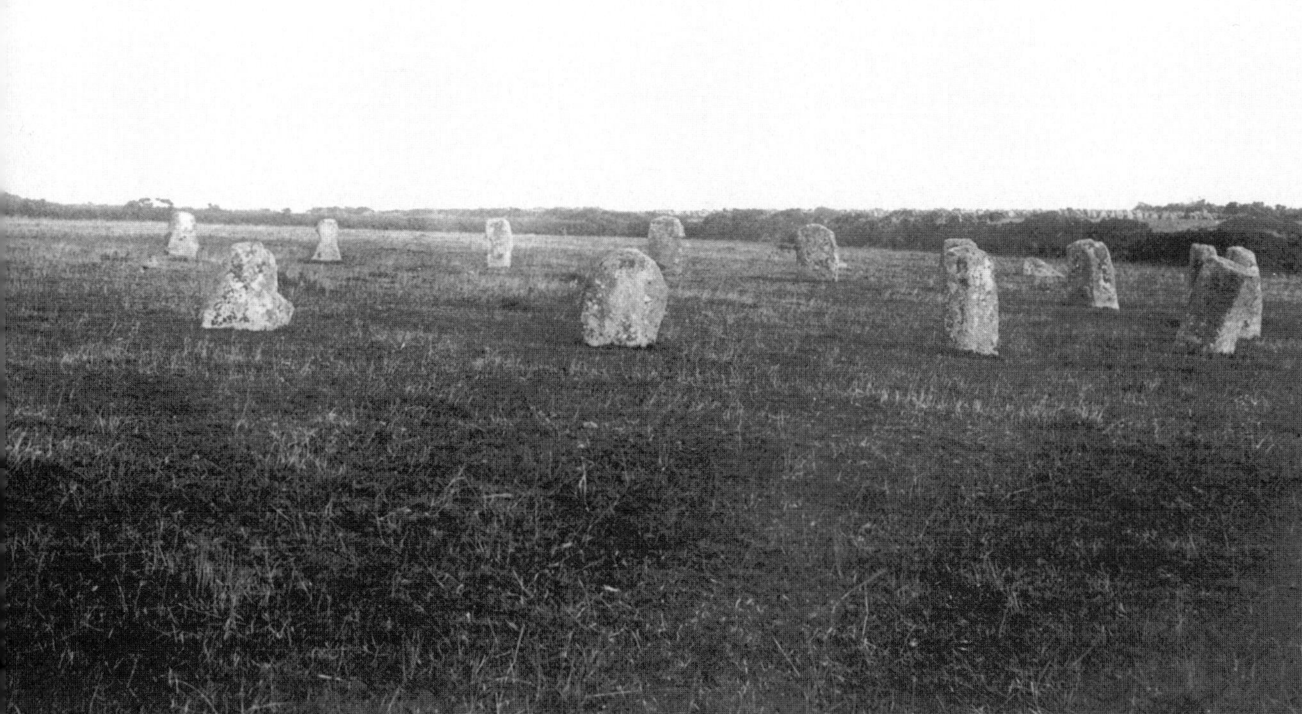

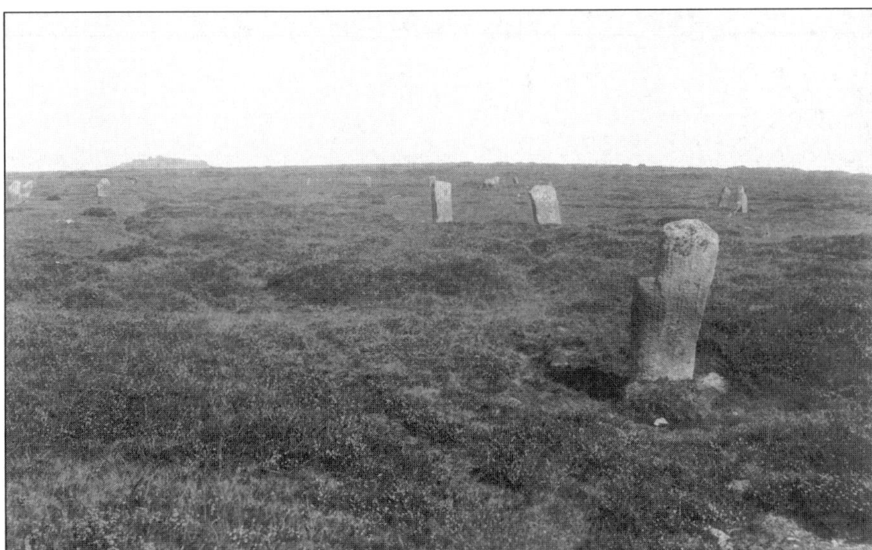

LISKEARD, THE HURLERS AND CHEESEWRING HILL 1900 45899

Three Bronze Age stone circles on Bodmin Moor are called the Hurlers, set amongst the old tin mines. They stand in line, and are all over 100 feet in diameter. It is unusual that the stones have been crudely shaped and are roughly of the same size. They are named 'Hurlers' because it is said that those who profaned the Lord's Day by hurling the ball were turned into stone. Cheesewring Hill can be seen on the horizon.

STONE CIRCLES

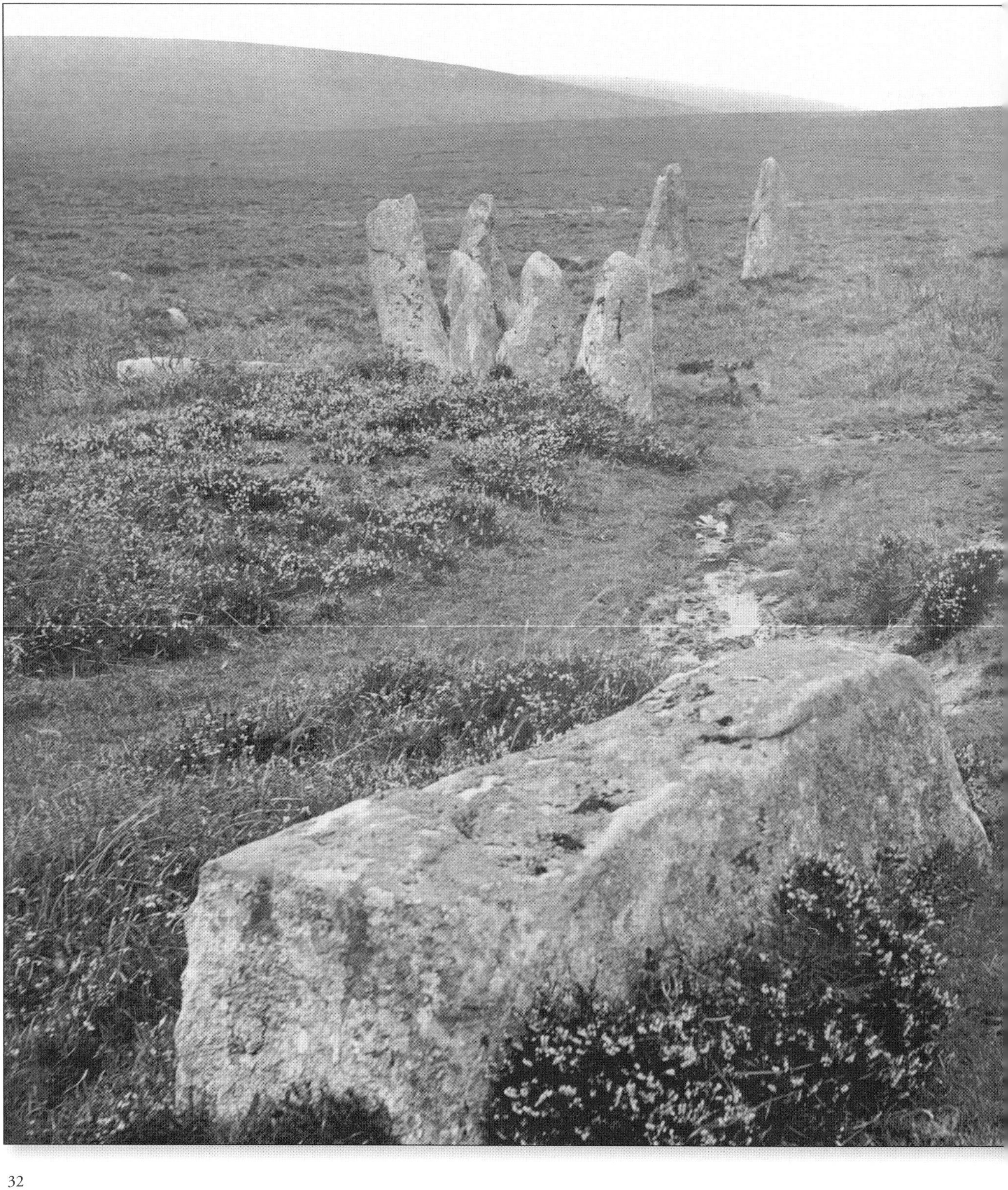

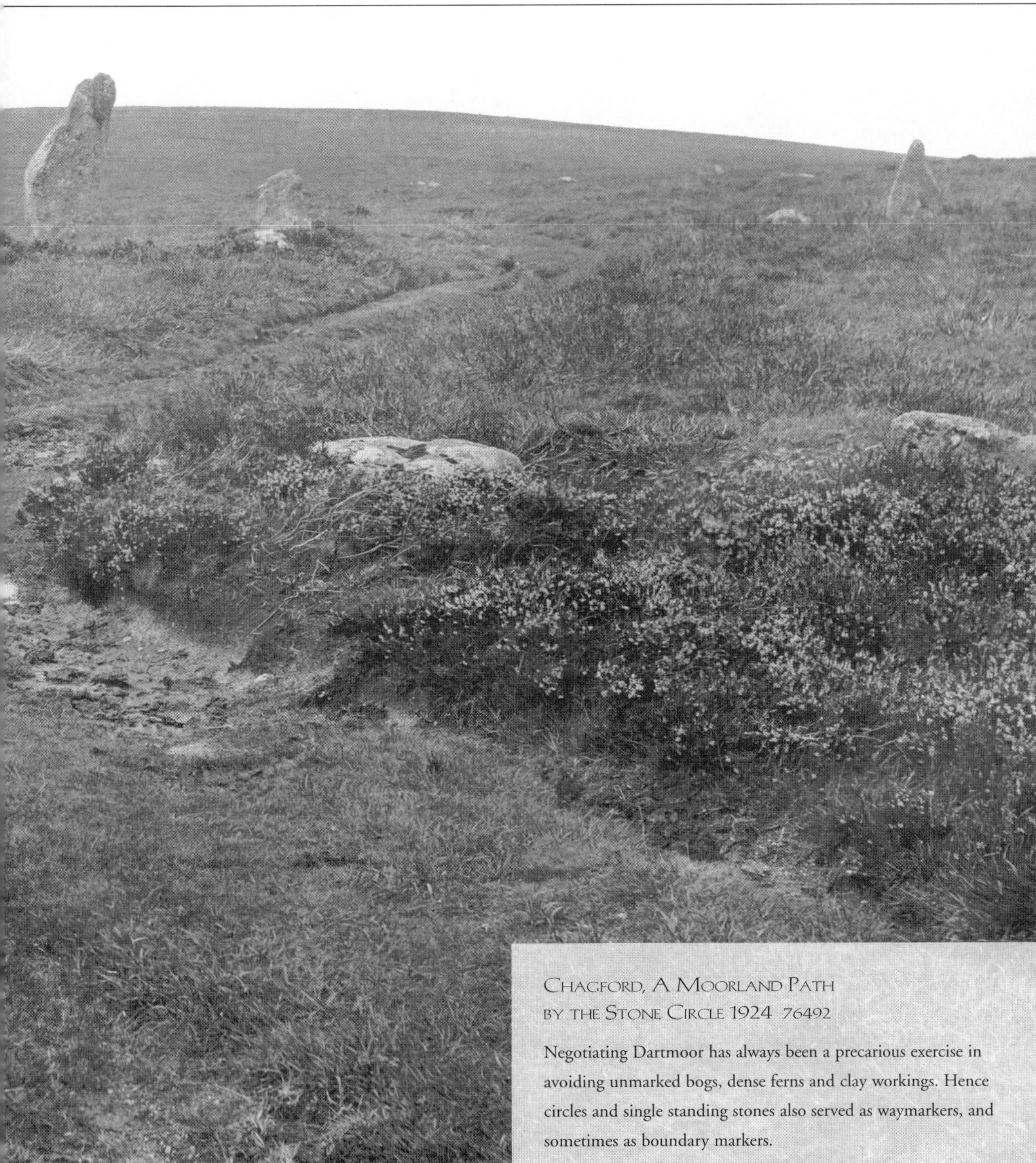

Chagford, A Moorland Path by the Stone Circle 1924 76492

Negotiating Dartmoor has always been a precarious exercise in avoiding unmarked bogs, dense ferns and clay workings. Hence circles and single standing stones also served as waymarkers, and sometimes as boundary markers.

STONE CIRCLES

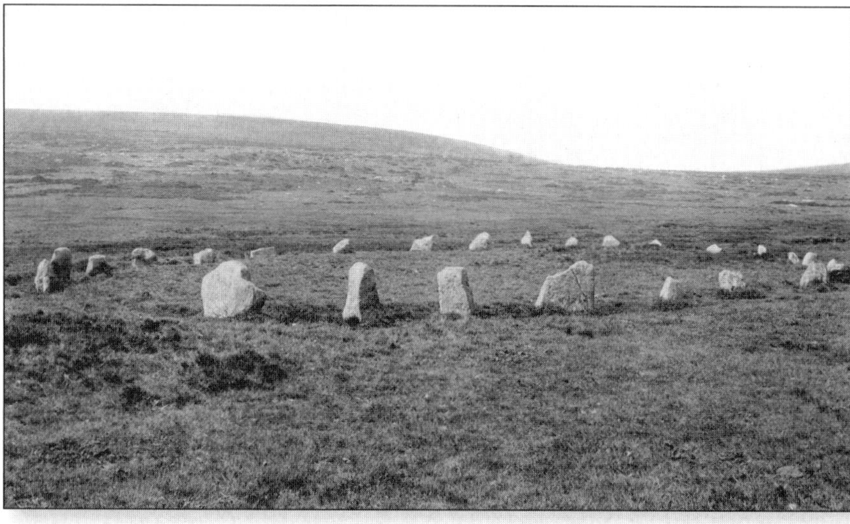

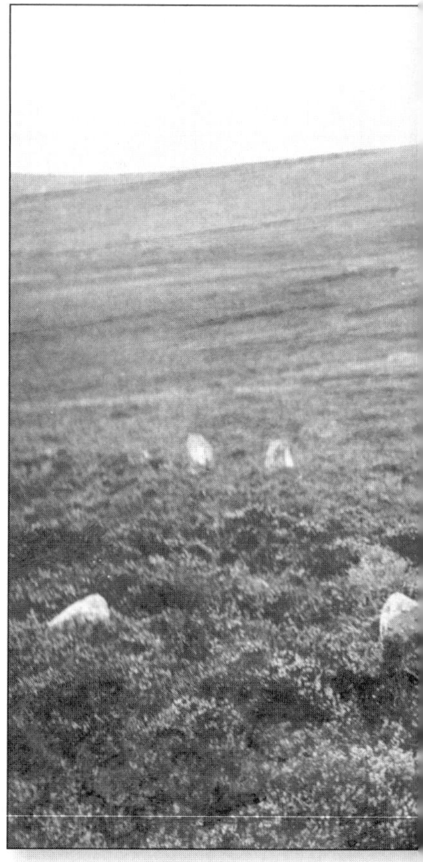

ABOVE: FERNWORTHY, THE SACRED CIRCLE 1907 58486

It is probable, given the number of stone circles found on Dartmoor, that a family or a group of families erected them for ritual worship, either to venerate the dead or for an astronomical purpose. The entire inner area of Fernworthy circle was found to have been strewn with charcoal. This could have come from pyres on which bodies were placed, or perhaps from burning autumn stubble.

ABOVE RIGHT: CHAGFORD, KESTOR ROCKS 1924 76490

Rising to 1433 feet, the boss of Kestor serves as a prominent landmark with its outlying granite rocky basin, as seen when approaching from Chagford.

RIGHT: CHIPPING NORTON, THE ROLLRIGHT STONES C1960 C288073

The integrity of the Rollright stones, which stand near the A34 in Oxfordshire, cannot be verified. There are today 77 stones that make up the circle, yet in the 17th century a drawing by John Aubrey shows only 25 standing stones. Time and man have ravaged the limestone uprights. They are not all original; some are the broken tops of stones, others have been wrongly re-sited. The stones evoke mystery and abound with folklore that even the famous Sir Arthur Evans (who excavated Knossos, Crete) recounts in some detail; unfortunately, space does not permit it to be included here.

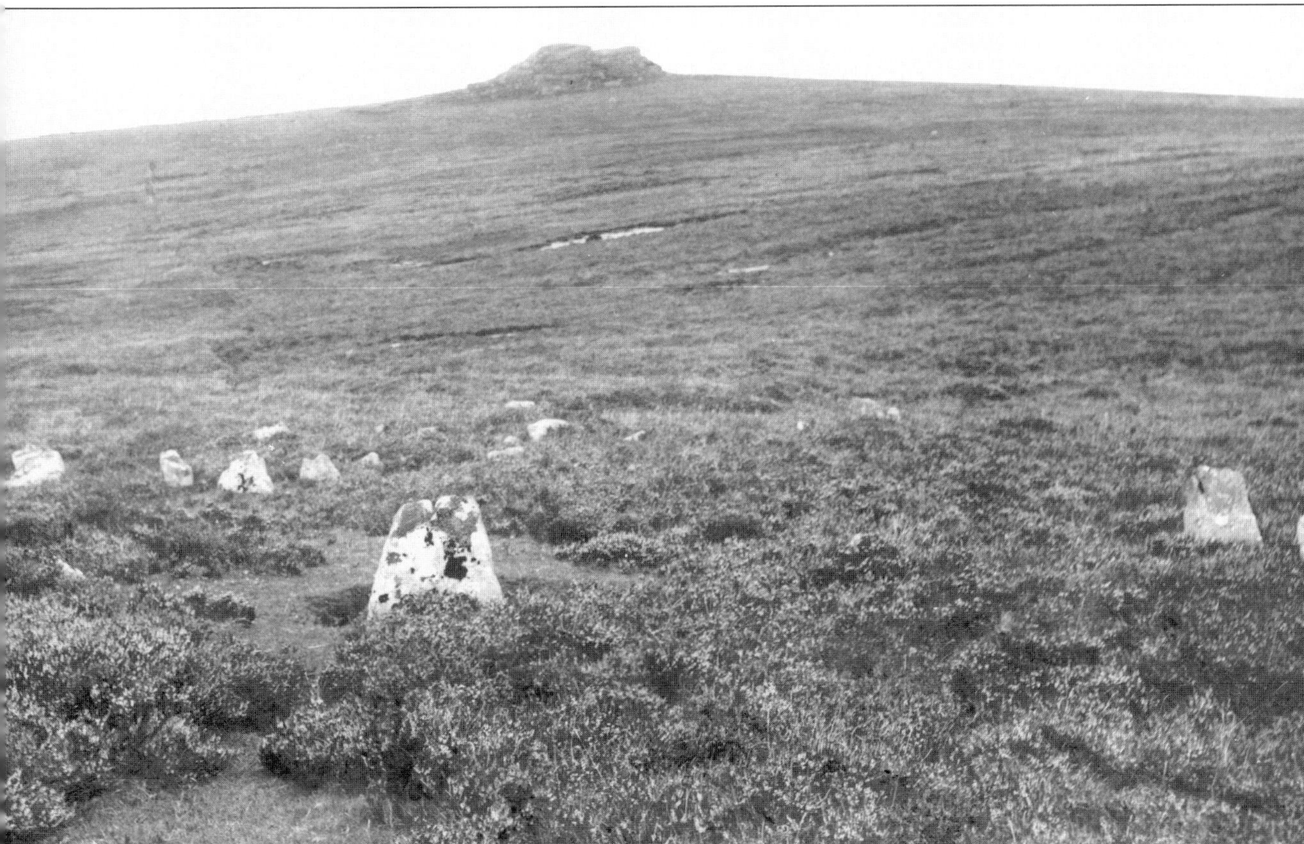

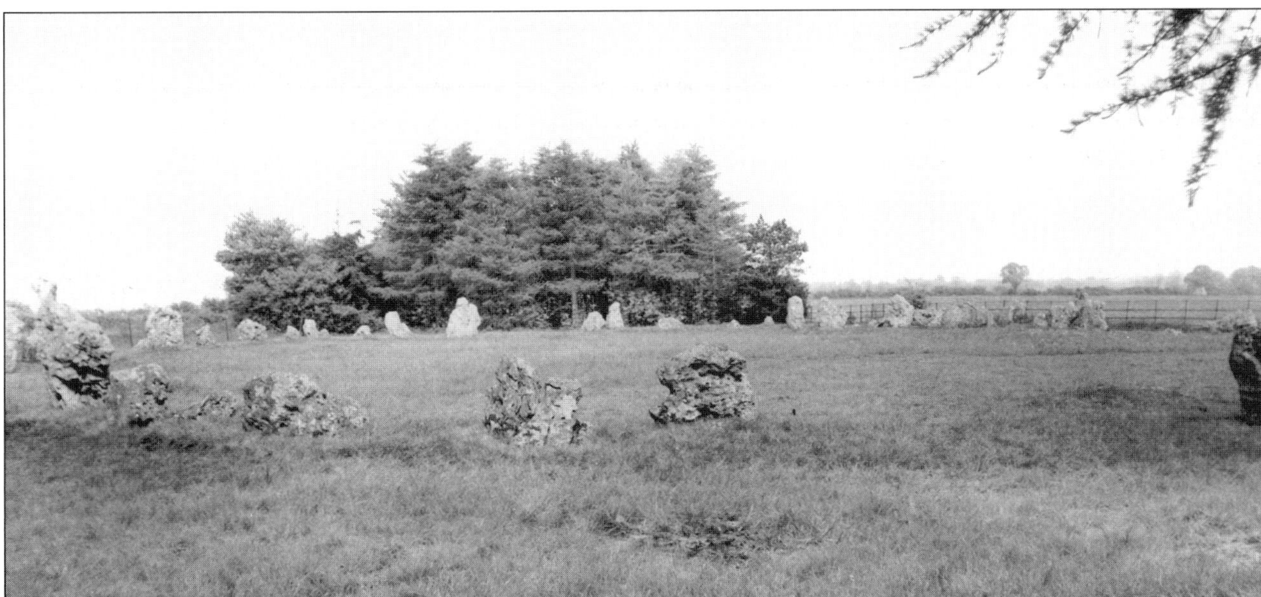

STONE CIRCLES

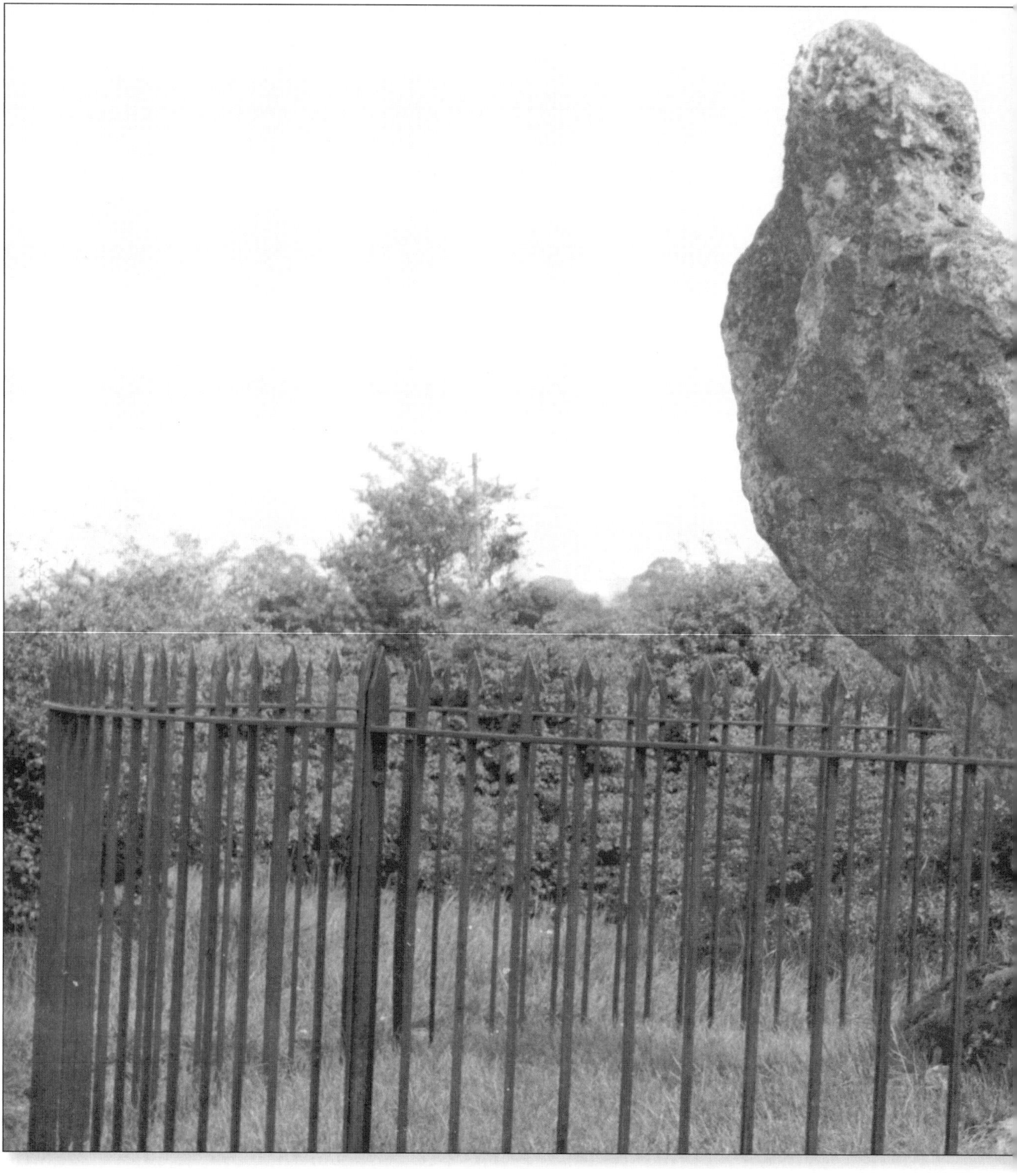

CHIPPING NORTON, THE KING STONE, ROLLRIGHT STONES c1960 C288070

Next to the circle is the railed King Stone, badly deformed by weather and people. The railings do little to enhance its setting. It was considered a magical stone where barren women would press their breast against the stone in hope of a child! Local people used to meet at the stones once a year for merrymaking, and in Tudor times there are reports of witches using the circle as a meeting place.

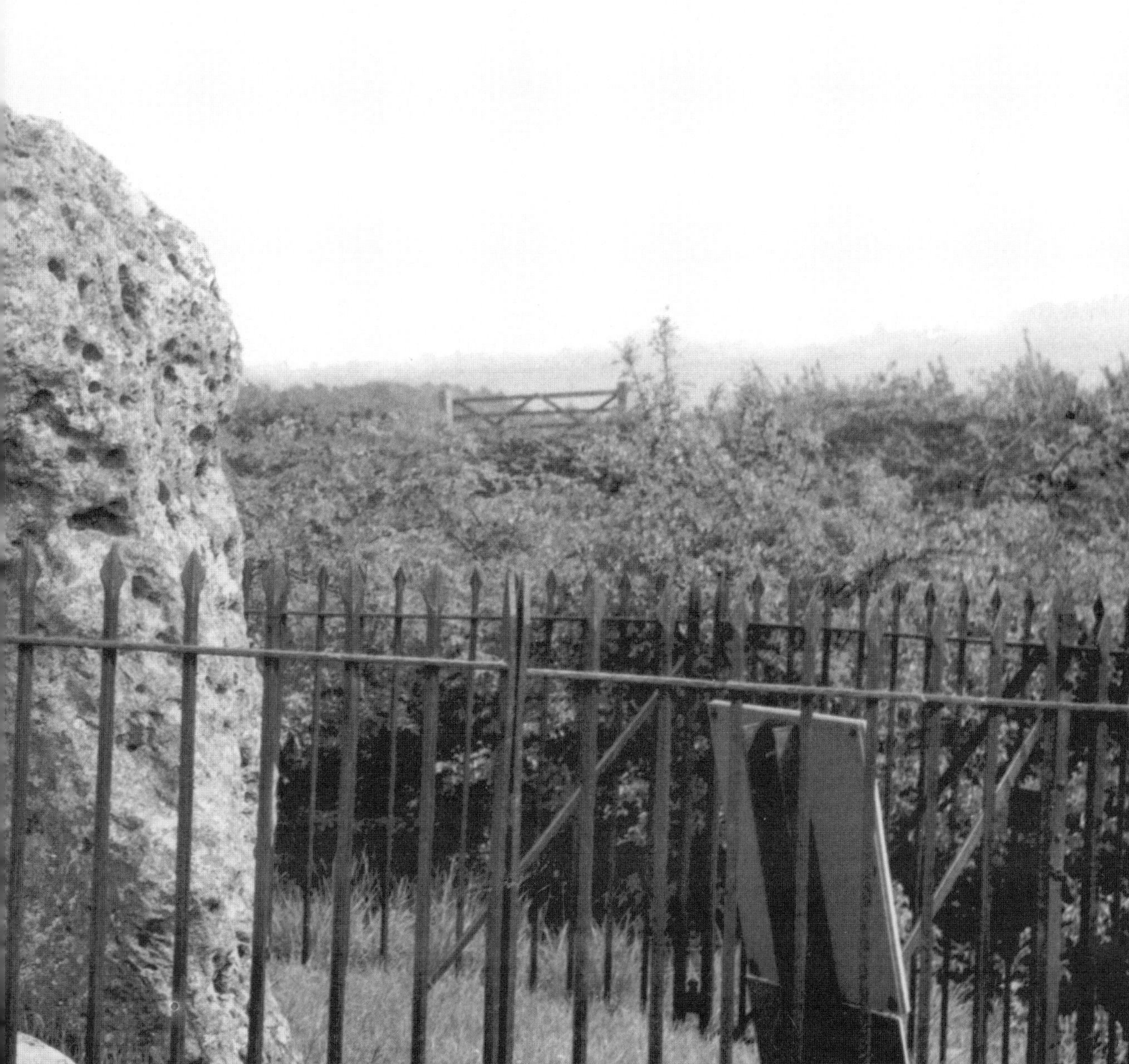

Stone Circles

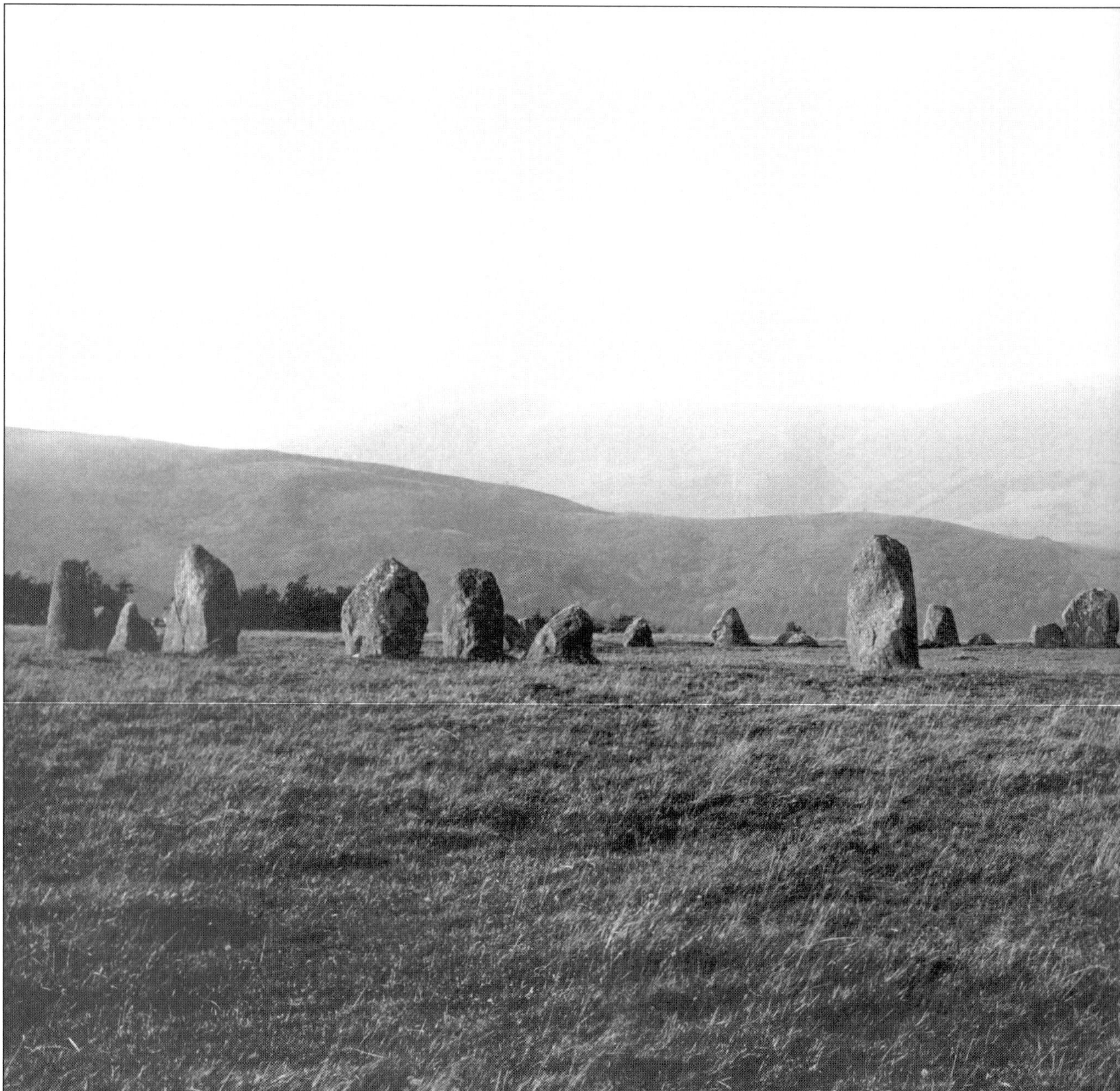

Right: Keswick, The Castlerigg Circle 1895 36950

Thirty-eight millstone grit stones form the circle, which is about 100 feet across. The circle has an attractive setting on a little rise against Castlerigg Fell. To the east there is an outlying stone, over which the sun rises at the spring and autumn equinoxes. To the south-west is another stone in the direction of the midwinter sunset, which is a far more useful calendar date for ancient agricultural communities.

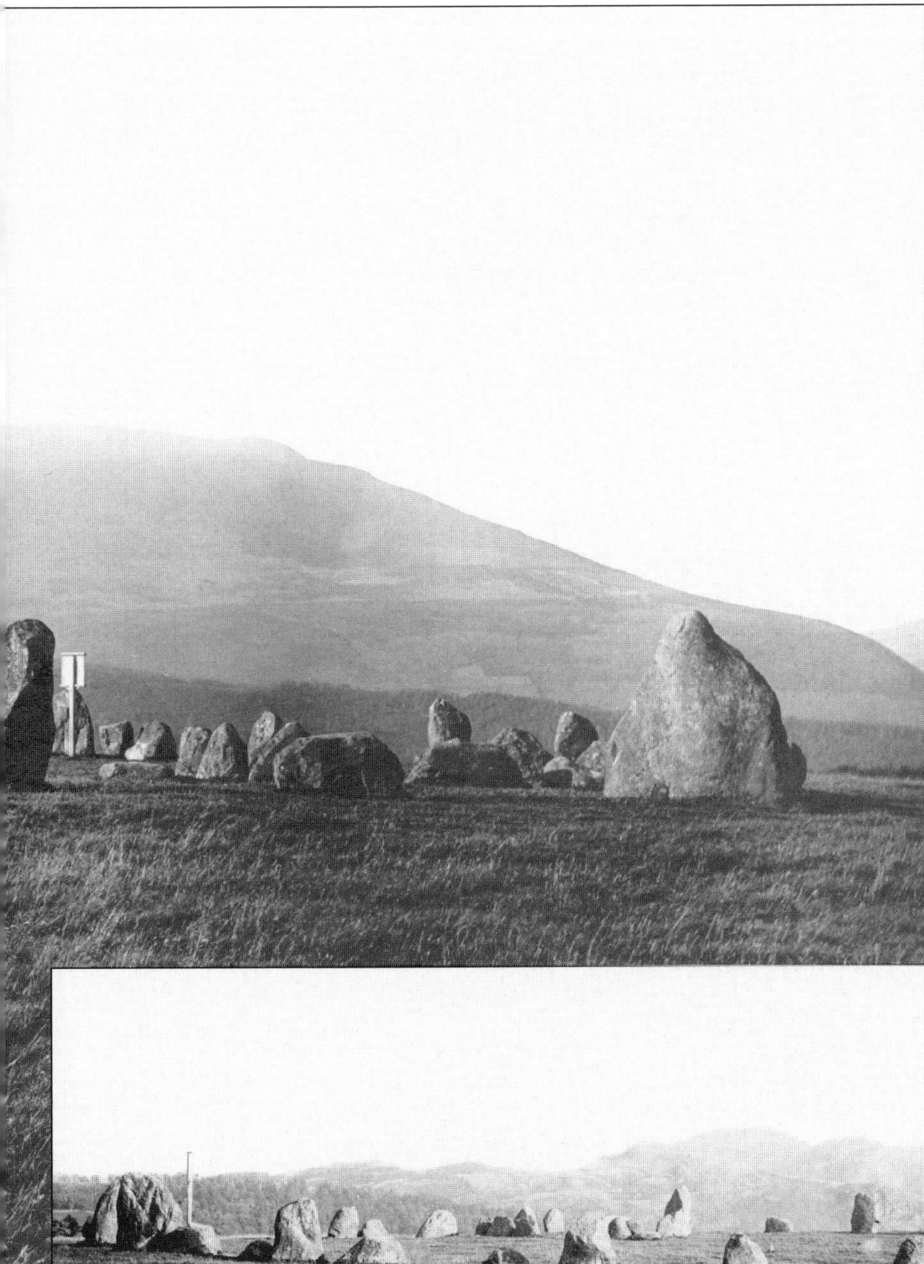

LEFT: KESWICK
THE CASTLERIGG CIRCLE 1895
36951

Set against the background of the Lakeland peaks, the Castlerigg circle, near Keswick, forms a beautiful setting for what is considered to be one of the oldest stone circles in England. It is also still known as the Druids' circle, though it was erected long before Druids ever existed on these shores.

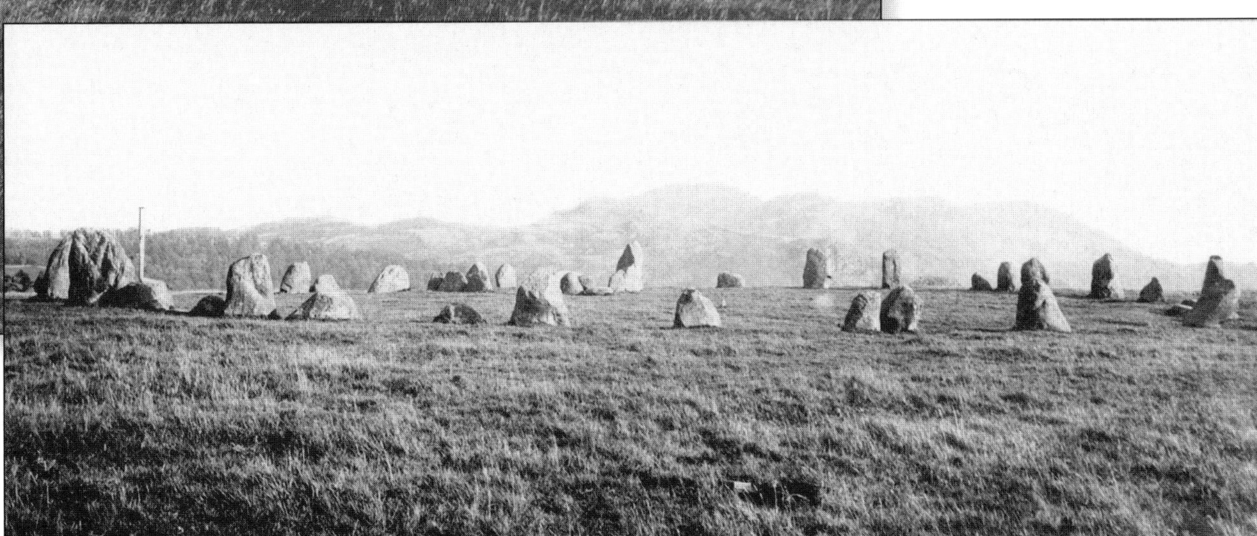

STONE CIRCLES

KESWICK, THE CASTLERIGG CIRCLE 1889 22090

At the northern end the two largest stones form an entrance; inside, just visible to the left of the photograph, on the eastern side of the circle, are the remains of ten stones arranged in an oblong, whose purpose is unknown.

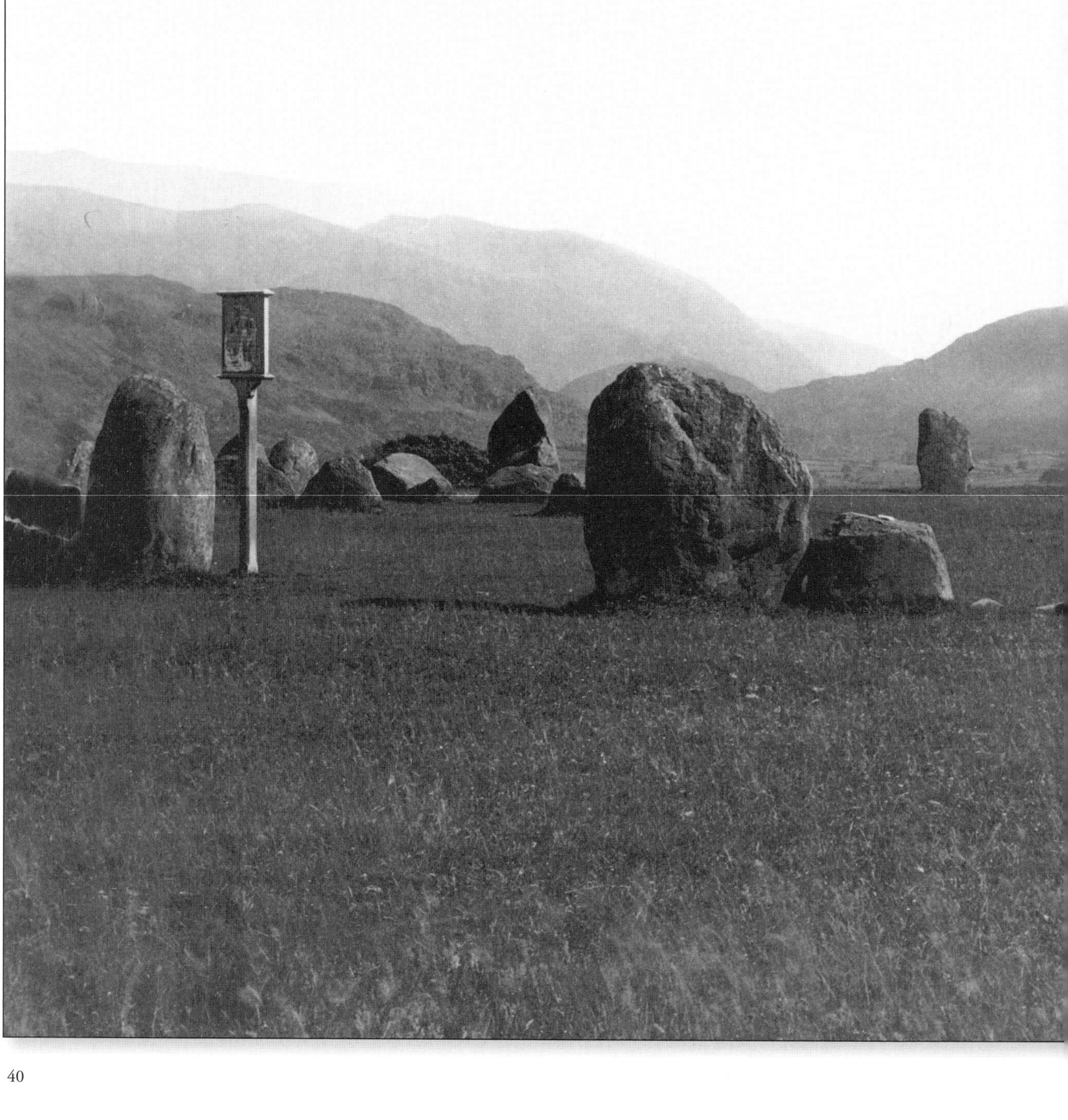

Stone Circles

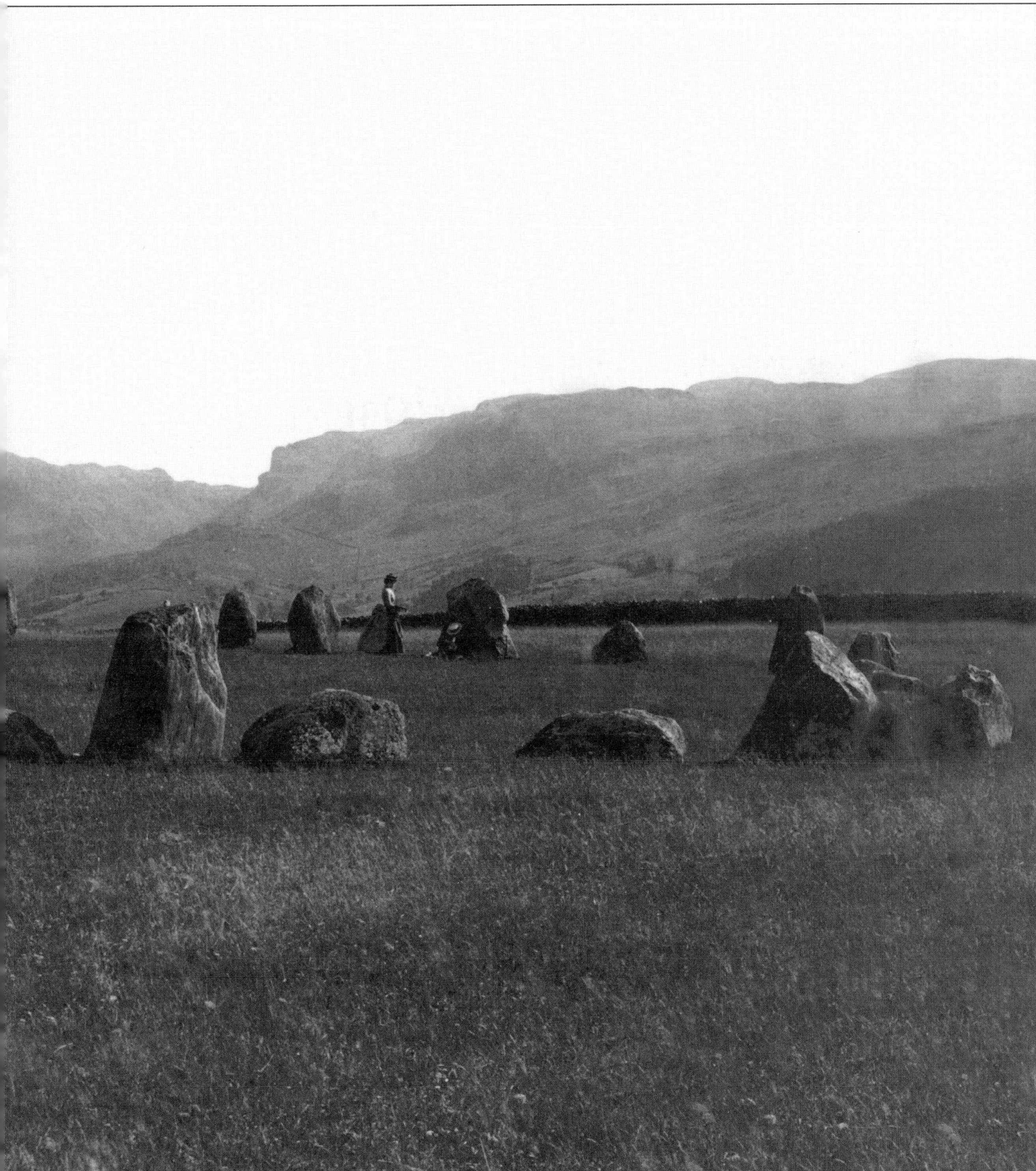

Burial Mounds

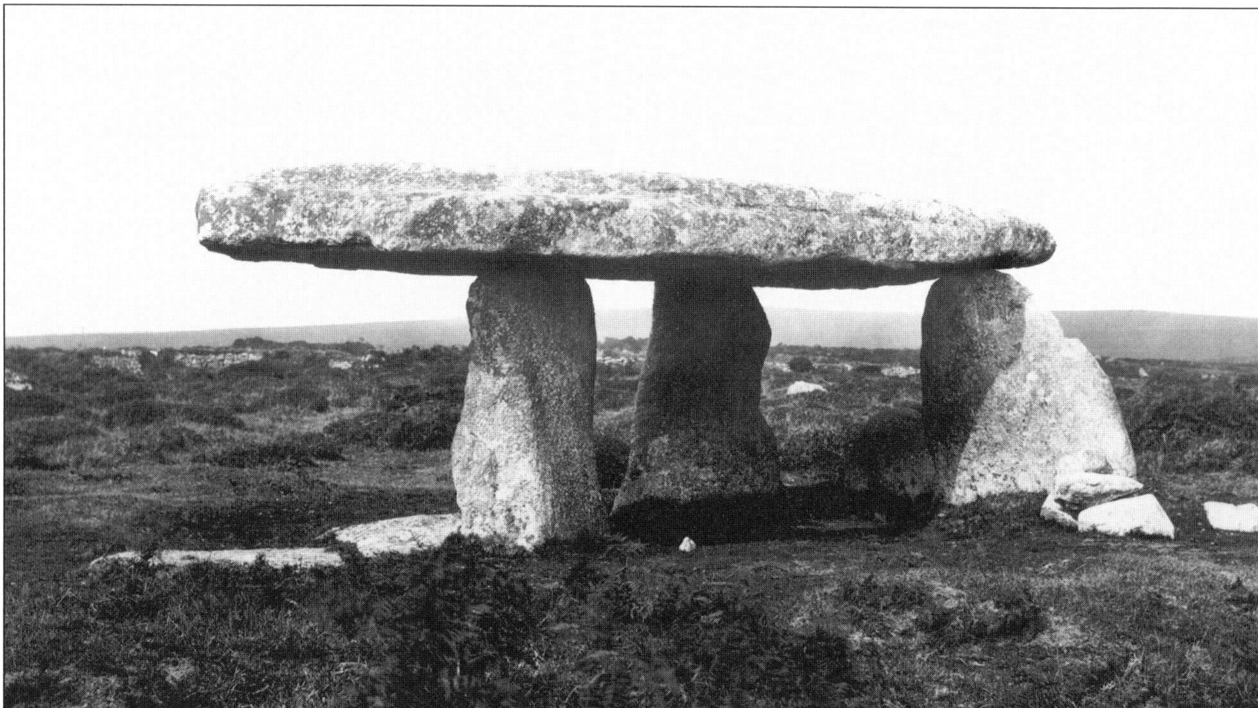

The burial mounds described here straddle the Neolithic and Bronze Age periods. The use of a chamber was commonplace until, late in the Bronze Age, the practice either became too labour-intensive or customs simply changed.

The Neolithic people in the west country built tombs with a single chamber; in Wessex, they could contain five or more separate compartments. Geography and the ease of readily-available building materials probably played a part in determining custom and practice. Unlike the practice in other areas, complete skeletons were not buried in these chambers, and thus few skulls have ever been discovered. The custom seems to have been to allow the body to decompose on funerary piles; then, after a ritualistic ceremony, the bones would often be scattered around a chamber or placed in convenient gaps in the stone walls. Over the chamber or chambers a massive earthen mound was piled, which could be clearly seen and recognised as a special resting-place for the bones of chieftains or important people.

Burials in the Bronze Age tended to differ, depending on whether burials belonged to the Early Bronze Age (the Beaker period) or the later Middle and Late Bronze Age. The Beaker Folk mostly buried contracted skeletons, to signify the re-birth or sleeping position, and the burial was generally accompanied by a beaker of hand-made pottery. In the case of the most famous barrow, Bush Barrow near Stonehenge, the skeleton of a man lying from south to north was found in 1808. At his side were two Bronze Age daggers, one with a wooden hilt decorated with thousands of minute gold pins. Near his leg was a mace, symbol of a chieftain perhaps, an axe and the remains of a wooden shield decorated with bronze. A lozenge-shaped gold plate was at his chest, and an engraved hook of hammered gold at his waist. This has been by far the most glamorous discovery of a Bronze Age tomb; it reveals how far man had progressed since the days of those early Neolithic settlers.

The Middle and Later Bronze Age people tended to cremate their dead and put the remains in an urn, which was often inverted and placed at the bottom of the barrow before being covered with the traditional earthen mound.

BURIAL MOUNDS

LEFT: LANYON QUOIT 1890 22985

Near the Madron-Morvah road in Cornwall, this Neolithic burial chamber was restored in 1824 when the capstone fell to the ground during a storm. It was most certainly originally higher, and would have had a large earthen mound over it. The chamber would probably have contained the bones of local chiefs.

BELOW: AVEBURY, SILBURY HILL 1902 48647

Silbury Hill, near Marlborough, is the largest man-made mound in Europe. It was once thought (justifiably at that time) to be a large burial mound for an important Bronze Age chieftain. Excavations, however, have revealed nothing of particular interest, other than the fact that it was started in August - the foundations revealed evidence of flying ants! It predates the Roman road, now the A4, whose early track can be seen in the photograph. In 1883 it was the first site in Britain to be classified as an ancient monument.

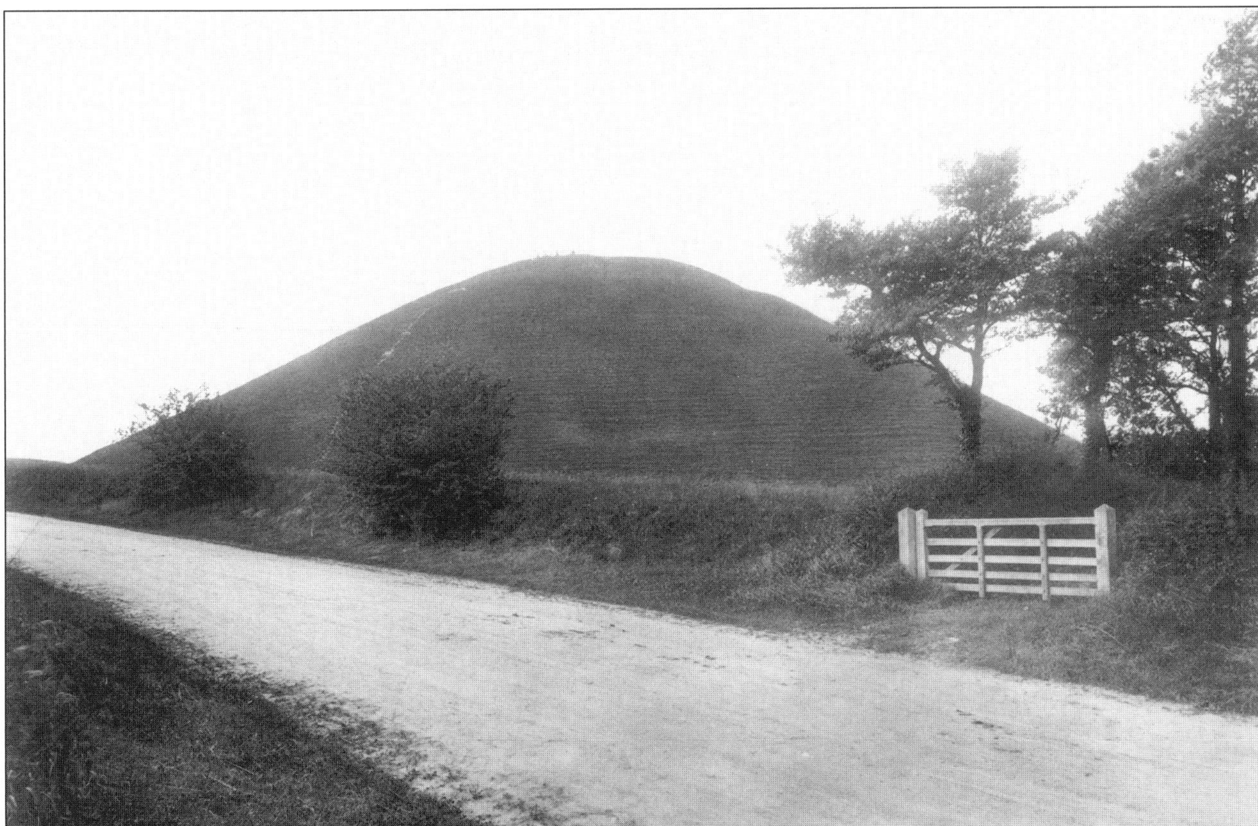

BELOW: LISKEARD, THE TRETHEVY STONES 1890 24475

Six uprights form the walls, and the massive capstone is 11. feet long. The name Trethevy means 'place of the dead'.

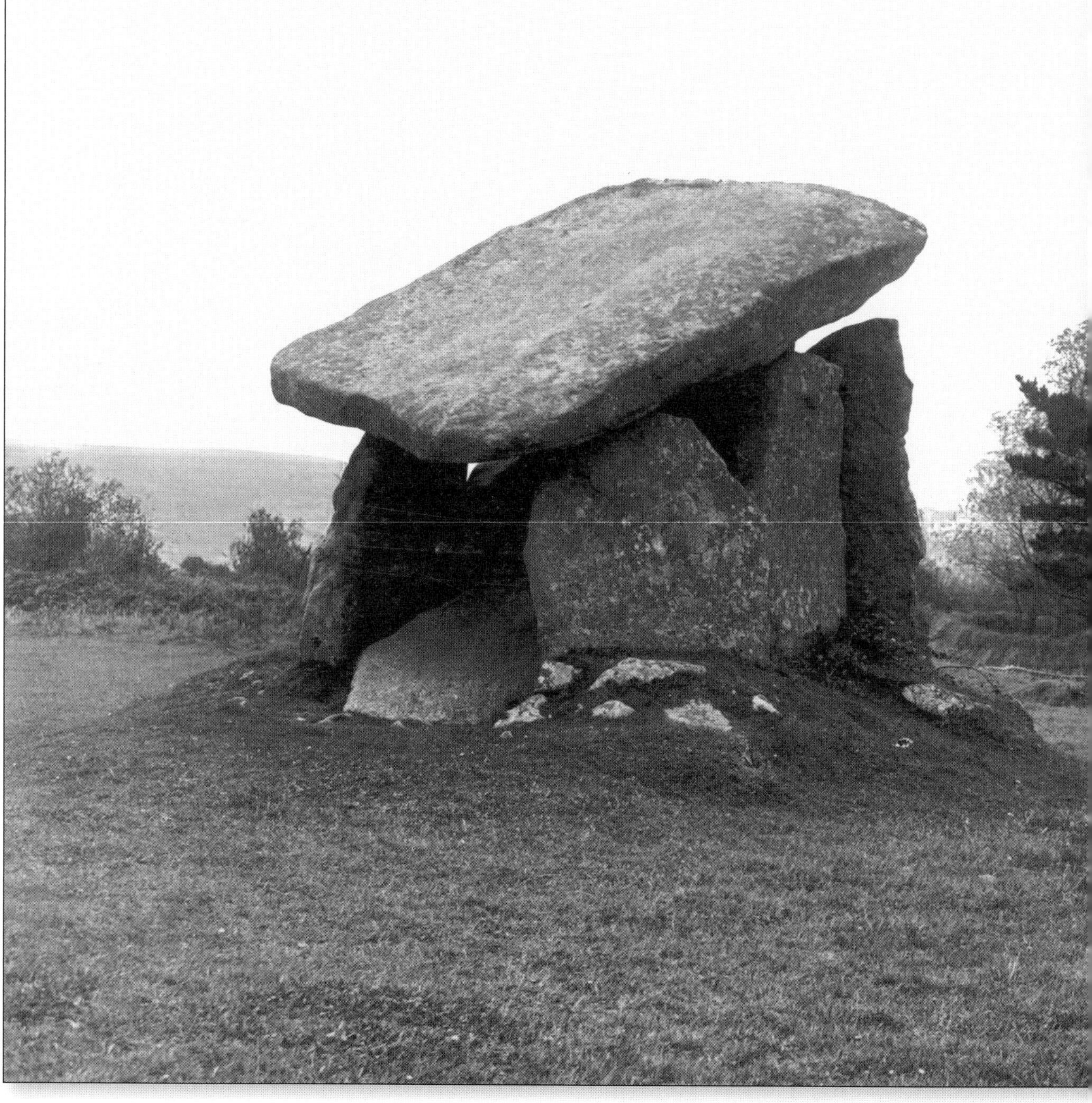

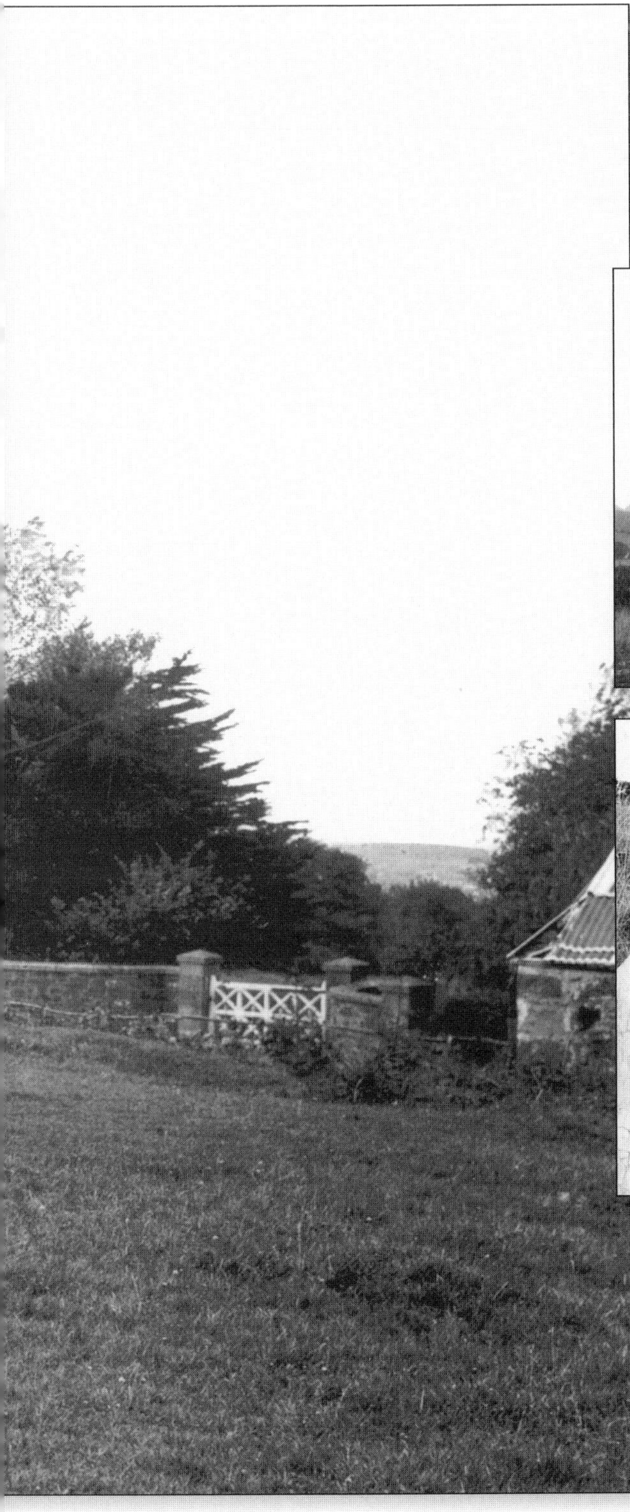

LISKEARD, THE TRETHEVY STONES C1960 L53018

On Bodmin Moor stands the spectacular burial mound Trethevy Quoit. It contained two chambers for the dead and was originally covered by a large oval mound; this was last recorded in the 19th century, but is now obliterated by man and time!

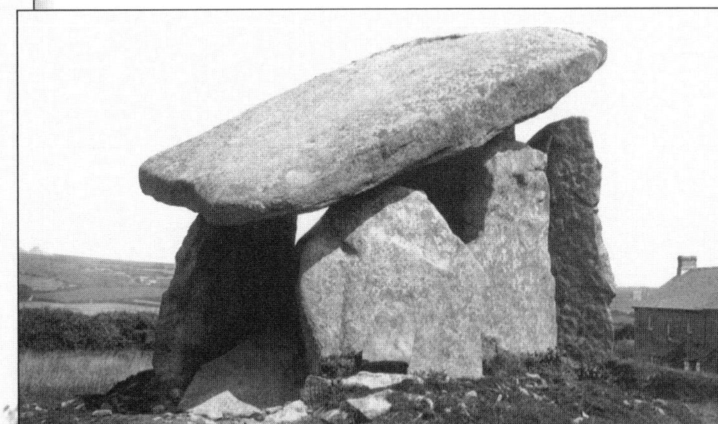

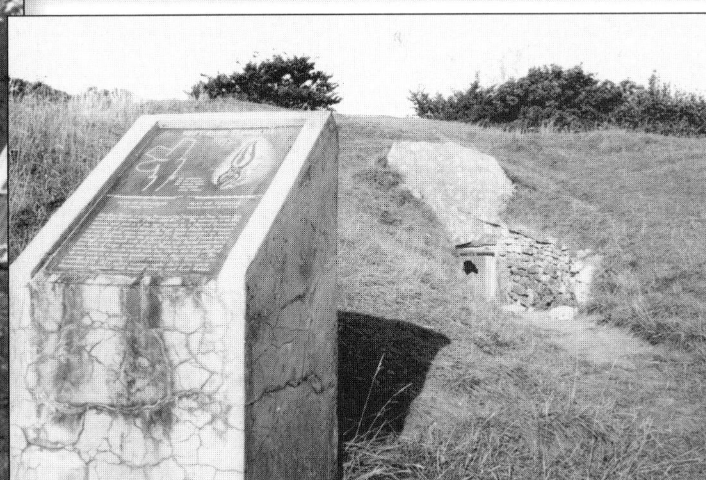

ABOVE: ULEY, THE TUMULUS C1960 U3008

Little can be appreciated of this magnificent burial chamber from this photograph. It is known as Hetty Pegler's Tump, and is in Gloucestershire. It contains five burial chambers opening from a central gallery in which decomposed bodies were placed. It belongs to the Neolithic period, and is a fine example of a long barrow. Its unusual name comes from the wife of its 17th-century owner.

BURIAL MOUNDS

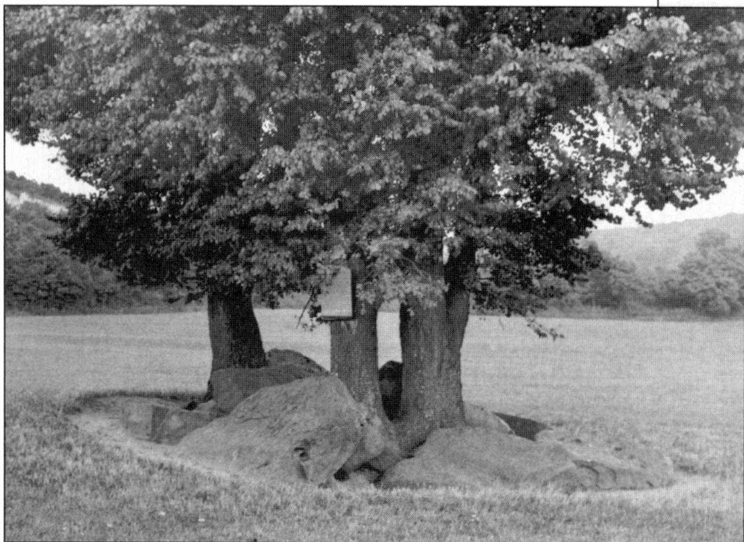

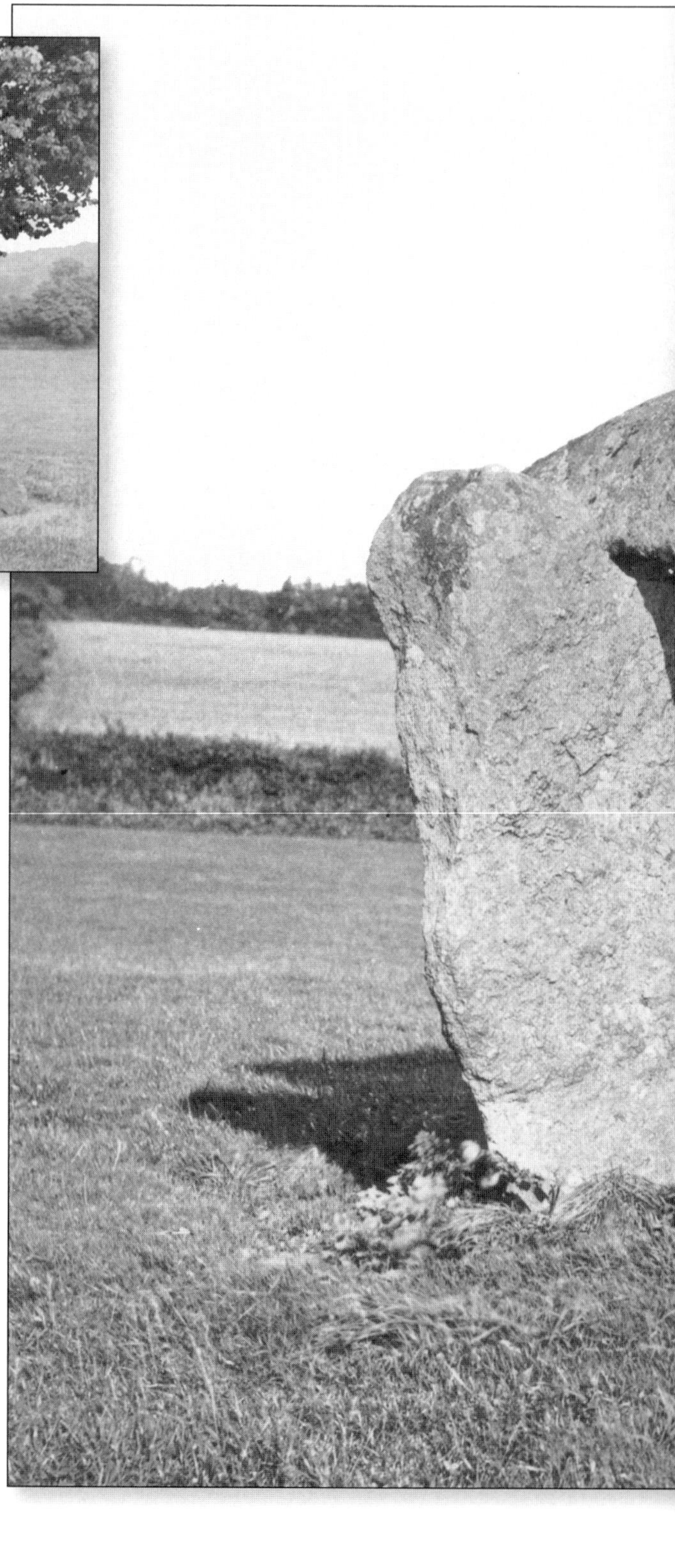

AYLESFORD, THE COUNTLESS STONES c1960 A85044

Beneath a clump of trees near Aylesford, Kent, is a confused group of sarsen stones, some twenty in number, which probably formed a Neolithic burial chamber 5,000 years ago. Now known as Little Kit's Coty House, the stones were believed to help barren women to conceive. It was also said that you could never count the stones more than once and come to the same total - hence its name.

CHAGFORD, SPINSTER'S ROCK c1871 5801

Spinster's Rock is in Devon, near Drewsteignton. The three uprights also give rise to its name: it is recounted that three spinsters erected this monument before breakfast! The covering mound has long since disappeared - it is believed that it was probably oval-shaped. In 1862 it was restored after collapsing.

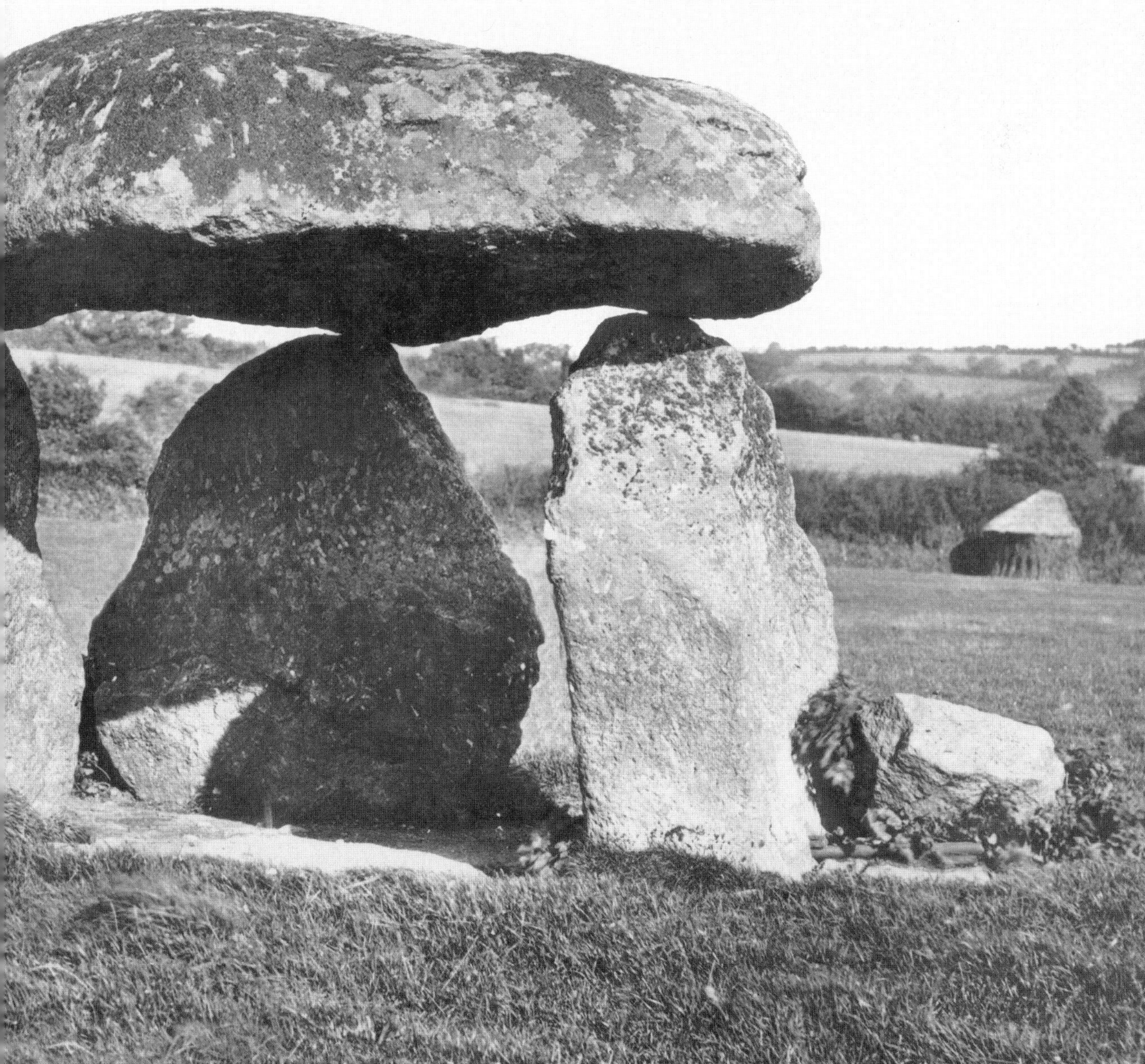

Burial Mounds

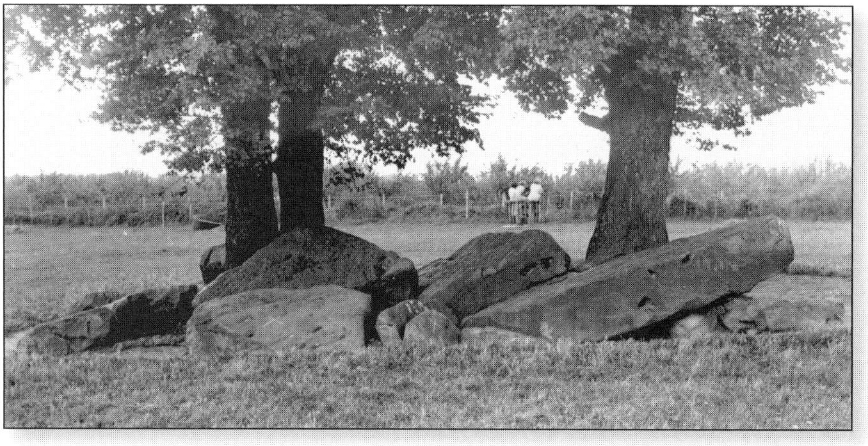

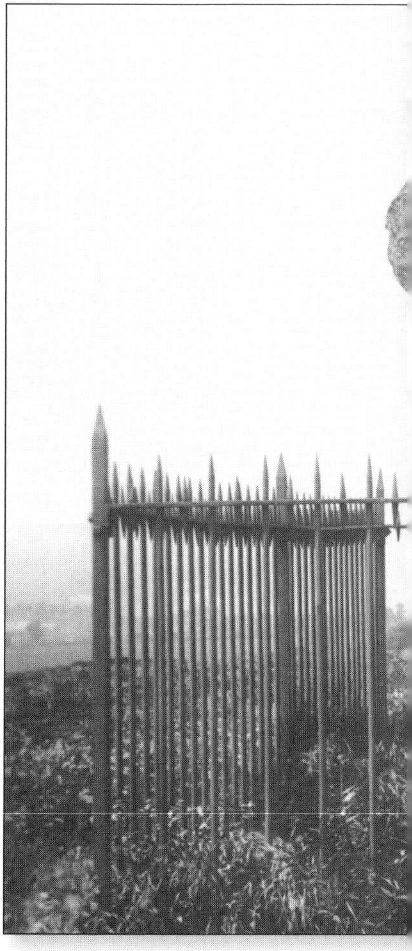

ABOVE: AYLESFORD, THE COUNTLESS STONES c1960 A85043

In the 1930s, traces of the mound covering the stones could still be traced. In the 17th century William Stukeley published a reconstruction of the stones, which were formed into a D-shaped structure. It is reported that a farmer knocked down the stones in 1690. The trees have now been removed.

ABOVE RIGHT: AYLESFORD, KIT'S COTY HOUSE 1898 41555

To the west of the A229 is Kent's most famous Neolithic burial chamber. The capstone measures 13 feet by 9 feet, and the earthen mound, which covered the stones, was 170 feet long. Legend has it that the burial mound was the tomb of Catigern, a British chief killed fighting the Saxons, although it is actually far older.

FAR RIGHT: AYLESFORD, KIT'S COTY HOUSE c1960 A85040

The ugly iron railings do little to enhance or exploit this fine dolmen; it is sad that it may well be the price society has to pay for preserving one of the oldest man-made monuments in Britain - it dates from about 5,000 years ago.

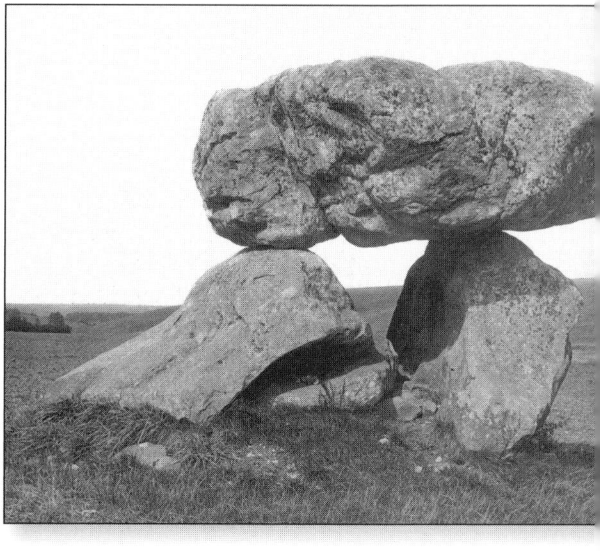

RIGHT: MARLBOROUGH, DEVIL'S DEN 1901 47674

Devil's Den, near Marlborough in Wiltshire, is an example of how the ravages of the plough is nothing more than intentional vandalism. Further, it is known that there were at least five more stones in the collection. What has happened to them? The stones have now been restored and partly concreted in place. This was once a magnificent chambered long barrow that was covered with a brilliant white chalk mound. It sits snugly in the Downs near to the Ridgeway and Avebury stone circle.

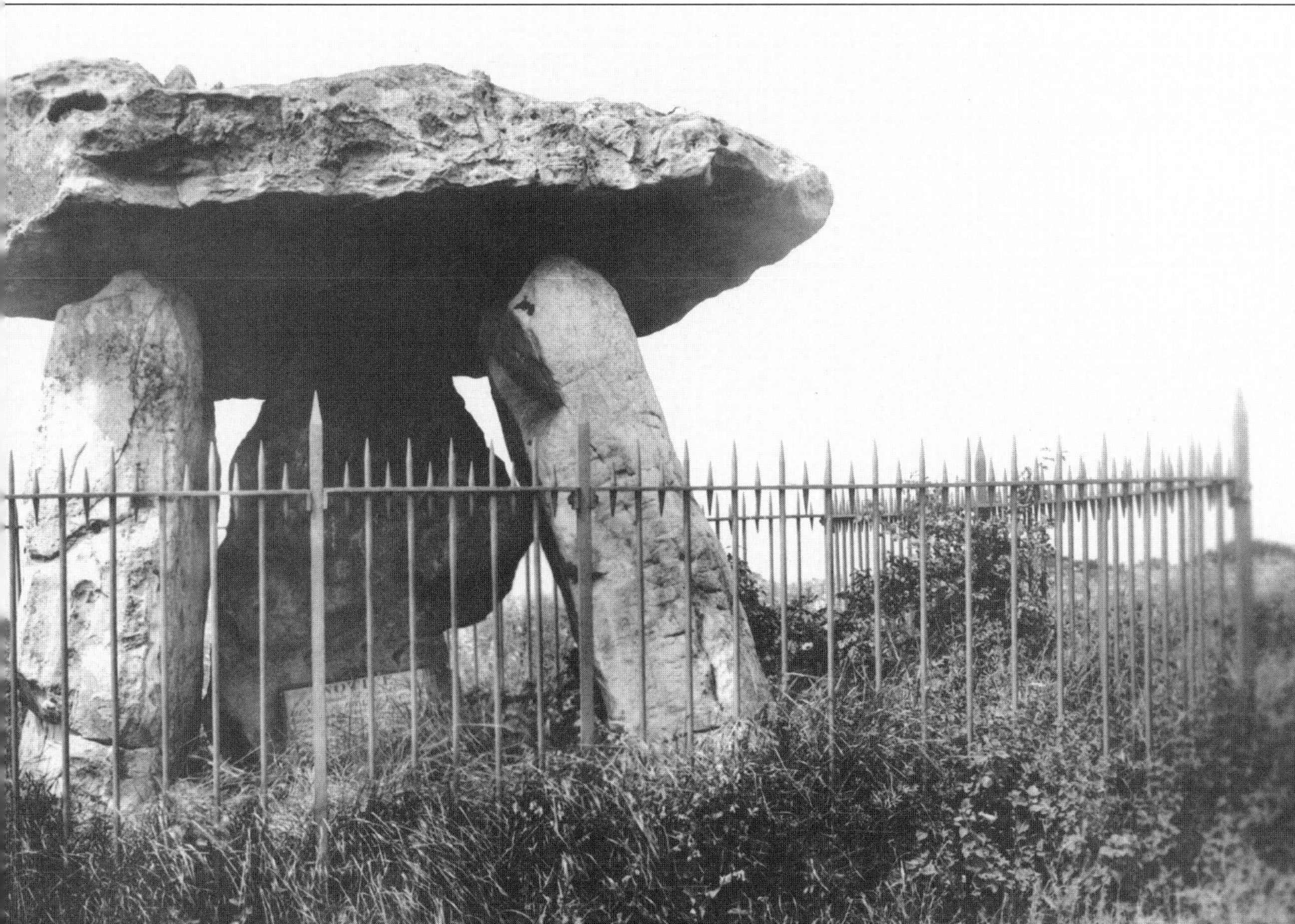

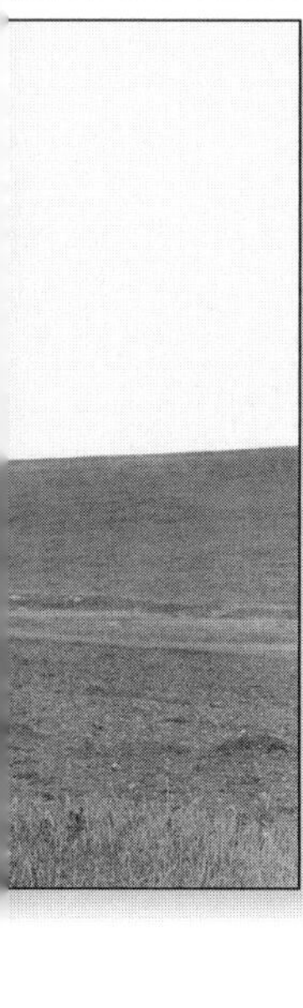

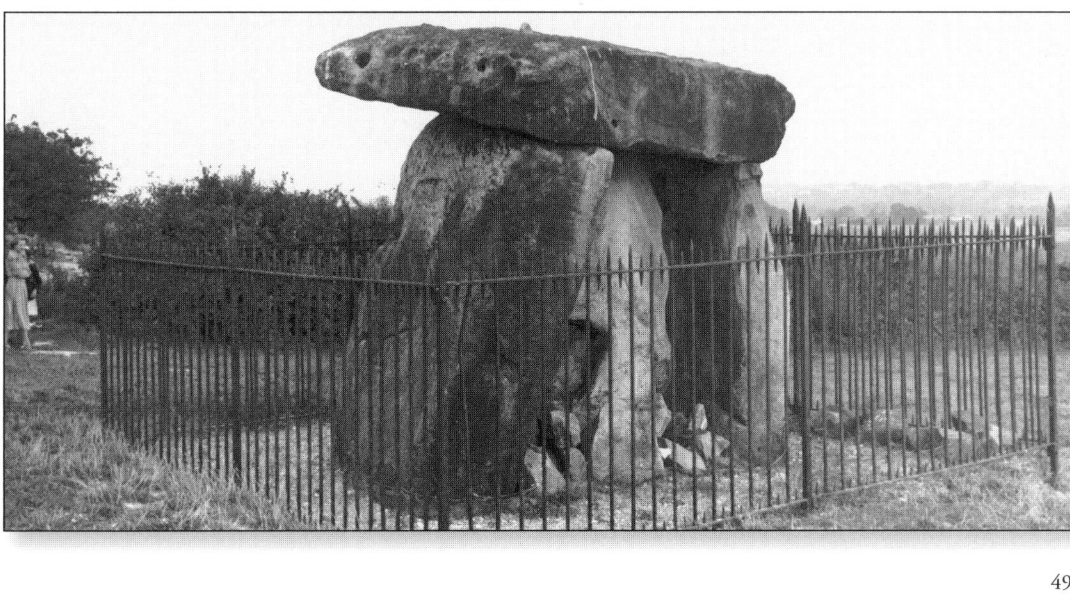

STANDING STONES

Standing stones are particularly associated with the Celtic peoples of Cornwall, Devon, Wales, Ireland and the northern part of Britain. Some stones are nothing more than geographical outcrops of an unusual or prominent nature to which legend and folklore has given a story that has become enshrined with the stone's very existence. Other stones demand more careful research, especially when they are associated with a particularly famous person: these stones are often inscribed with Latin script, and belong to the Romano-British period. Others are much older, and can be dated from the Bronze Age. Some are engraved with cup-and-ring markings - still an unsolved mystery - and can be found throughout Celtic culture. The variety of the stones' geographical position invites yet more conjecture. Those found in lonely spots on the Cornwall or Devon moors must surely be some form of way-marker, which may indicate the way to a stone circle or, in more recent times, to a church. Others, which may occupy a more prominent position, still baffle the archaeologist. However, a link with some form of astronomical alignment cannot be lightly dismissed. The people who erected these stones were much more in contact with the movement and understanding of the stars, sun and moon: therefore, predicting full moons, eclipses and the shortening or lengthening of the days were of vital importance to their beliefs and livelihood.

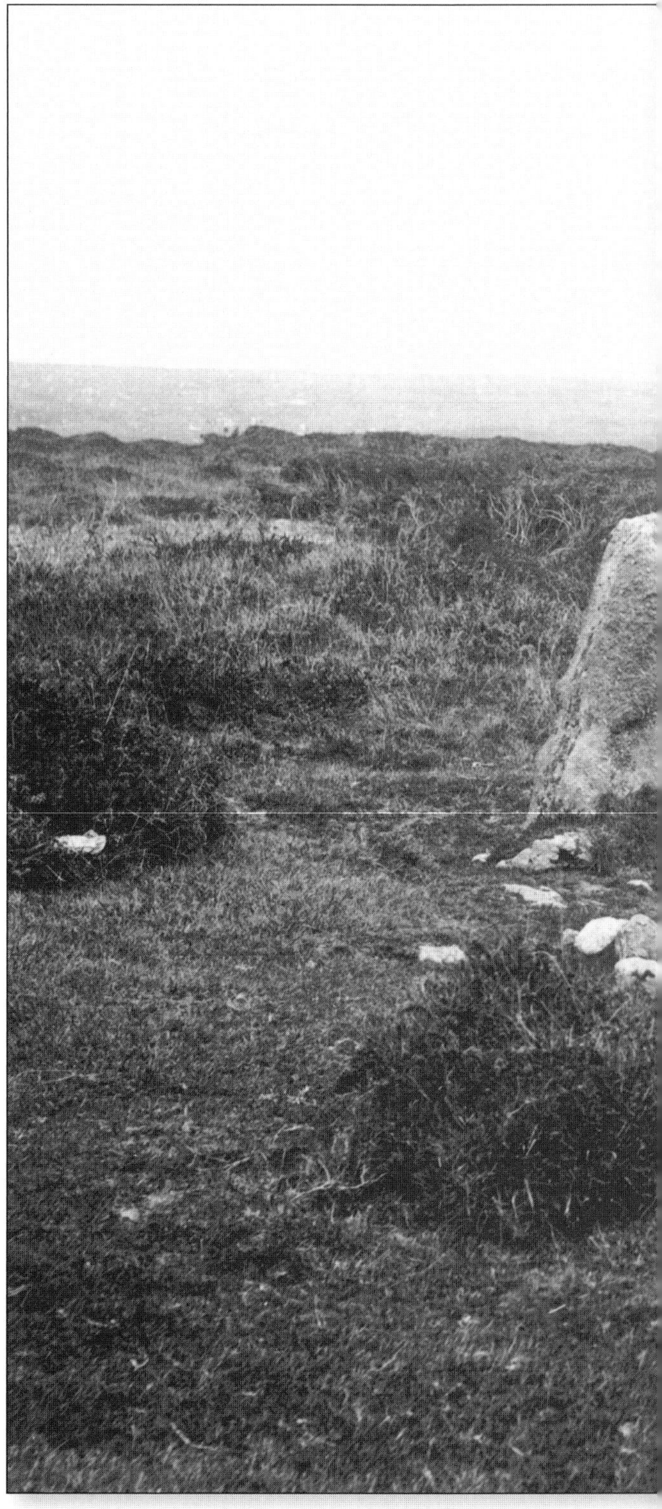

MEN AN TOL 1890 22986

Men an Tol means 'stone of the hole'; this most famous of Cornish landmarks probably belongs to the Neolithic period. Inevitably, legend and myth concerning its use abound: it is said that children were passed through the hole to cure rickets and skin diseases. Adults who were sufficiently slim could ward off fevers by crawling through the hole nine times against the sun! Since this photograph was taken, the site has been tidied and the ground worn smooth by visitors. Some historians claim that the holed stone was the entrance to a Neolithic tomb. Perhaps: but the phallic nature of the stones seems to point strongly to other ritual customs.

& STONE CIRCLES STANDING STONES

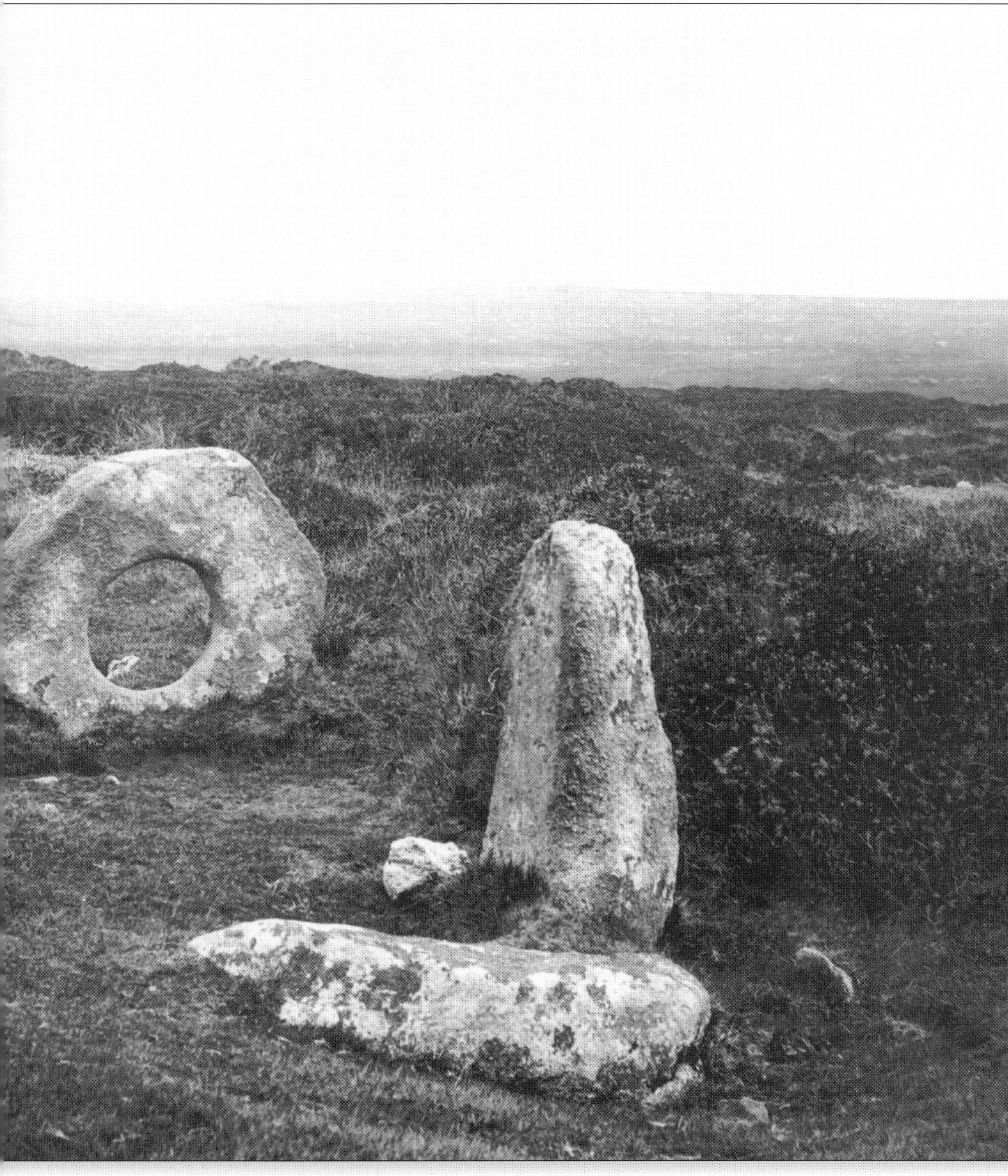

STANDING STONES

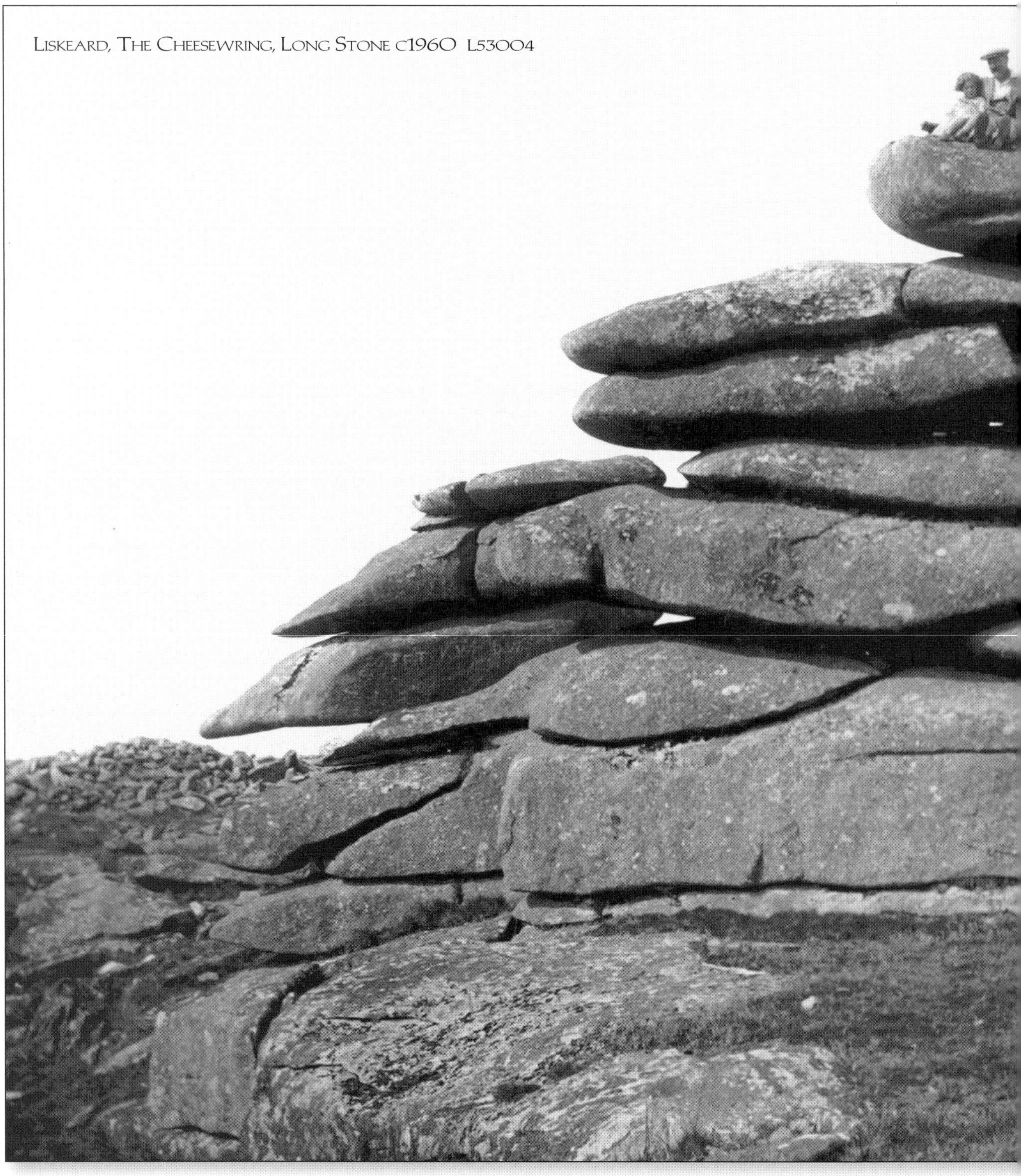

LISKEARD, THE CHEESEWRING, LONG STONE c1960 L53004

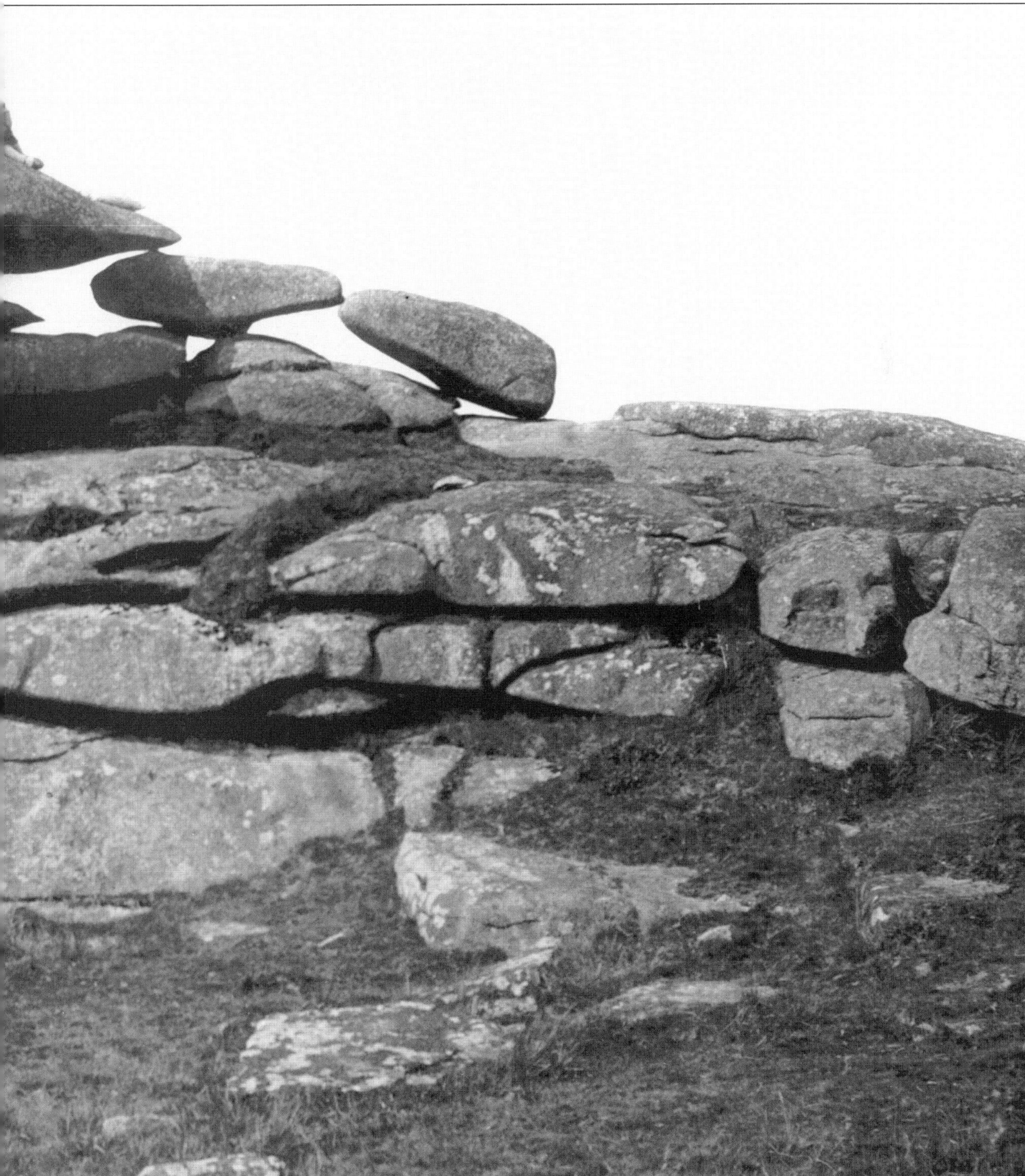

LISKEARD, THE CHEESEWRING 1908 59772

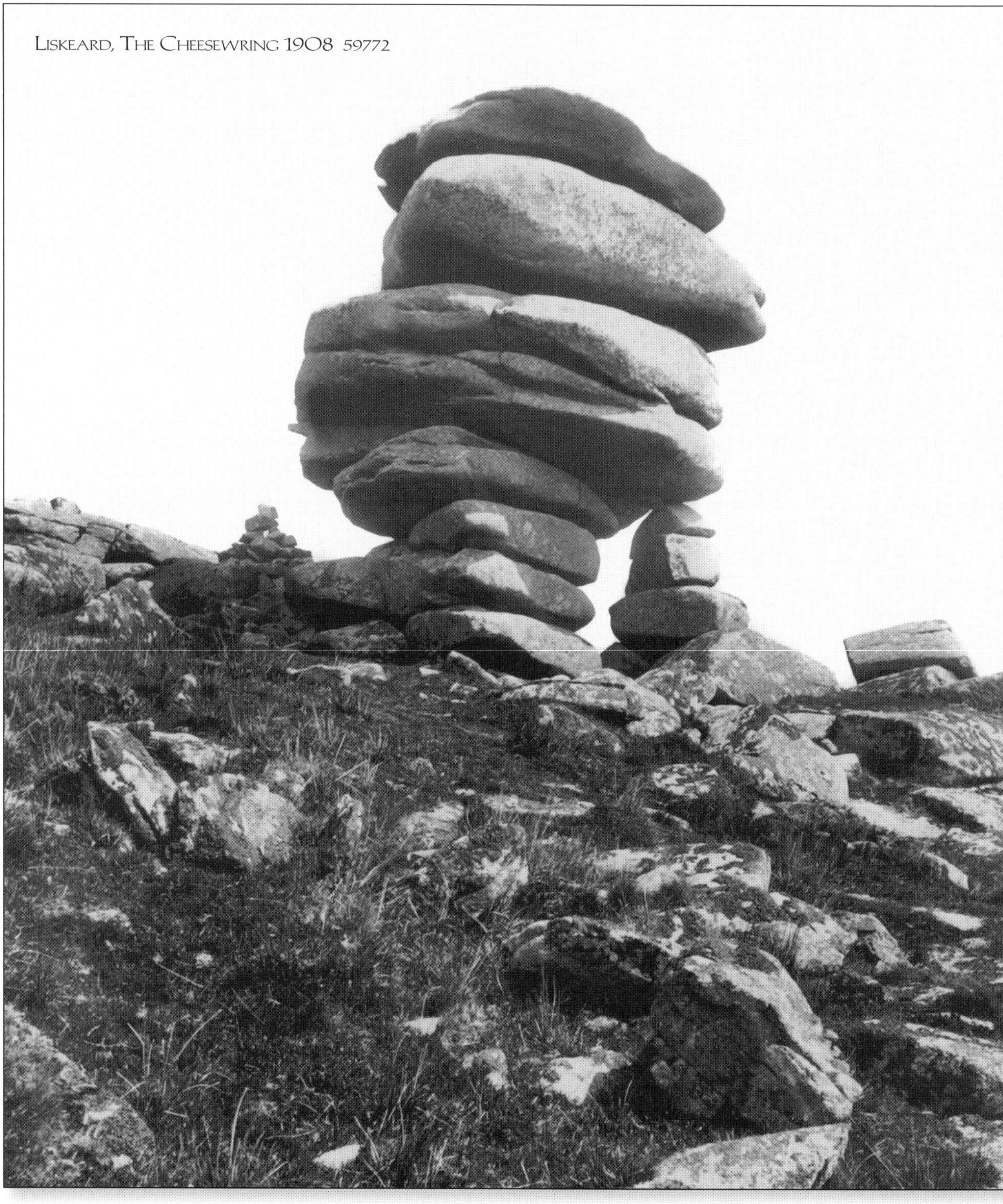

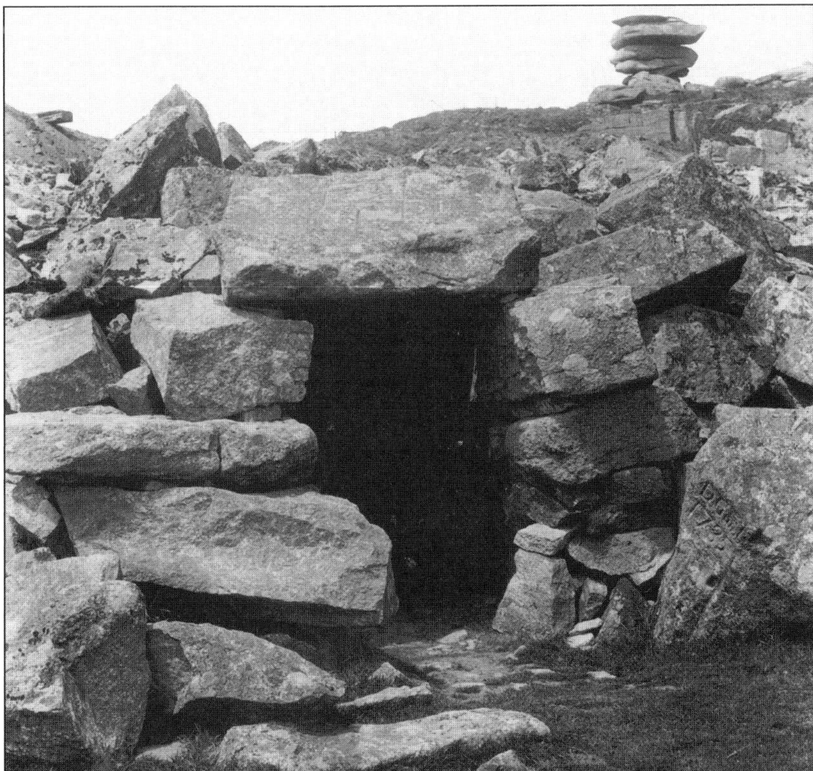

LEFT:
LISKEARD, THE CHEESEWRING, DANIEL GUMB'S HOUSE 1908 59773

The granite stone of Bodmin Moor supports a natural oddity, the impressive outcrop known as the Cheesewring. The summit of the hill encloses a stone fort probably associated with the Bronze Age. The work of nature and man sit comfortably together.

BELOW:
REDRUTH, CARN BREA
THE MONUMENT 1891 29855

Surrounding this monument to Lord de Dunstanville, erected in 1836, are the famous Carn Brea remains, near Redruth. They consist of possibly the oldest known Neolithic village in England, and are dated about 3700BC. It subsequently became home to Iron Age inhabitants, who left behind their circular huts and fort ramparts.

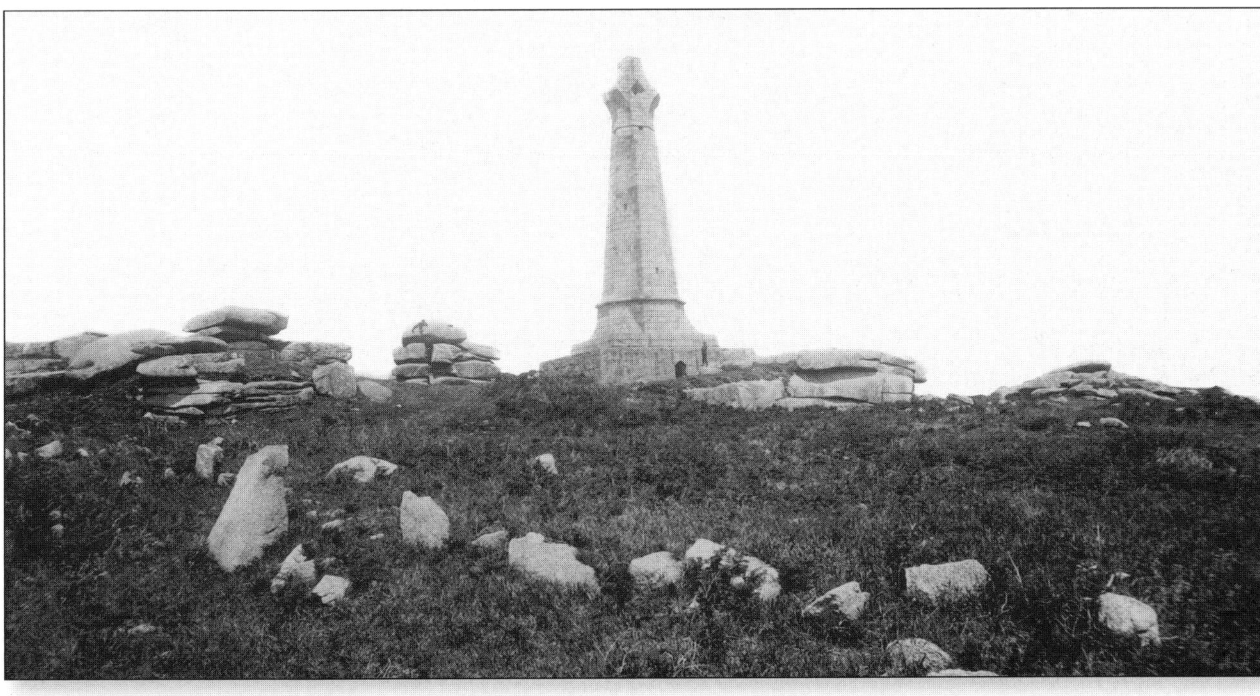

Standing Stones

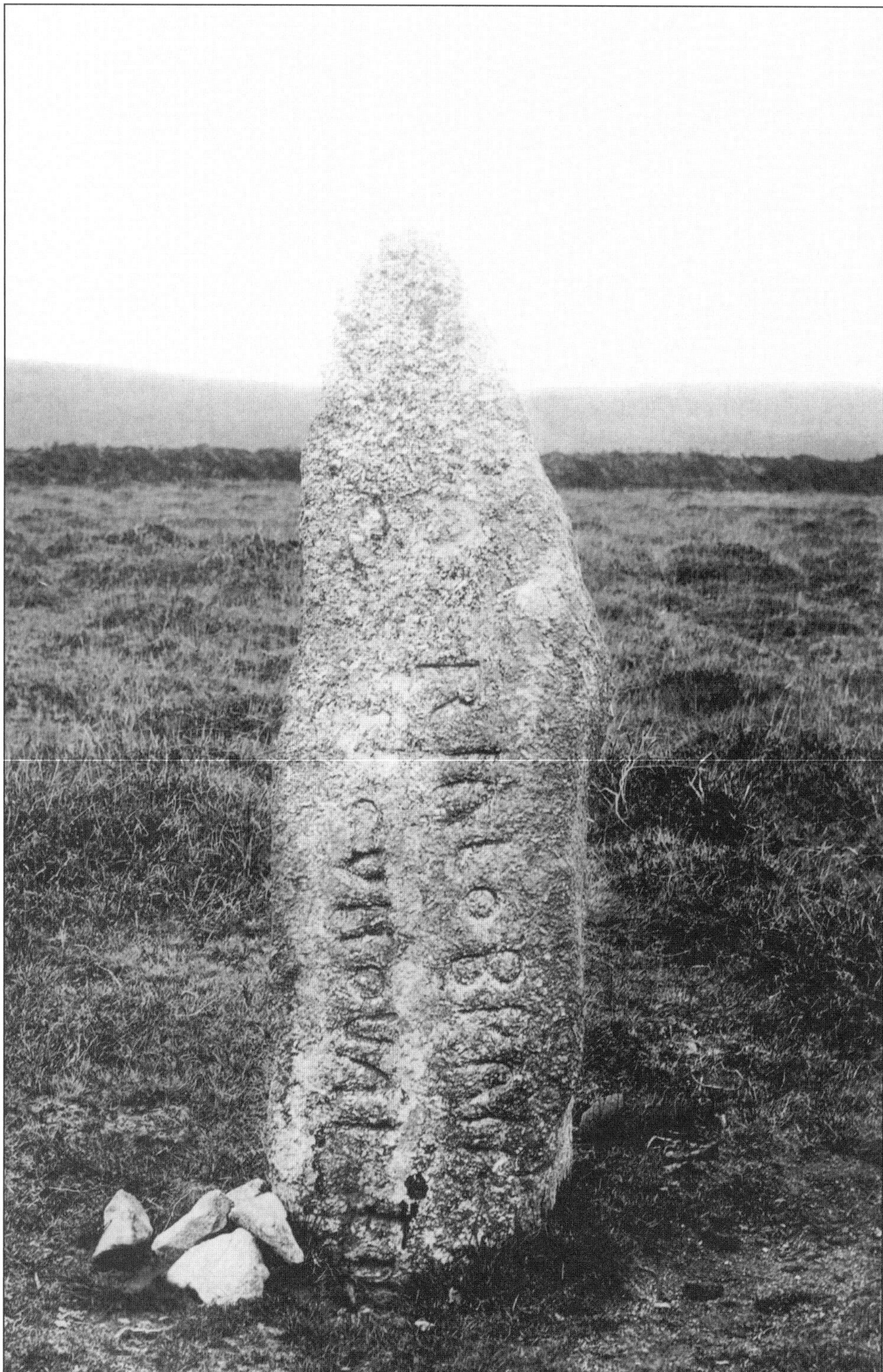

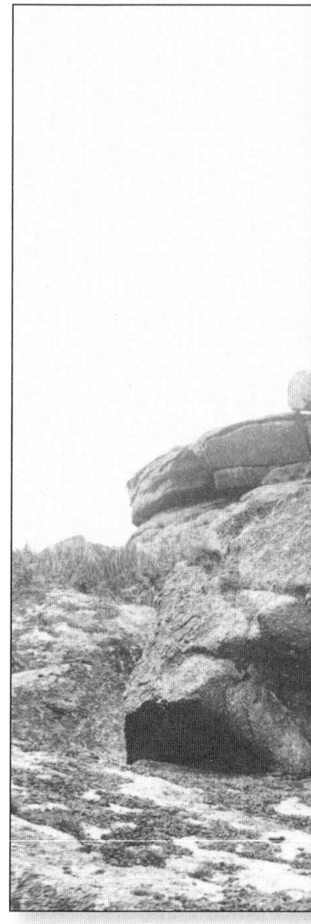

LEFT:
MADRON, MEN SCRYFA 1890 22987

Near the village of Madron, to the north of Penzance, is the 8-foot tall Men Scryfa,which means 'written stone'. It contains a vertical inscription 'Riolobran son of Cunoval' and dates from the 6th century. It is an impressive yet sad monument standing lonely on the bare moor; its meaning is a mystery.

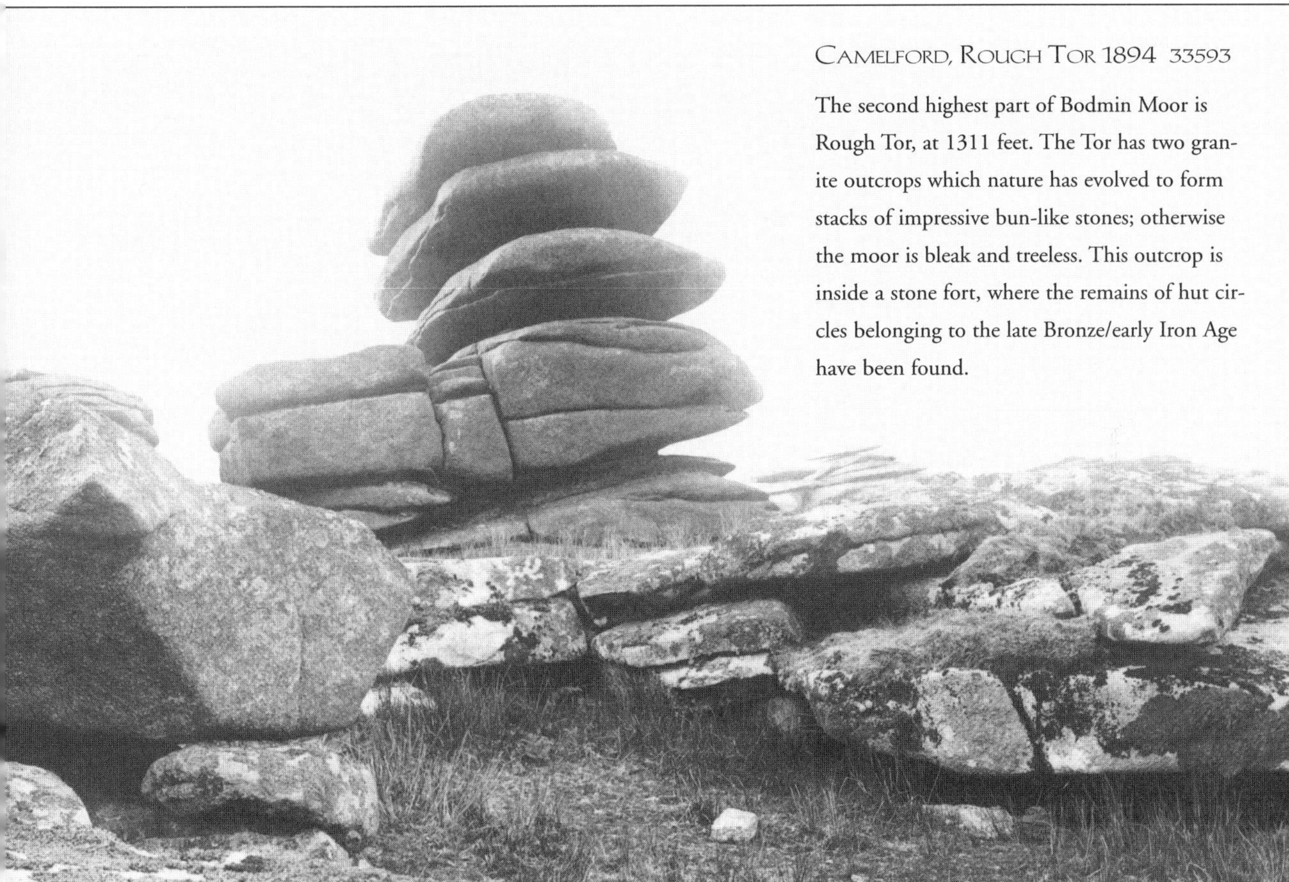

CAMELFORD, ROUGH TOR 1894 33593

The second highest part of Bodmin Moor is Rough Tor, at 1311 feet. The Tor has two granite outcrops which nature has evolved to form stacks of impressive bun-like stones; otherwise the moor is bleak and treeless. This outcrop is inside a stone fort, where the remains of hut circles belonging to the late Bronze/early Iron Age have been found.

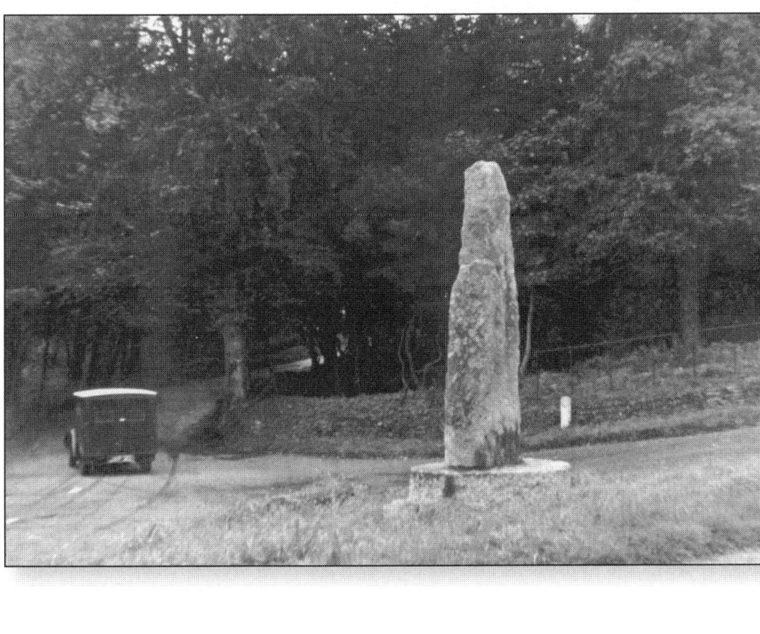

LEFT: FOWEY, THE ANCIENT INSCRIBED STONE AT FOUR TWININGS C1955 33593

This 7-foot-tall inscribed stone stands on the B3269 road, and was moved to its present position from Castle Dore. It is reputed to be of the 6th century. Though the inscription is now too difficult to read, it was said to be 'here lies Drustans, the son of Cunomorus'. Some believe that this refers to Sir Tristram of Lyonesse, who was immortalised in several medieval Arthurian romances.

Standing Stones

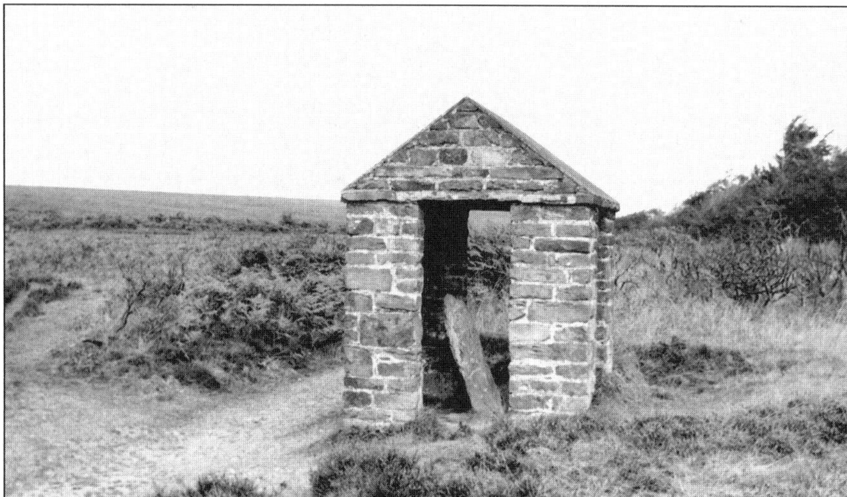

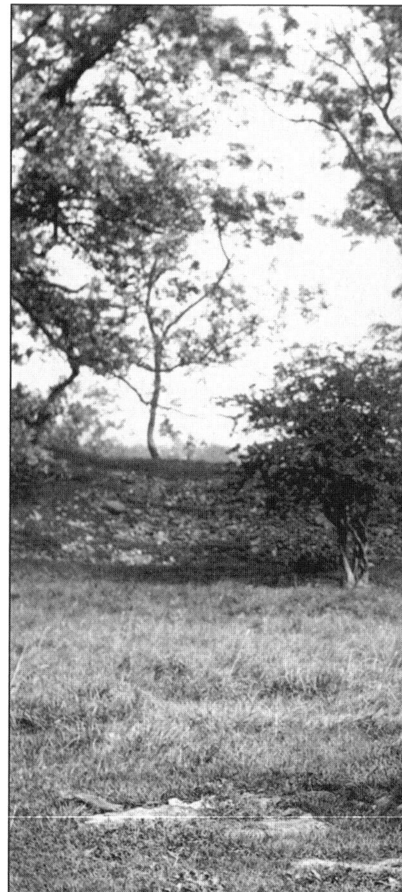

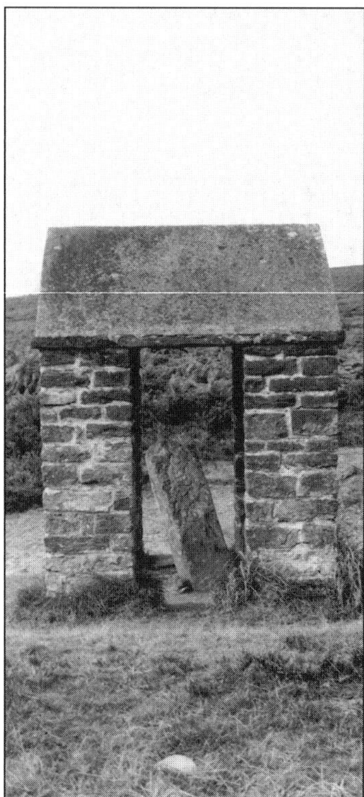

ABOVE: EXMOOR, THE CARATACUS STONE, WINSFORD HILL c1960 E51018

This well-preserved stone (now in the care of the National Trust) is inscribed in Latin 'Carataci Nepus', that is, 'nephew of Caradoc'.

LEFT: EXMOOR, THE CARATACUS STONE c1960 E51017

Caradoc was a British chief who fought against the Romans after they invaded Britain in AD43. He is also known as Caratacus, Caractacus or Caradog.

ABOVE RIGHT: EAMONT BRIDGE, MAYBURGH HENGE 1893 32935

Just south of Penrith, Mayburgh Henge is a circular bank of earth and stones of about 1.5 acres, with one 10ft stone at the centre. It is thought to have been built between 1000BC-2000BC. There were four standing stones at the centre during the 19th century.

FAR RIGHT: LLANBEDR, TWO LONG STONES 1892 30212

Near Llanbedr, about 3 miles from Dyffryn in Wales, are two standing stones, one over 10 feet high. The stones are now enclosed with railings. The Bronze Age Celts almost certainly erected the stones, but their purpose is a mystery.

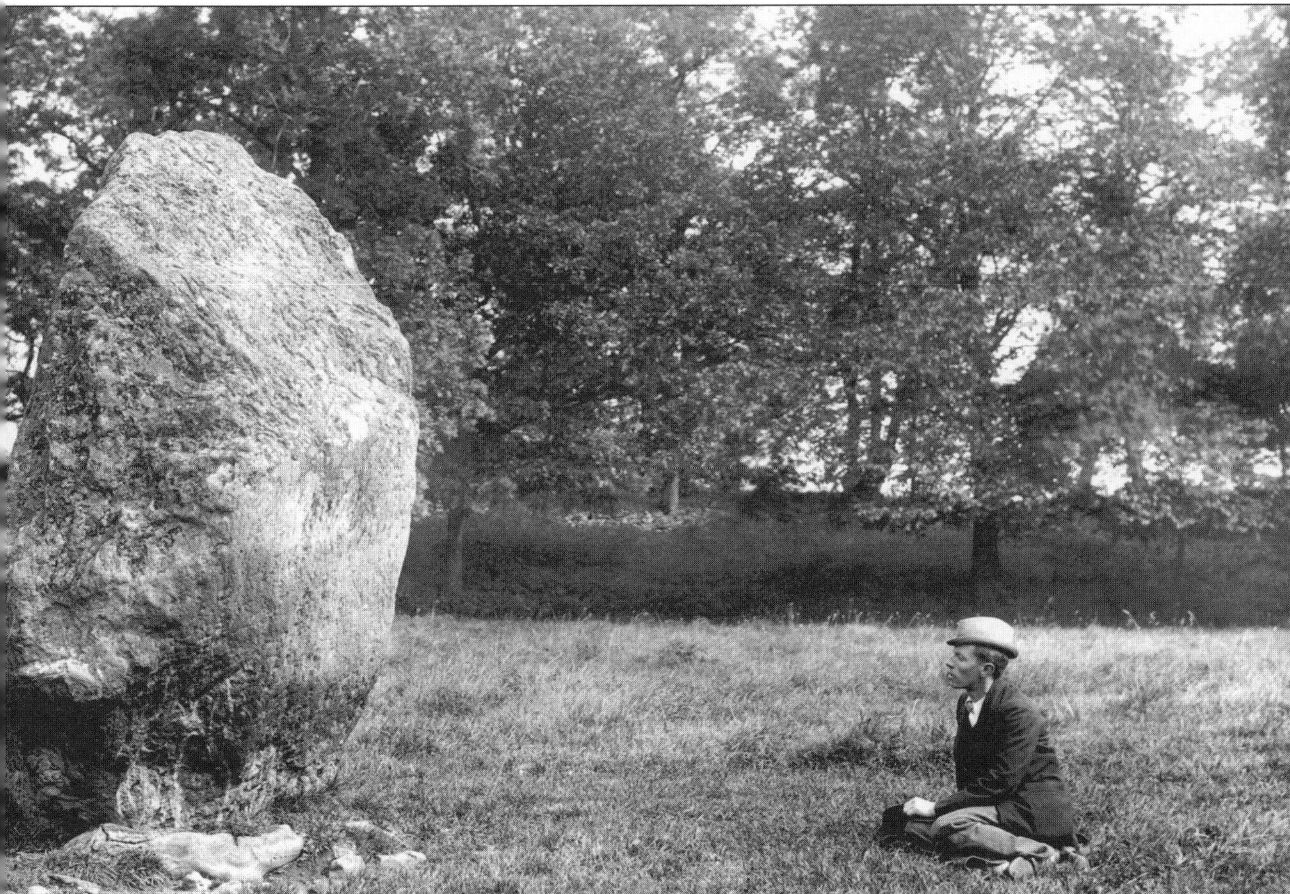

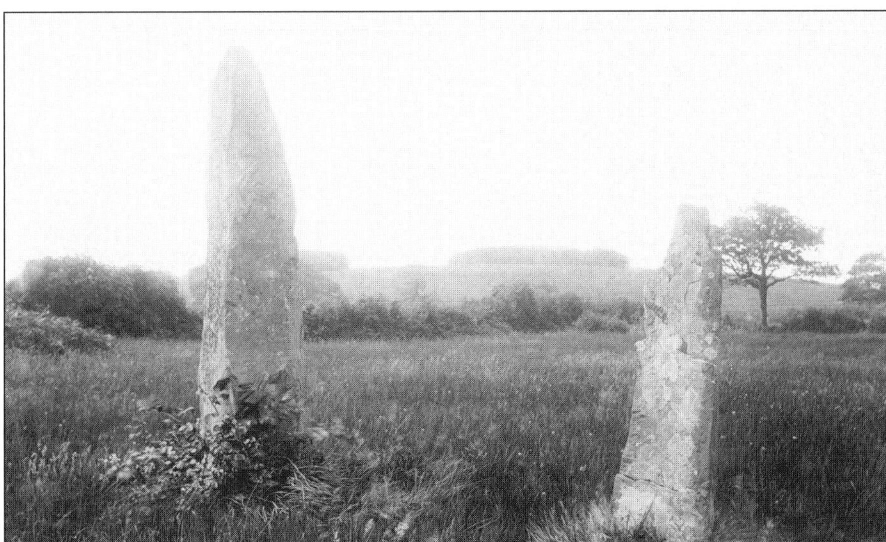

Standing Stones

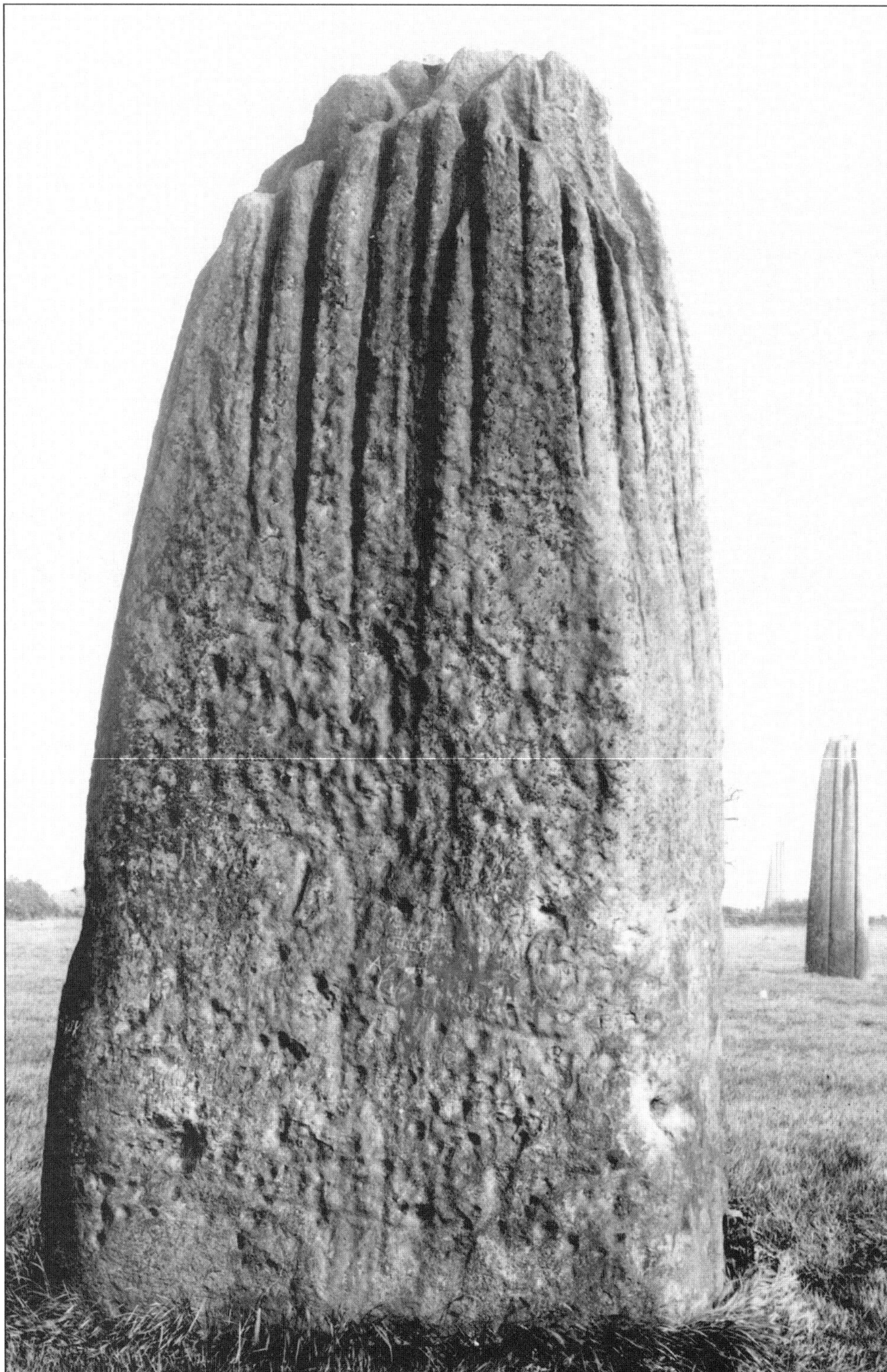

Boroughbridge
The Devil's Arrow
1895 35295

The Devil's Arrows is nowadays composed of three stones. They stand in North Yorkshire, close to the A1: it is one of the most famous prehistoric monuments in the county. Originally four in number, the stones were brought here from Knaresborough, about six miles away, in 200BC. They range from 18 feet to 22 feet in height (taller than most of the Stonehenge uprights) and weigh more than 20 tons each. The unusual deep and curiously fluted grooves are believed to be the result of weathering. They stand in a line running north to south and at intervals of 200 to 370 feet. The stones' power and influence has perhaps been diminished since the creation of a nearby housing estate, which has hardly contributed to the mystery and presence the stones once commanded.

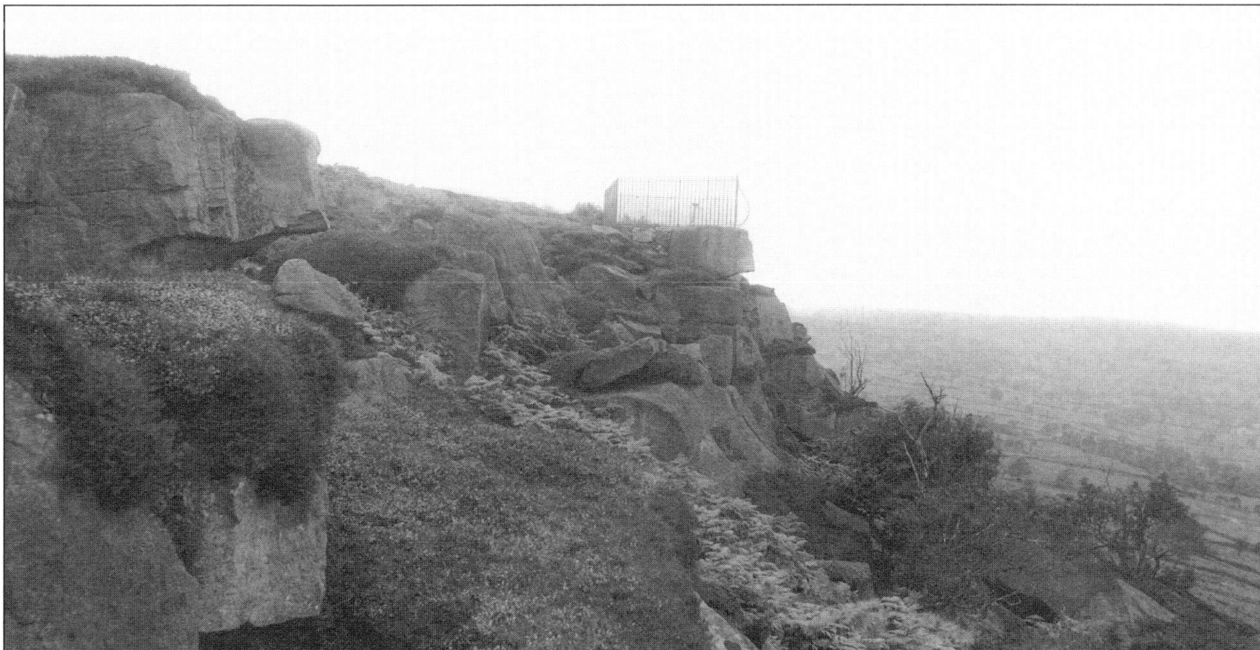

ILKLEY, THE SWASTIKA STONE 1916 *67342*

Overlooking Ilkley is the Swastika Stone, so called because of its attractive engraved markings; in reality, they barely resemble the emotive 20th-century swastika symbol. Believed to be associated with cup and ring culture, the design, on millstone grit, is a shallow indentation between a half and one inch deep and eighteen to twenty inches wide but sixteen to nineteen feet high. Although speculation tends to believe the design is a fertility symbol, its meaning remains an enigma.

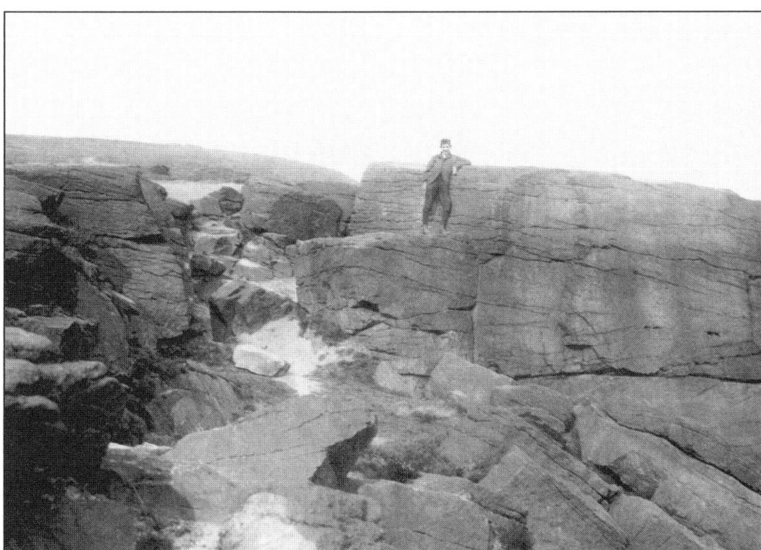

LEFT: BINGLEY, THE DRUIDS' ALTAR 1894 *34759*

The Druids' Altar is a naturally large millstone grit formation on the edge of, and overlooking, the Aire valley conurbation, with Bradford to the east and to the west the eastern end of the Yorkshire Dales. The top of the rock is marked with cup and rings, typical of many such marked rocks on the adjacent moors. Disraeli is reported to have addressed the Young Conservatives here in 1844; nearby, it is said that the Chartists held meetings. The purpose of the 'Altar' has been celebratory - recently a beacon was lit here at the coronation jubilee - or as a meeting and picnic spot.

Hill Forts & Roman Britain

Many of the obvious landmarks that command our attention when in the countryside are the Iron Age hillforts. More often than not they are found on a natural promontory that the Iron Age Celts converted to a fortified enclosure. Today they are ideal for picnics and those who wish for a tranquil and pleasant setting.

After about 700BC, the rich civilisation of the Bronze Age gradually assimilated people from the continent; amongst other things, they brought with them new techniques in metal and the use of iron. It is still not clear whether this was a sudden invasion of these shores or a slow and gradual assimilation brought on by hundreds of years of trading with the continent. Certainly, the appearance of hill-forts and the use of iron, the change in pottery styles and the change in burial habits marked a noticeable and identifiable cultural change. Later, in about 100BC, another invasion from the Belgium area occurred. Landing in Kent, these people were known as the Belgae; they brought with them a more warlike and different culture. The change in culture was immense: gold, silver and bronze coins were now in use, and wheelmade pottery made its first appearance. During this period the might and threat of the Roman Empire also

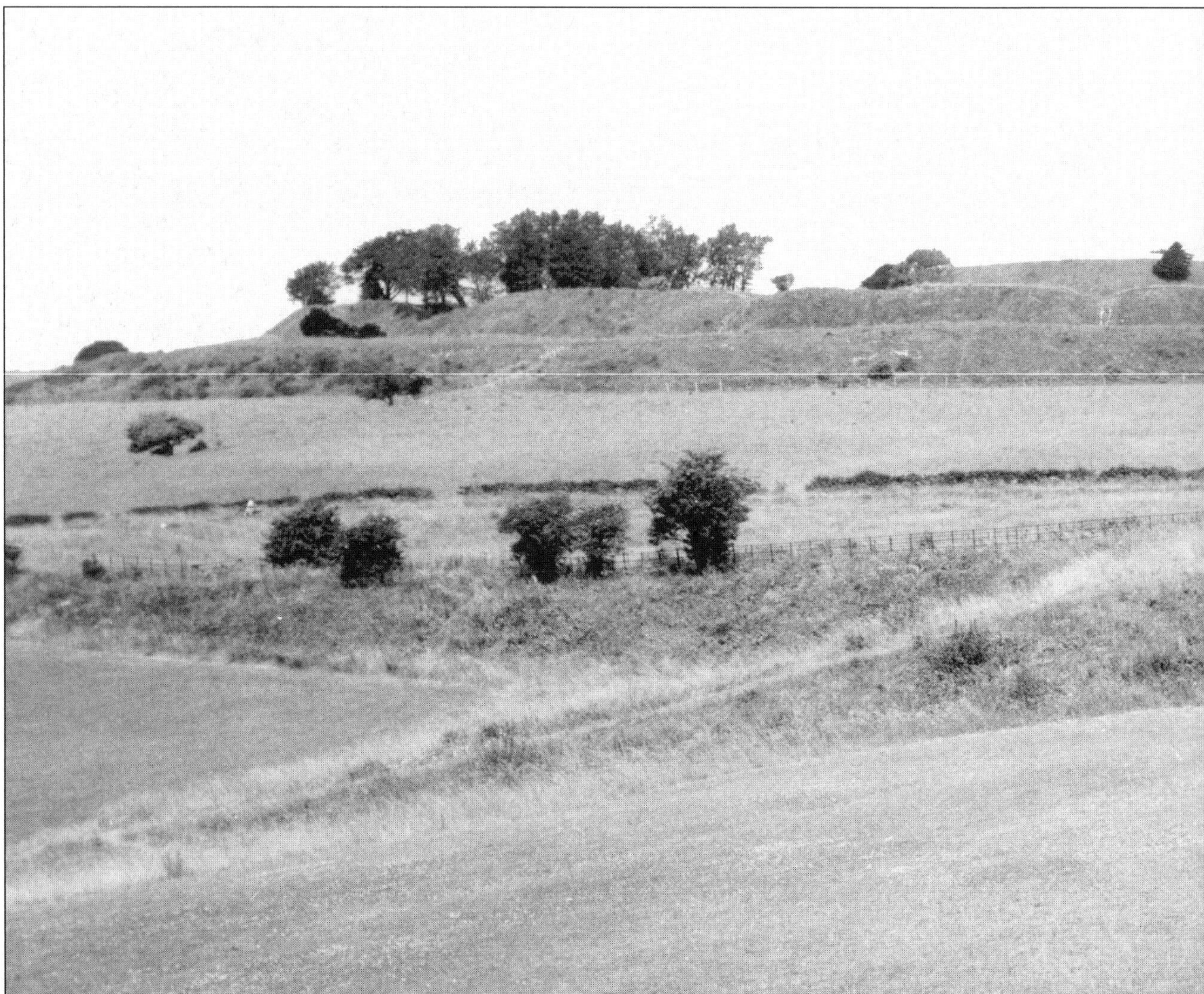

came closer, and in 54BC Julius Caesar led a brief expedition to these shores. For the first time names of tribes and leaders became known, including the Atrebates and Catuvellauni in the south and the Brigantes in the north. Druidism was the favoured religion with, under leadership of the Druid priesthood. (Stonehenge was probably long since abandoned, and the Druids have no historical connection with it). For a hundred years prior to the Roman invasion under Emperor Claudius in AD43, many of the hillforts were reinforced to strengthen their defence. When the Claudian invasion happened, fighting amongst those who decided to resist was fierce, as the excavations at Maiden Castle revealed. Most tribes recognised the threat from the Romans; some were prepared to bow to their will, whilst others would decide to take on the might of the Roman army. Boudica was such a leader - in AD60 she led a revolt in southern England and ransacked Colchester, Verulamium and London. After AD60 the whole of southern England, with the exception of the area west of Exeter, was conquered: and Britain settled down to enjoy the benefits of colonisation.

OLD SARUM c1955 O58168

Old Sarum is a hillfort built by the people of the Iron Age, who came to Britain from around 500BC. Its spectacular ramparts and ditches enclosed their community. The inner rampart would have had a wooden stockade. This fort is also the junction of four Roman roads and, after the Norman invasion, was the original Salisbury until the 13th century when a 'new town' was built.

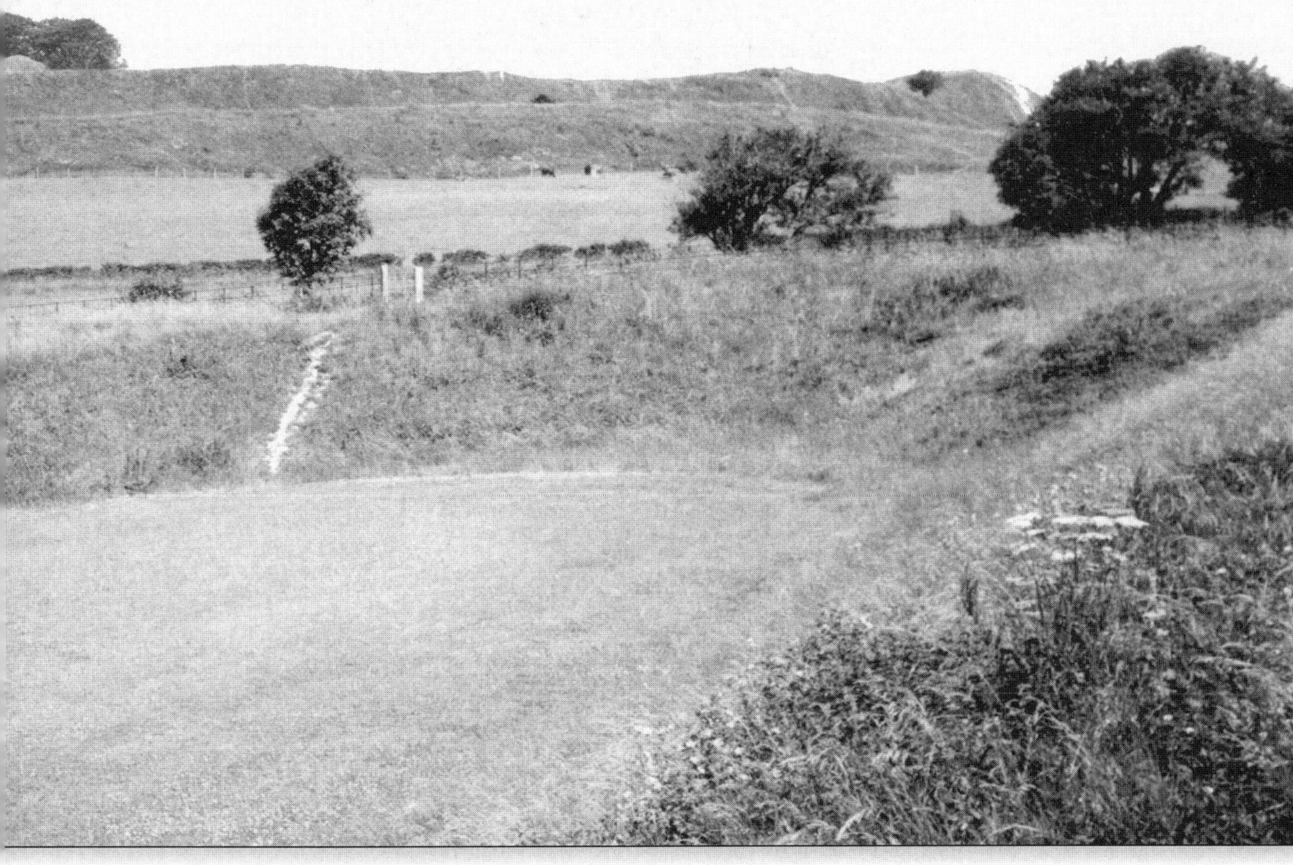

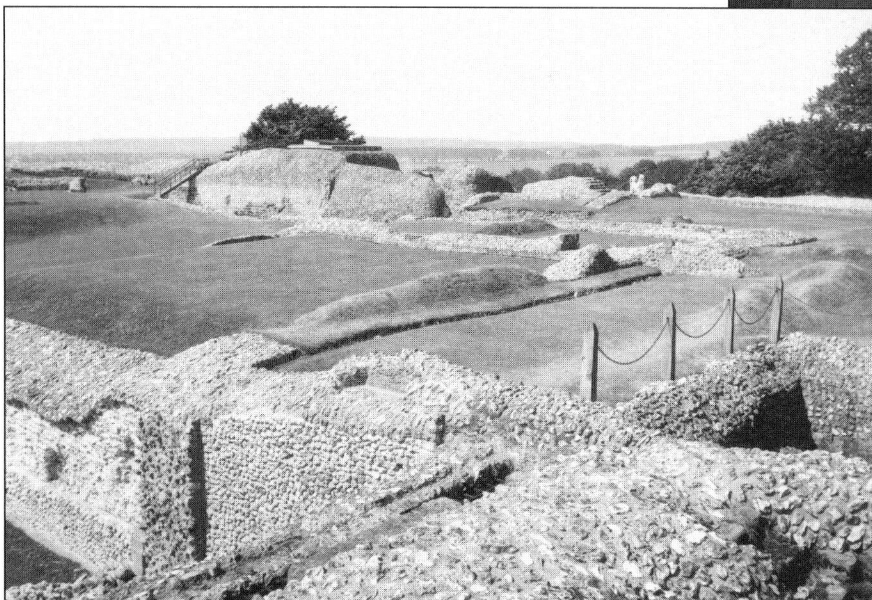

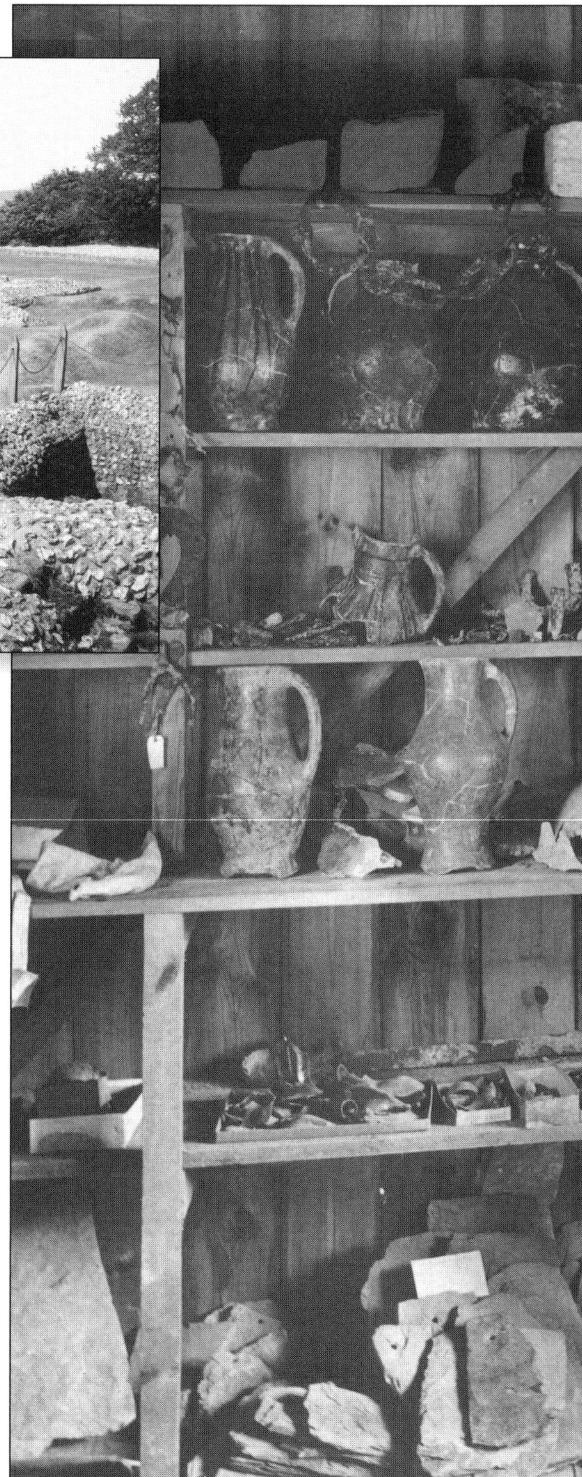

ABOVE: OLD SARUM c1955 O58173

As was the case with many other hillforts, the Roman army proved too efficient for the Celtic defenders. Six hundred years later, another invading army made Old Sarum its defensive home: the inner fortifications now contained a Norman castle and a cathedral. The site was windy, cold and harsh, and the monks were continually falling out with their Norman masters. This prompted them to obtain permission from the Pope to build a new cathedral a few miles away, now the site of the famous Salisbury cathedral. The use of flint was a cheap and essential building material, as can be seen here.

RIGHT: OLD SARUM, OBJECTS DISCOVERED DURING THE EXCAVATIONS 1913 65303

Medieval vases, iron keys, Norman stonework and animal bones bring together Old Sarum's troubled and relatively short-lived past.

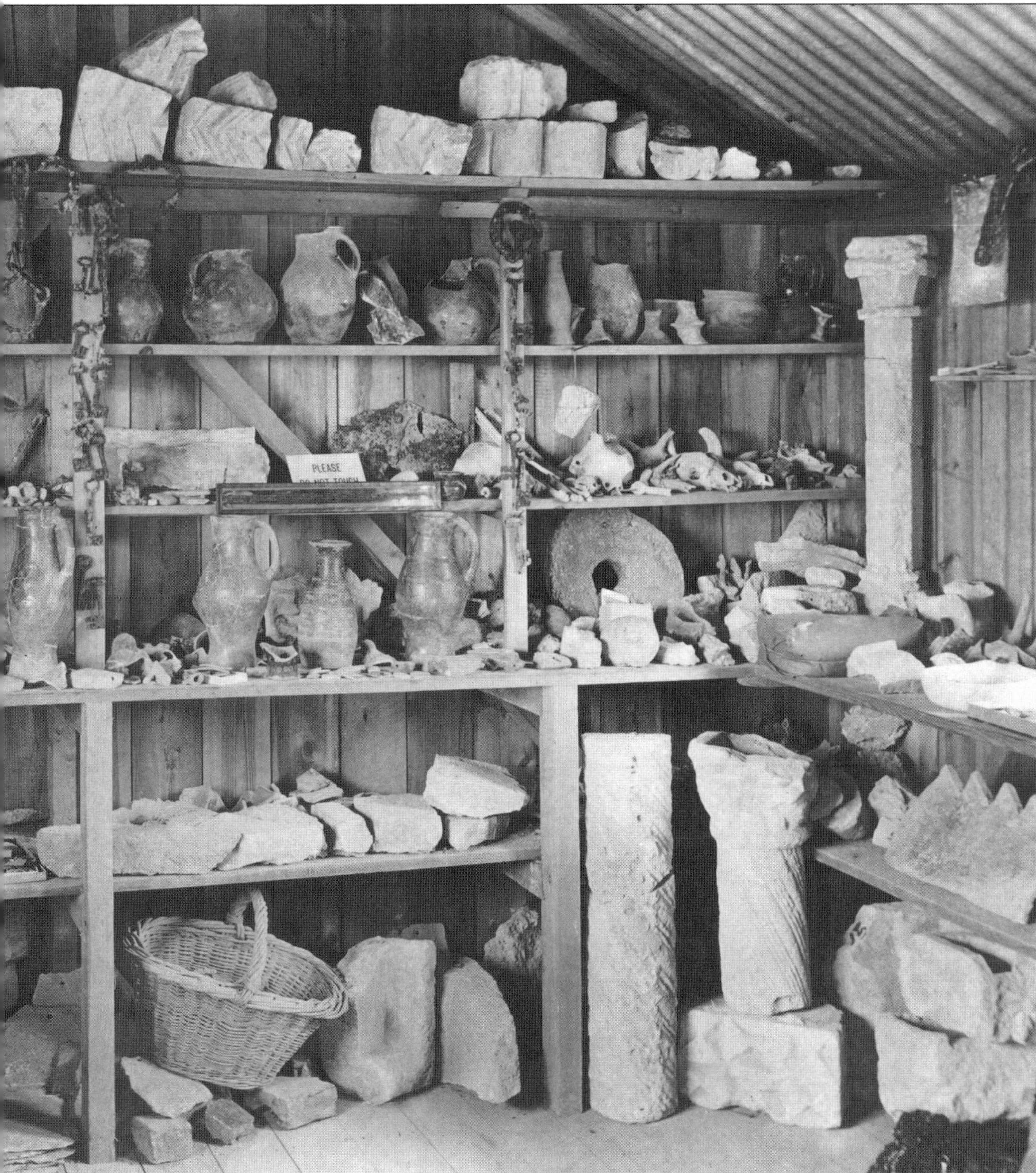
PLEASE

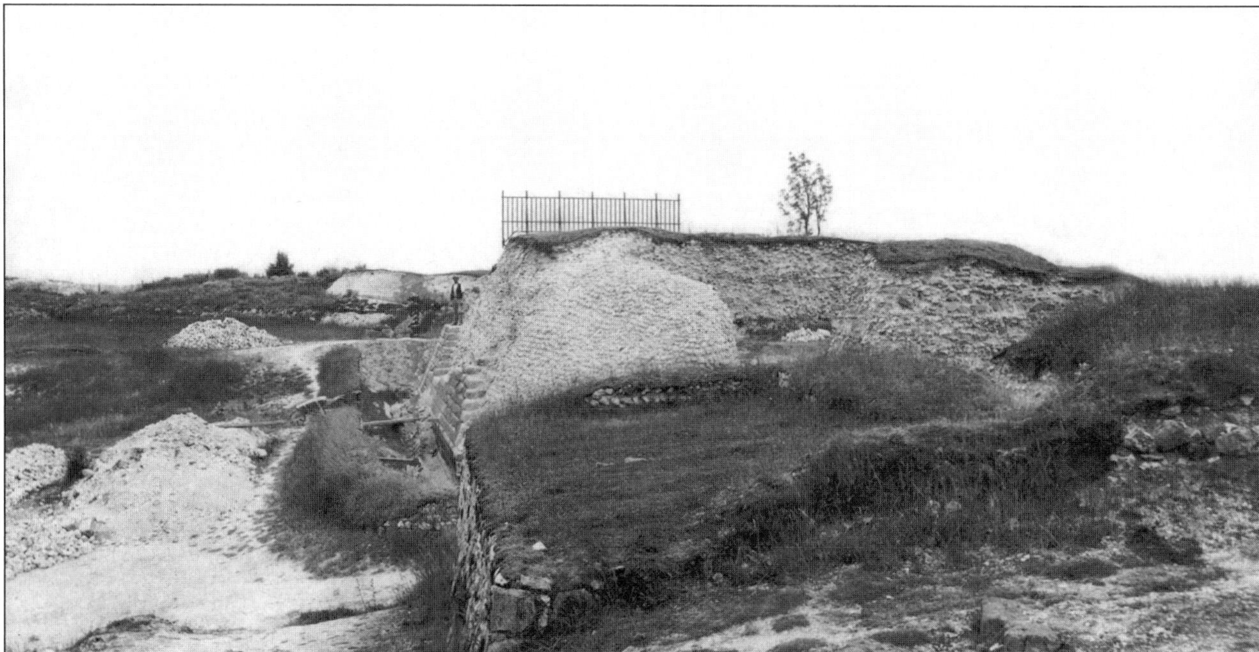

OLD SARUM 1913 65302

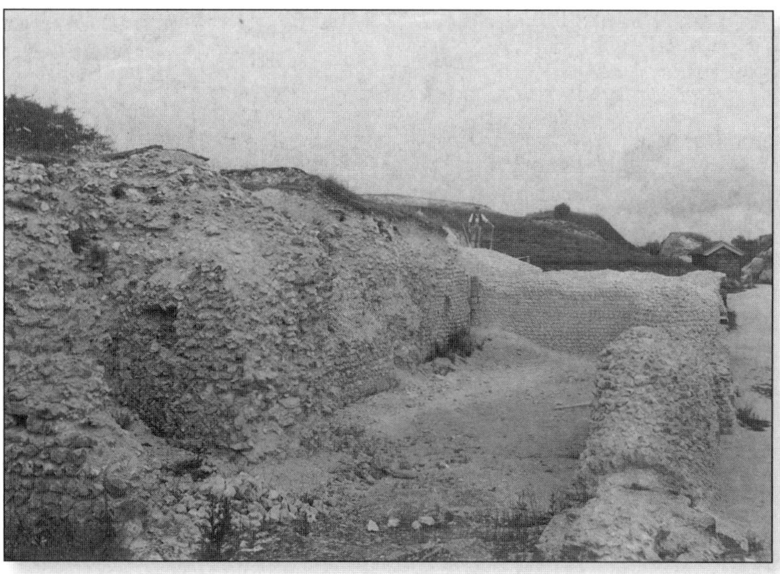

OLD SARUM, THE KITCHEN 1913 65295

It is sad that the massive flint walls that were excavated in 1913 have, through archaeological excavations, ceased to exist.

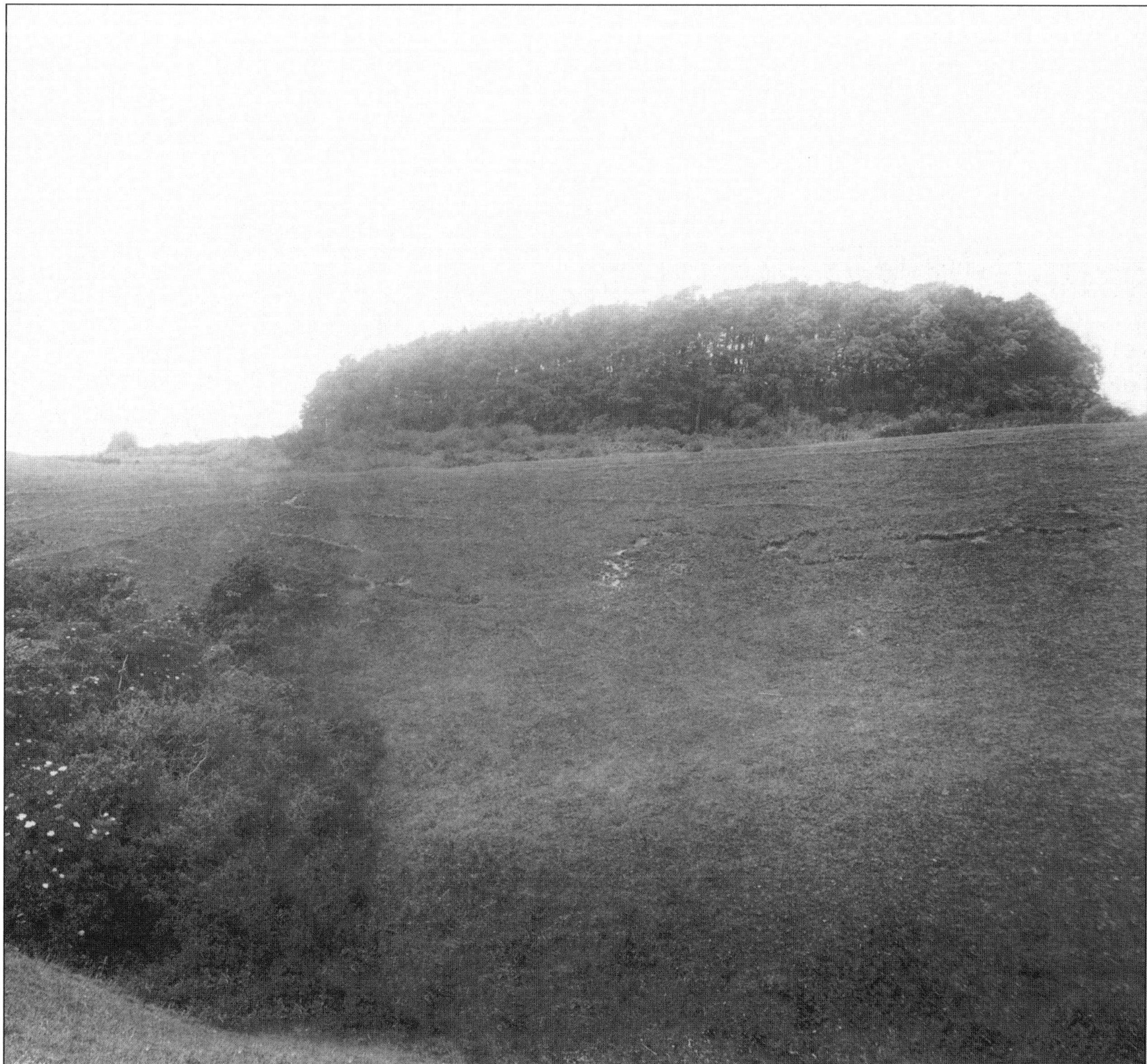

BADBURY RINGS 1899 43722

Now a tree-clad hilltop fort, this is another example of the many forts built by the Iron Age people. To date it has never been excavated. It stands at the junction of two Roman roads, the Ackling Dyke running from Dorchester to Old Sarum, and the Bath to Poole road, although there is still doubt that the latter was ever completed. Legend suggests that this may have been the site of King Arthur's battle at Mount Badon where he killed 960 people in a single day!

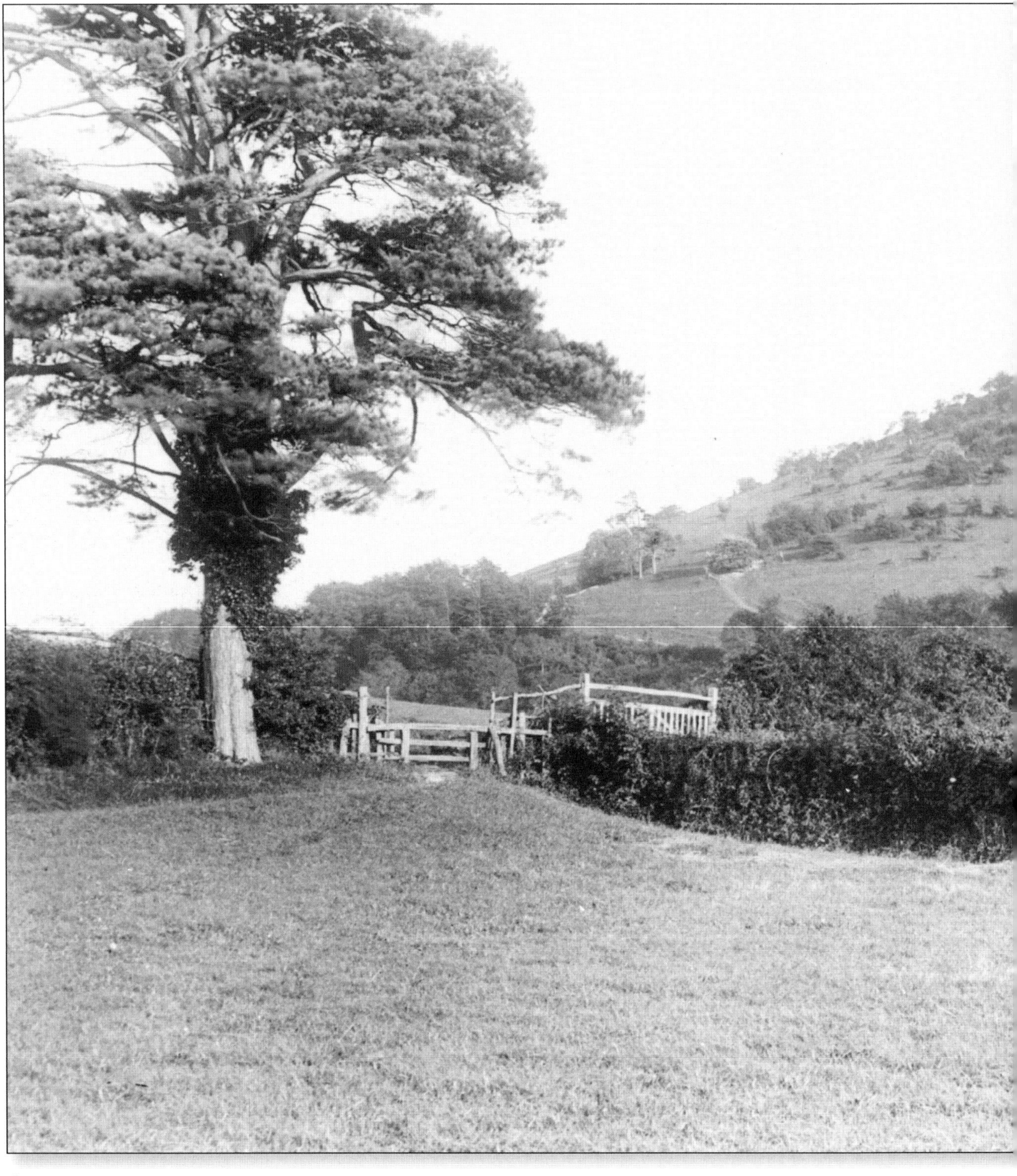

CHANCTONBURY RING 1894 34416

In Sussex is the small hillfort of Chanctonbury Ring. It is now festooned with beech trees, planted in 1760, and for which it has a local reputation. The inner compound contains the remains of two Roman buildings; proof that this too succumbed to the might of the Roman army.

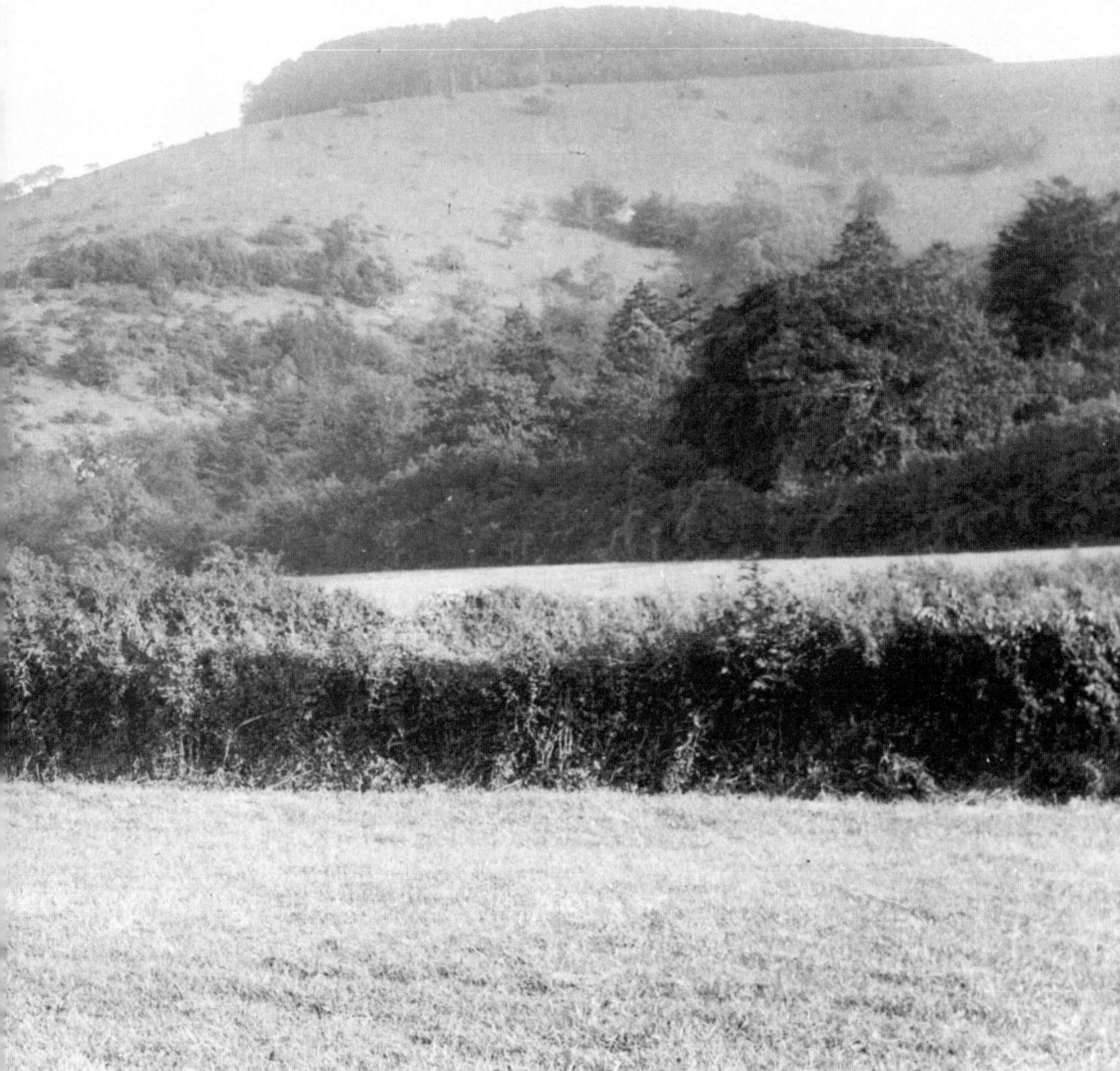

Hill Forts & Roman Britain

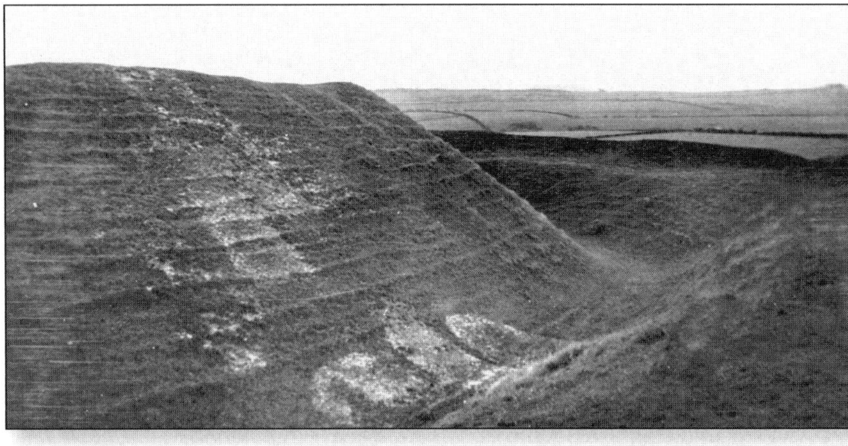

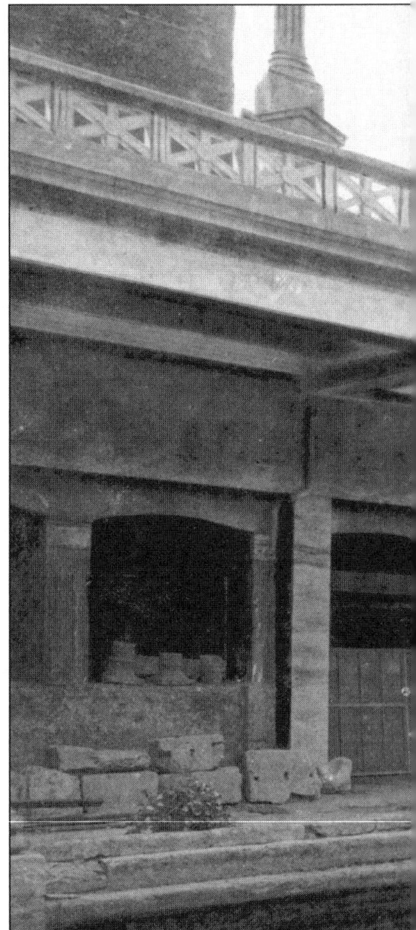

ABOVE: DORCHESTER, MAIDEN CASTLE EARTHWORKS C1950 D44008

This photograph hardly does justice to the most magnificent of all British hillforts. Sir Mortimer Wheeler excavated it between 1934-38. Despite three different phases of improving the fort and its defences, it still proved no match for the 2nd Legion commanded by Vespasian who took the fort in AD44. Excavations revealed 54,000 sling-stones, which in the end were inadequate weapons against Roman discipline and experience

ABOVE RIGHT: BATH, THE ROMAN BATHS 1897 40789

This is the Great Bath after the first excavations and restoration started in 1880: it was originally built in the 1st century AD. The flat bottom is lined with 45 sheets of Mendip lead. It is still fed by hot mineral waters from a continuous spring; it is hard to imagine that the water seen today fell as rain on the Mendip Hills 10,000 years ago.

FAR RIGHT: BATH, THE ROMAN BATHS, SCULPTURE FROM THE TEMPLE OF MINERVA 1907 57725

This wonderful pediment from the temple of Sul Minerva contains the famous Gorgon's Head. It has Celtic and Roman features, and is part of a sculptured shield. Today its total meaning is not clear, since the head, though closely similar to the female Gorgon, is male with flowing hair, blazing eyes and has similarities with the sea gods Oceanus and Neptune.

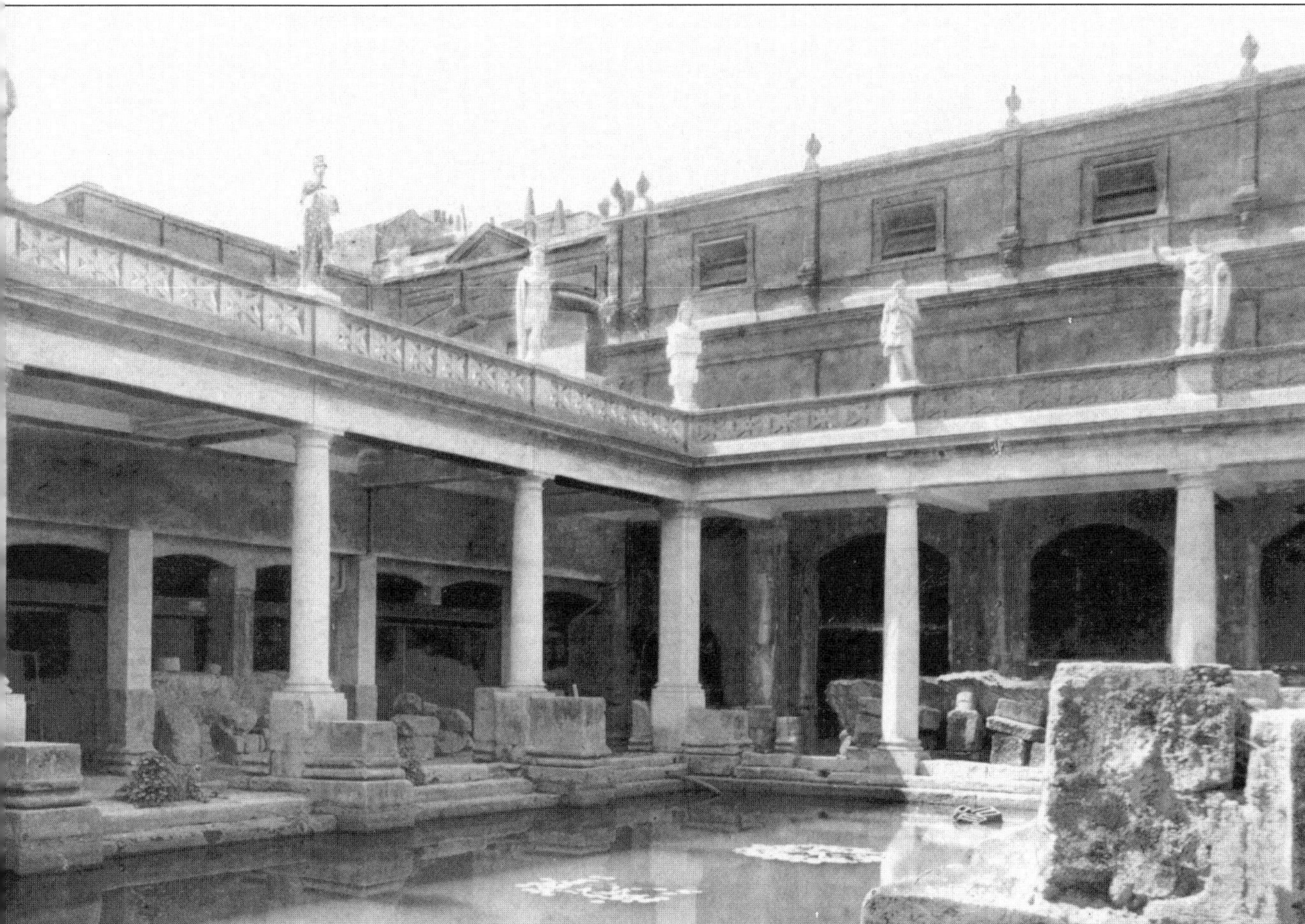

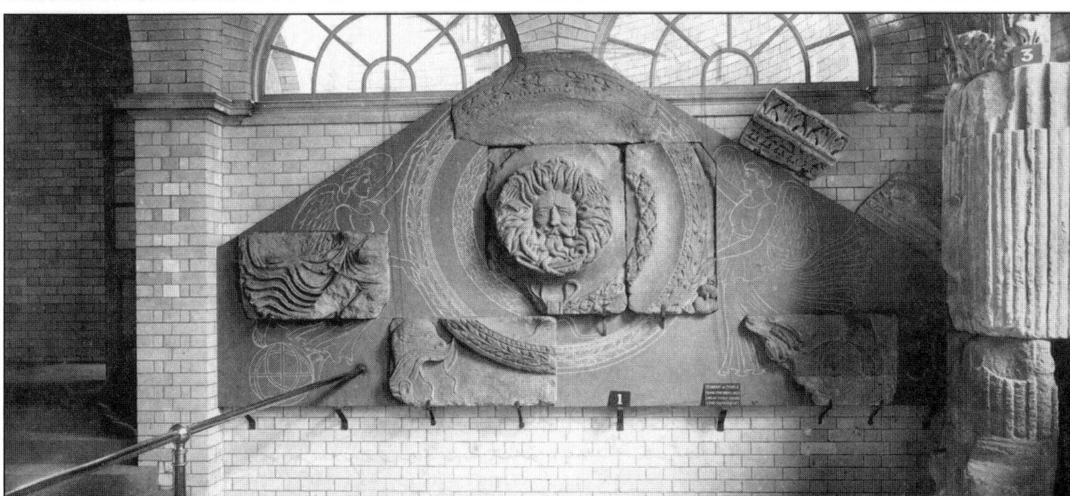

Hill Forts & Roman Britain

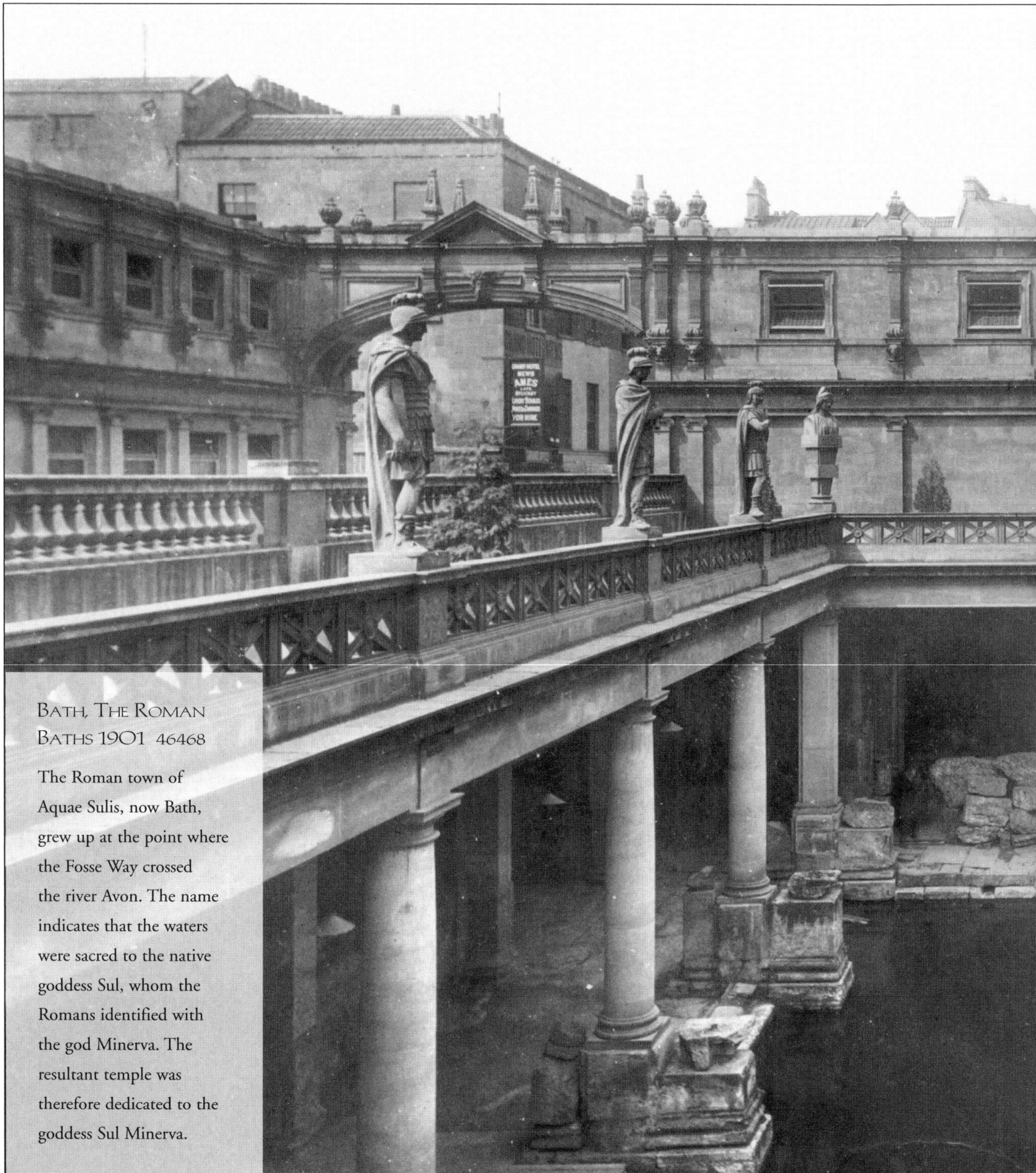

BATH, THE ROMAN BATHS 1901 46468

The Roman town of Aquae Sulis, now Bath, grew up at the point where the Fosse Way crossed the river Avon. The name indicates that the waters were sacred to the native goddess Sul, whom the Romans identified with the god Minerva. The resultant temple was therefore dedicated to the goddess Sul Minerva.

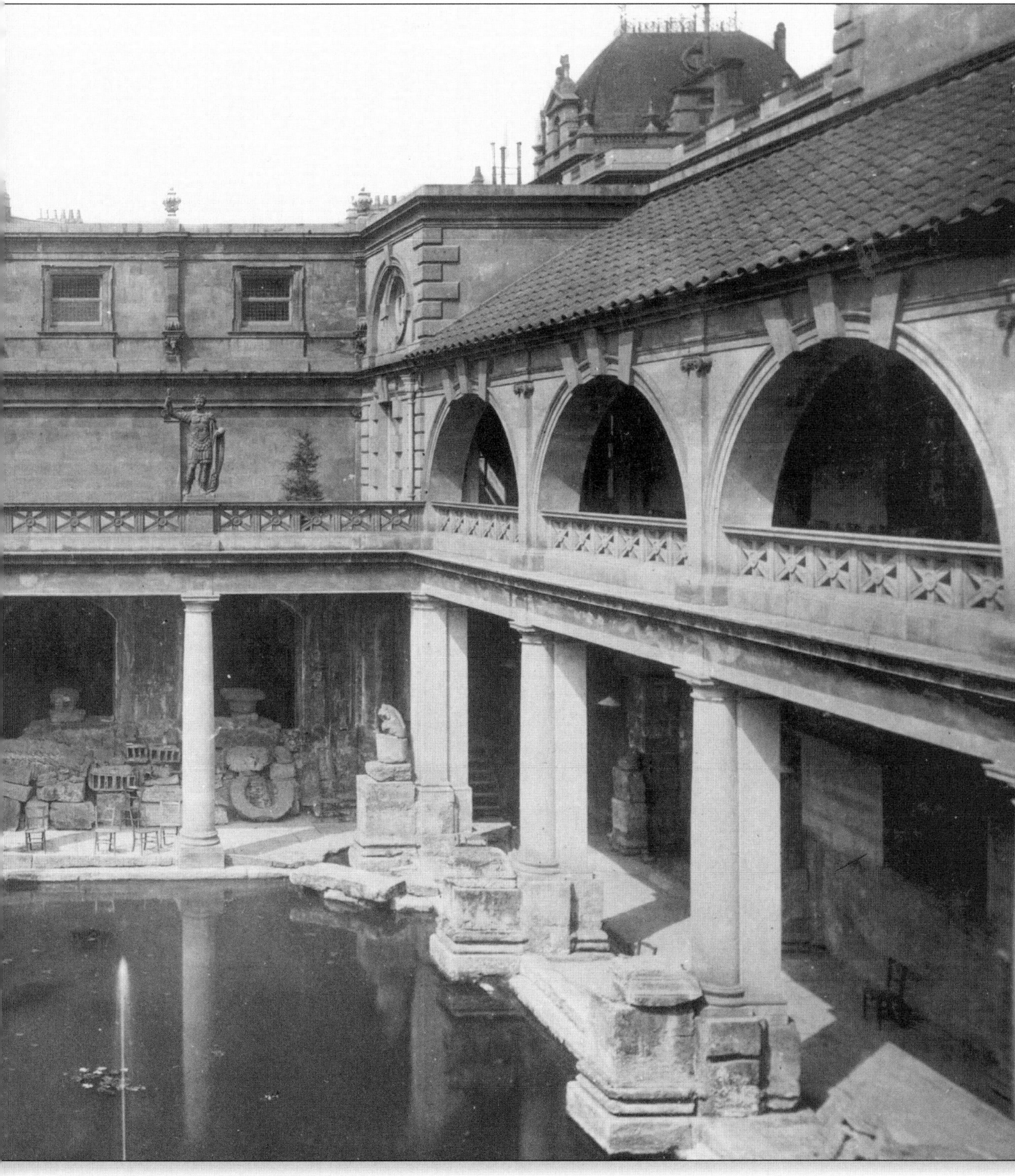

Hill Forts & Roman Britain

Gilsland, The Roman Wall 1924 *76661*

Gilsland Wall is in fact part of Hadrian's Wall. This was constructed as the northern frontier between Scotland and Britain and remained so for some two hundred years. This section is a narrow part of the wall, since orders were received in AD125 to reduce its width. Hadrian's Wall stretched from Wallsend to Bowness, a distance of 73 miles.

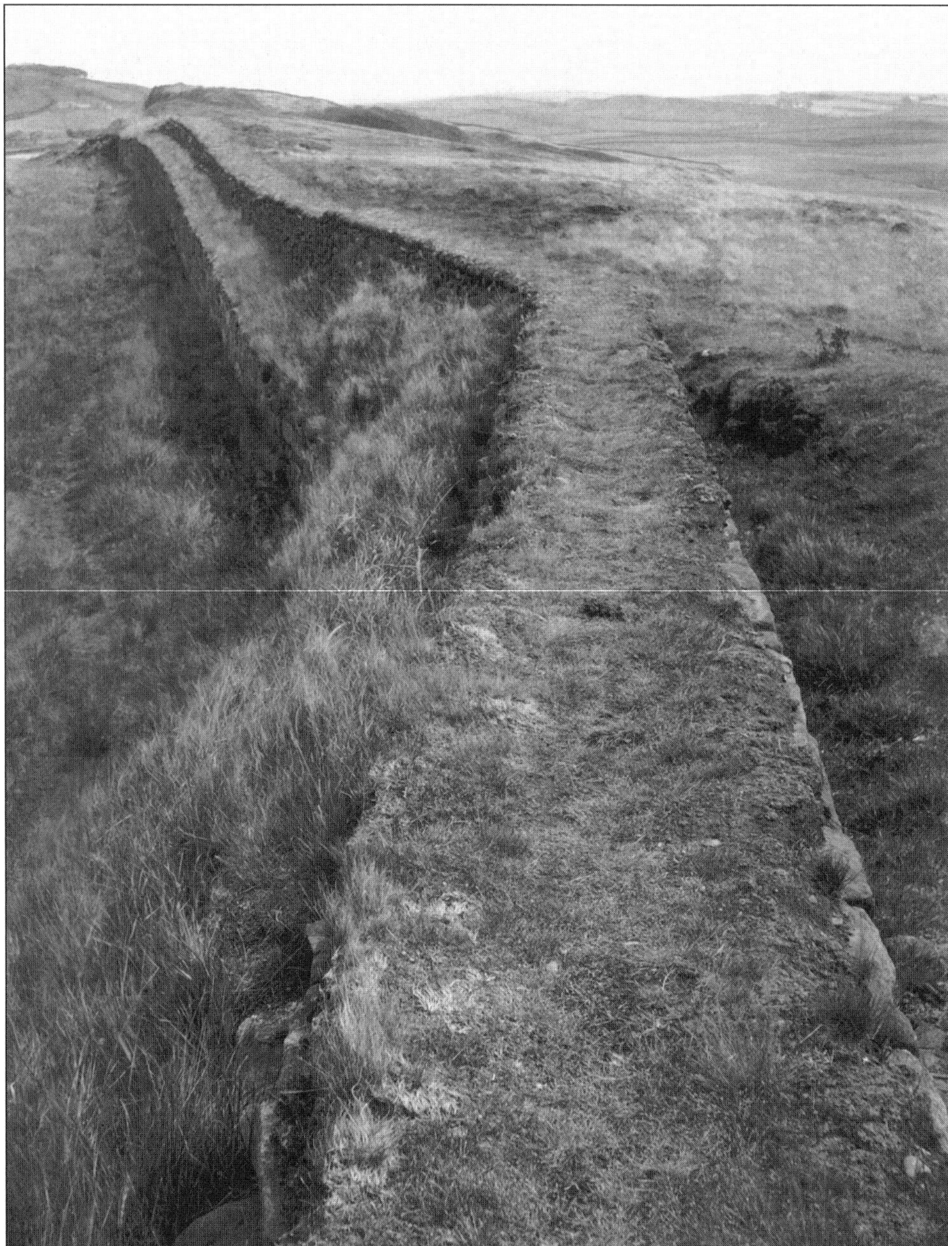

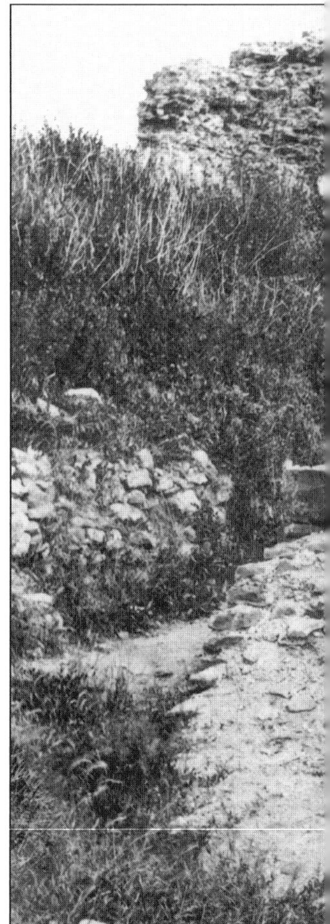

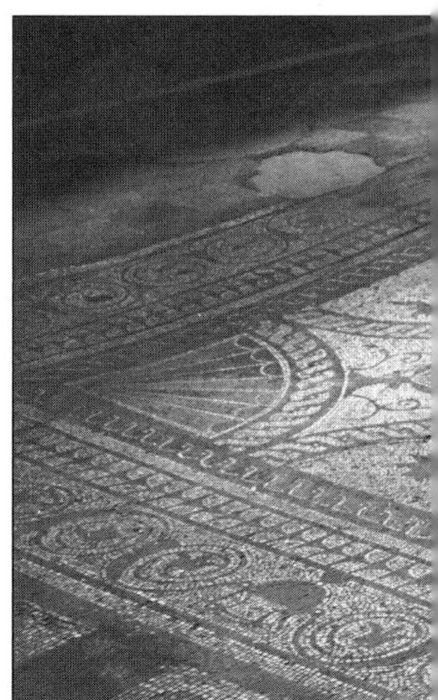

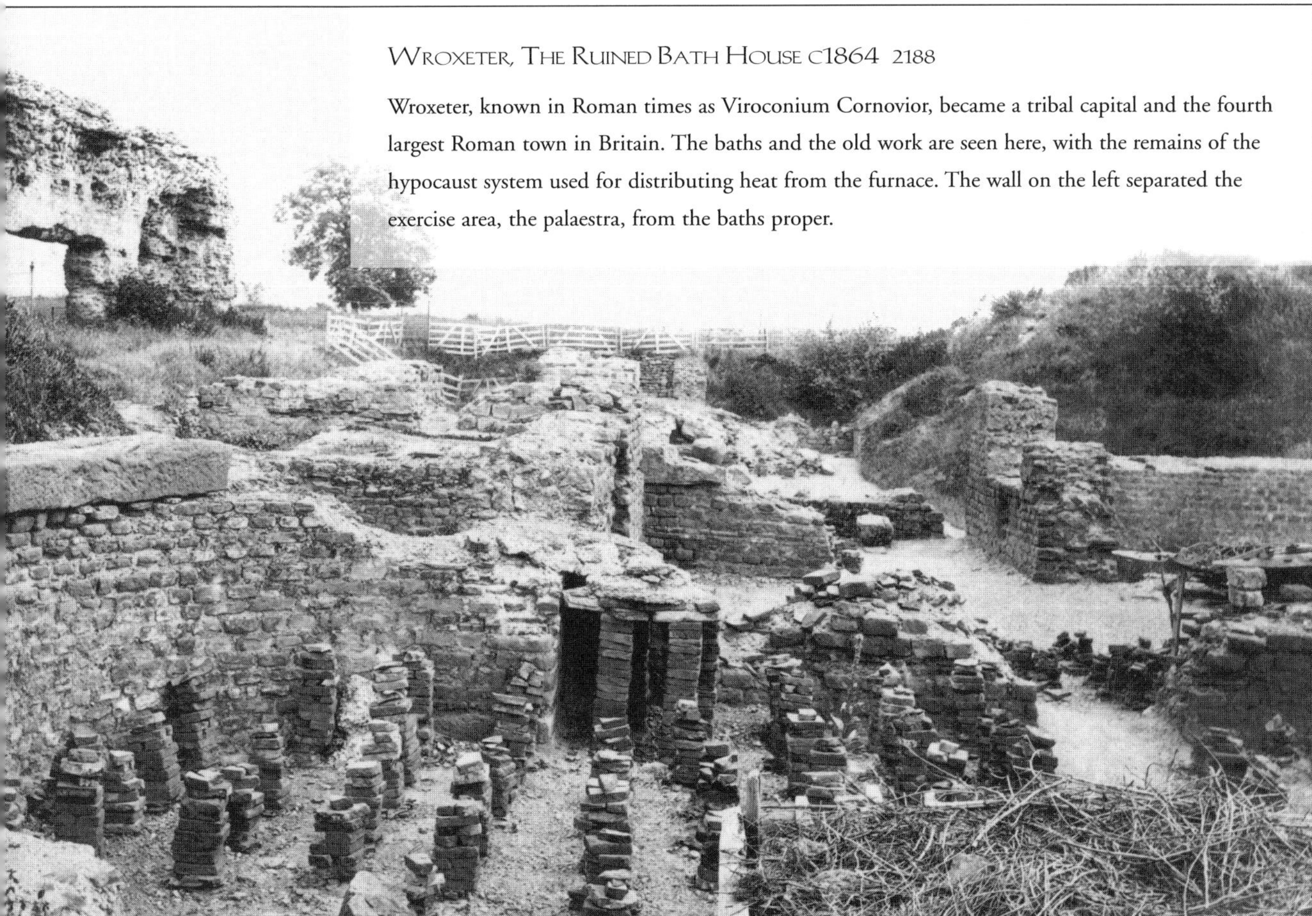

WROXETER, THE RUINED BATH HOUSE C1864 2188

Wroxeter, known in Roman times as Viroconium Cornovior, became a tribal capital and the fourth largest Roman town in Britain. The baths and the old work are seen here, with the remains of the hypocaust system used for distributing heat from the furnace. The wall on the left separated the exercise area, the palaestra, from the baths proper.

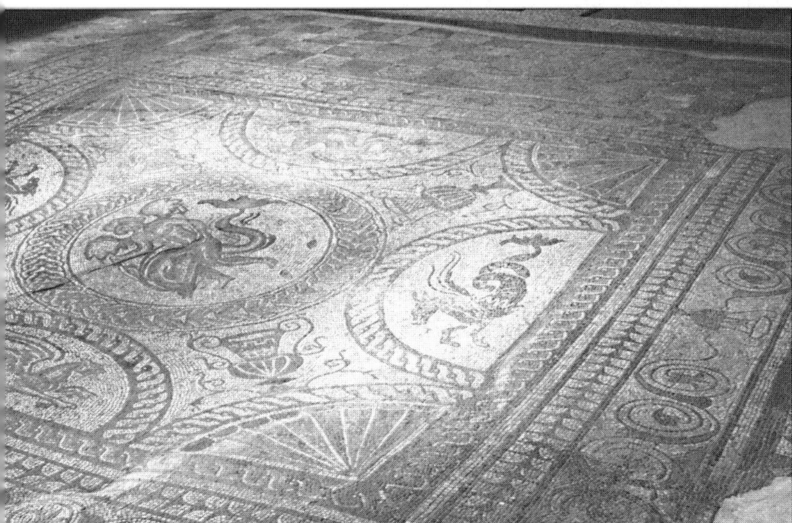

FISHBOURNE, THE ROMAN PALACE C1960 F132002

Fishbourne in West Sussex is by far the most impressive Roman building in Britain, and is rightly called a palace. It was probably built for a British chieftain, Cogidubnus, who was on the best of terms with the Romans. It is an early building which was started about AD75. The mosaic floor pictured shows in the centre a winged cupid riding a dolphin, with sea panthers and sea horses in the surrounding semi-circles.

Hill Forts & Roman Britain

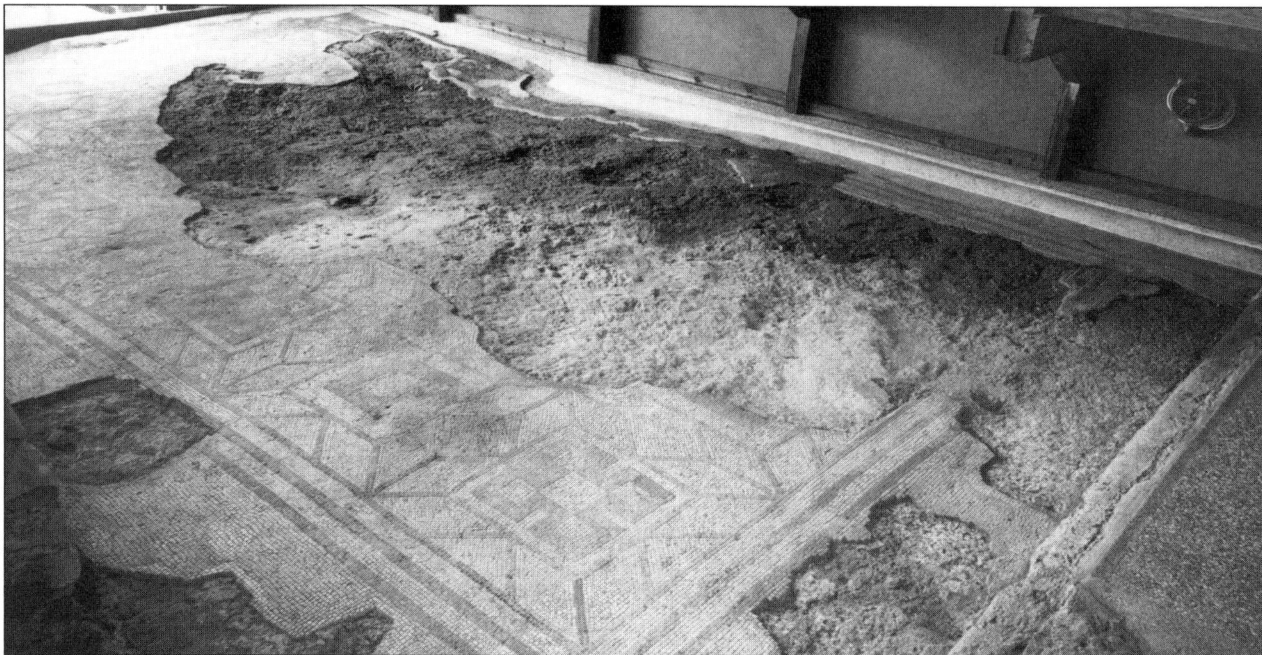

FISHBOURNE, THE ROMAN PALACE c1960 F132021

The building was palatial, and would have been comparable to those of Rome itself. The rooms had painted friezes and many mosaics, some of the earliest in Britain. There was a colonnaded courtyard, a reception hall, Roman columns and a scented garden. The mosaic shown is of geometric design; it consists of thousands of tessellated fired pottery, of various colours, which were laid into soft mortar.

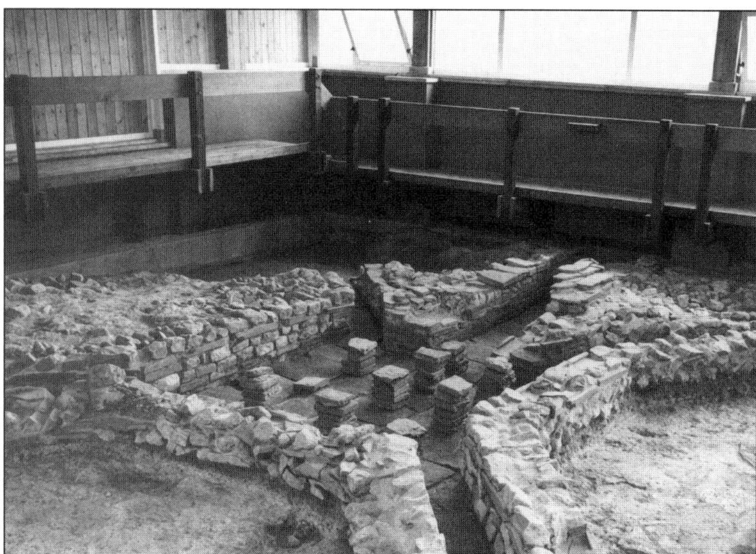

FISHBOURNE, THE ROMAN PALACE c1960 F132017

This photograph shows part of a hypocaust (underfloor heating) system and the remains of mosaic floors.

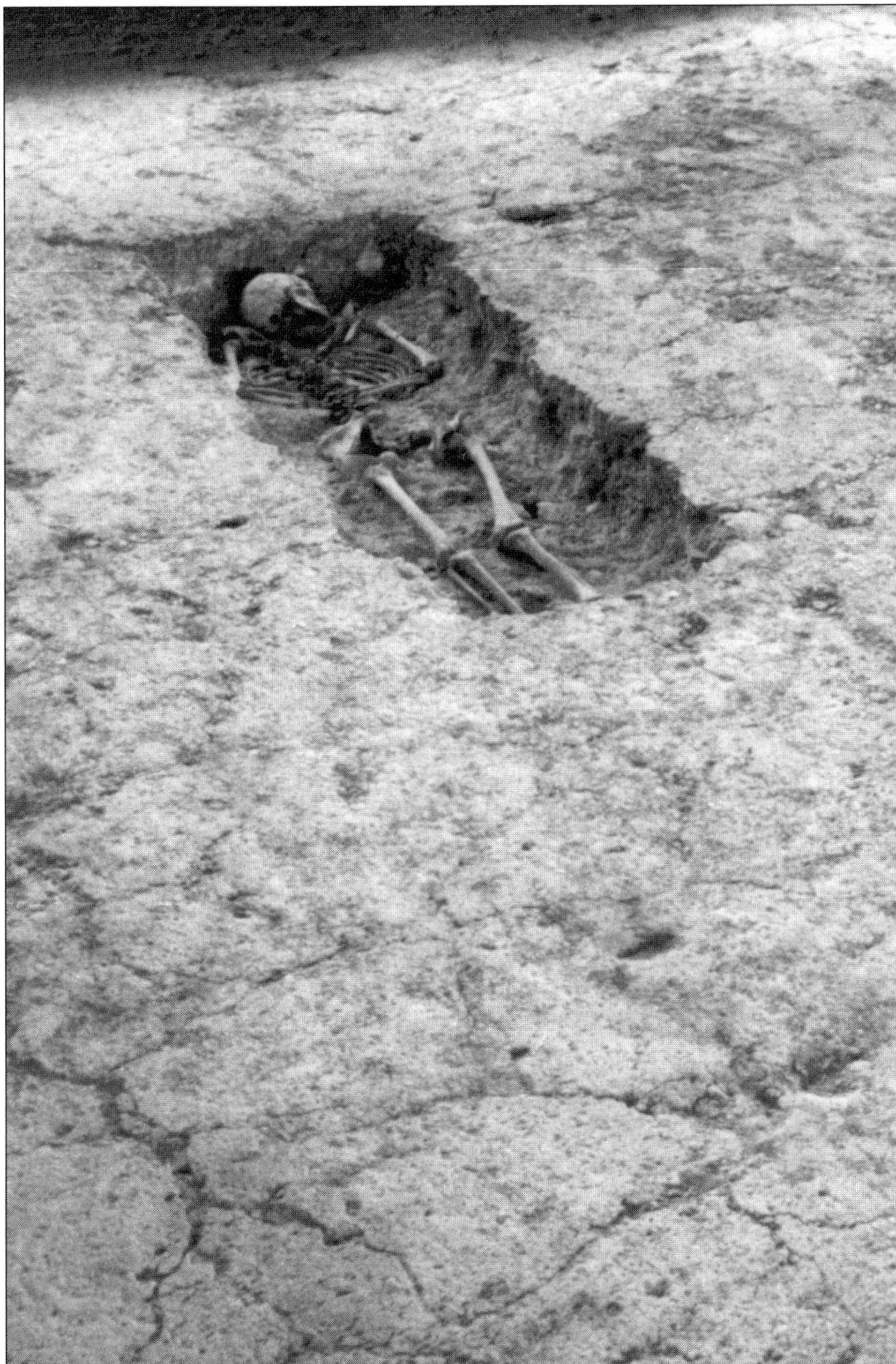

FISHBOURNE
THE ROMAN PALACE
C1960 F132008

At the end of the 3rd century a disastrous fire brought the Palace to an end. It was not until 1960 that the laying of a water main brought about its discovery. For whatever reason, the skeleton shown here was buried in the ruins of the building some time after its destruction.

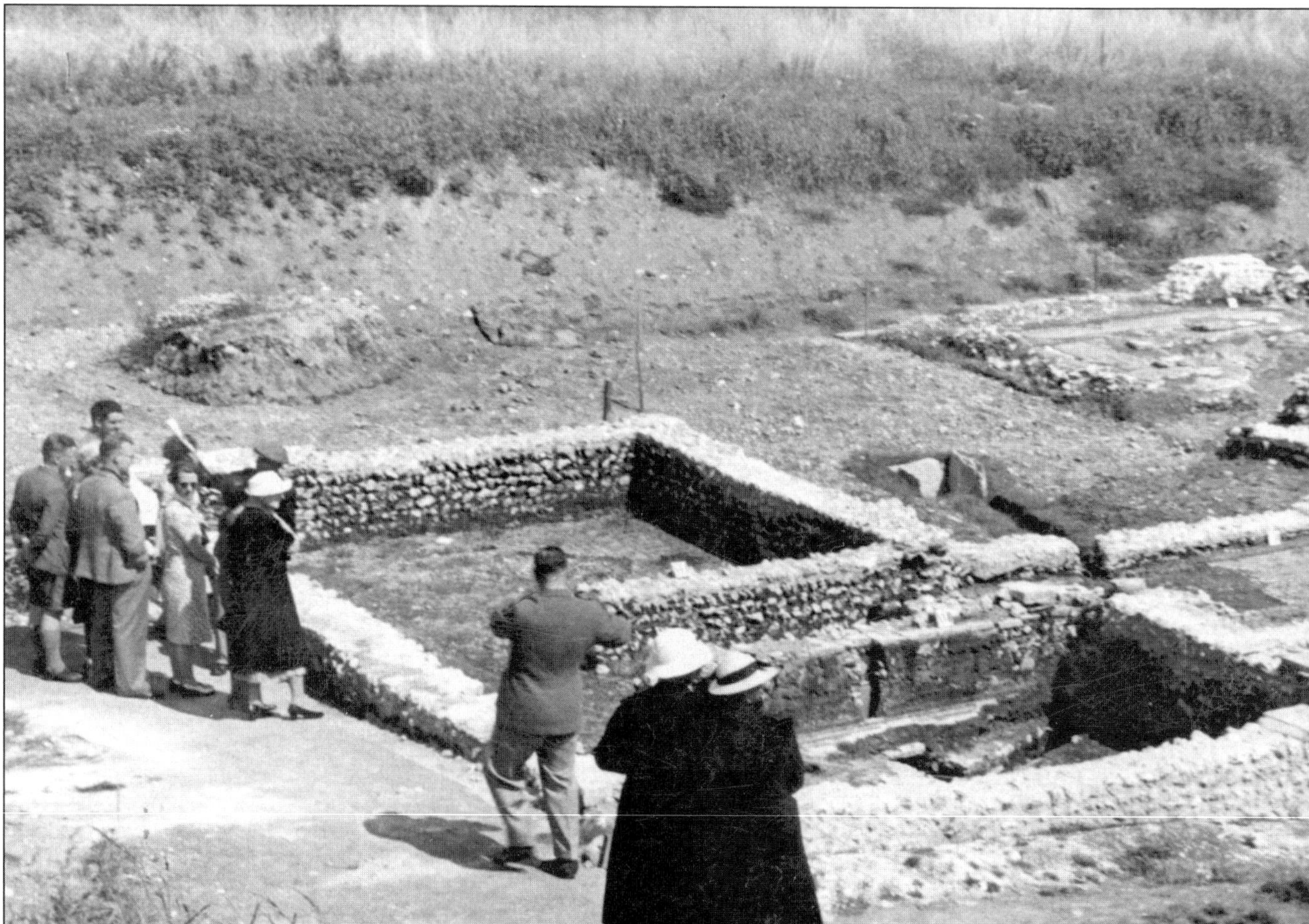

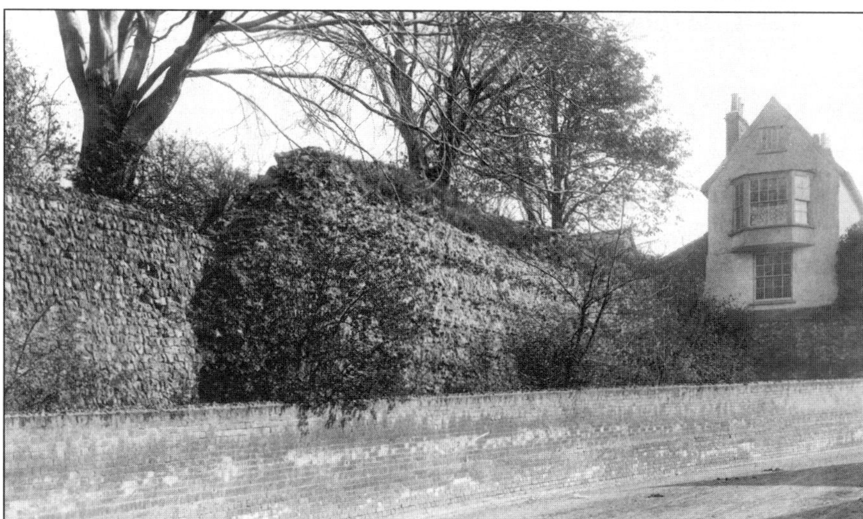

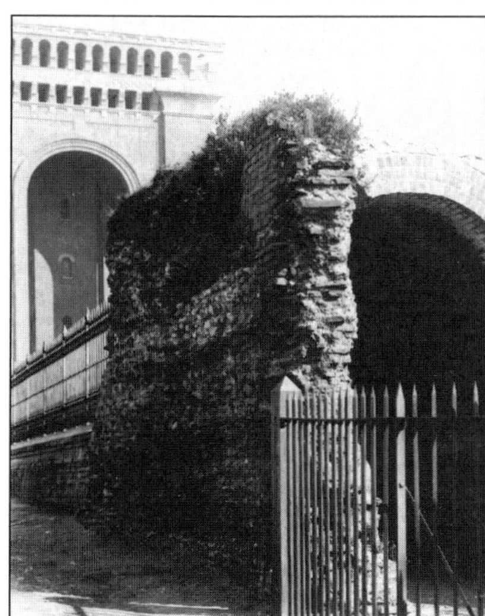

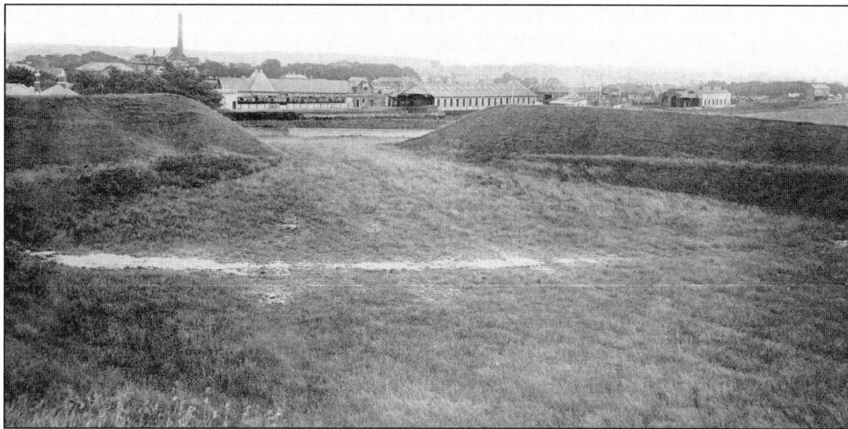

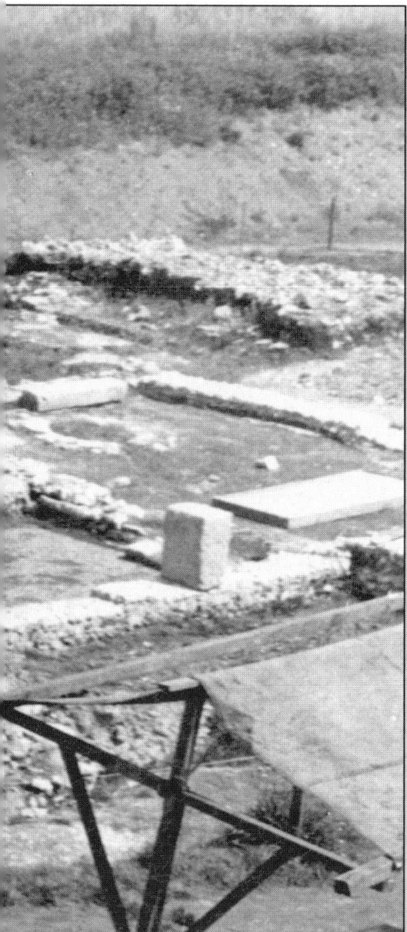

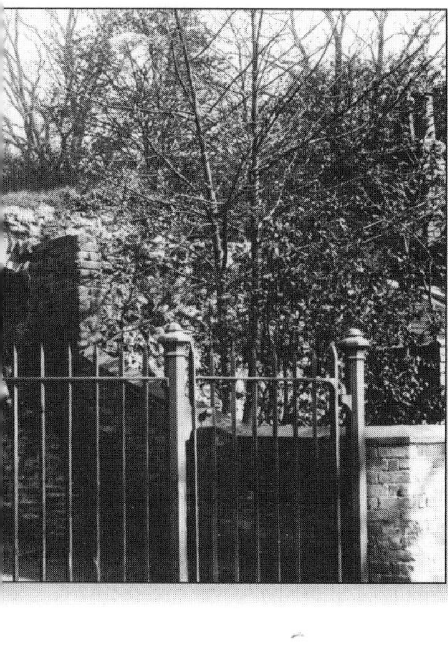

Above: Dorchester, The Amphitheatre 1891 28521

Very little of the Roman occupation of Dorchester, Durnovaria, remains. However, the amphitheatre was a converted hillfort, known as Maumbury Rings, a substantial circular bank with a pair of opposing entrances. These banks were built 4,000 years ago in the early Bronze Age, long before the Roman invasions in AD43. Here, Roman and British spectators witnessed fighting gladiators, men fighting against animals, and sometimes drama productions.

Above Left: Dorchester, Roman Excavations 1939 D44001

Little can be usefully gleaned from the remains shown here, but it is known that Dorchester was a centre for a school of mosaicists in the 3rd and 4th centuries. Their work has been recognised in local villages on stylistic grounds.

Bottom Left: Colchester, The Roman Wall 1892 31531

According to Tacitus, the Roman historian, the first Roman settlement at Colchester, Camulodunum, was built as a colony for retired soldiers; it was dedicated to the emperor Claudius, after the defeat the British chief Caractacus (see also page 58). However, Queen Boudica, who led the last British revolt against the Romans, soon burned it to the ground. The last survivors of the colony were burnt or massacred in the Temple of Claudius.

Left: Colchester, The Roman Wall 1892 31530

After Boudica's revolt, the Romans rebuilt Colchester within a hundred years. Consequently, it was one of the first Roman-British towns to have complete city walls.

Celtic Crosses

Celtic culture existed most strongly in Cornwall, Wales, Scotland and Ireland; today it can be traced through language, custom, religion and monuments, especially the Celtic crosses that can still be seen and enjoyed.

How did this separate identity come about? From AD313, when the Roman emperor Constantine legalised Christianity, Celtic Christianity could command followers without fear of prosecution. Constantine's story is an interesting one. On the eve of an important battle in northern Italy at Milvian Bridge, it is said that he, a pagan, had a dream in which he saw the Chi-Rho sign (the first two letters of Christ's name in Greek) and was told: 'In this sign conquer'. He changed the Roman Labarum, a banner with a wreath-like circle, to include the Chi-Rho sign. He won the battle, and thereafter Christianity was permitted throughout the empire. It is interesting that Constantine did not become converted himself until he was on his deathbed in AD330 - he clearly wished to hedge his bets!

It is this Chi-Rho sign and the crucifixion that has dominated Celtic Crosses. It was not always so, since early Christians often used the symbol of the fish or the peacock as a form of religious identity. However, this is the origin of the sign of the cross that appears on many stone crosses today.

The purpose of such crosses is not immediately obvious. Some appear now in churchyards, but they should not be confused with gravestones; nor should it be taken for granted that they always occupied the position in which they are now seen. Most probably many were markers pointing the way for travellers to a particular Christian site, be it the home of a reclusive saint or a secret meeting-place for worship. Some were commemorative in recognition of a saint or an early king. Others still present a puzzle to historians.

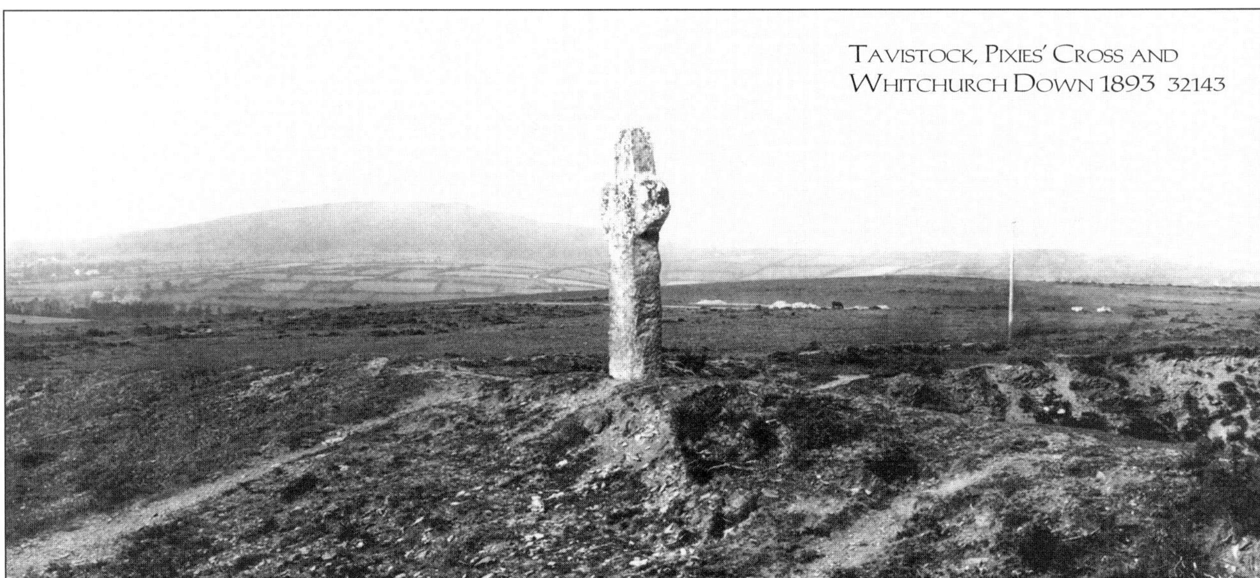

Tavistock, Pixies' Cross and Whitchurch Down 1893 32143

Celtic Crosses

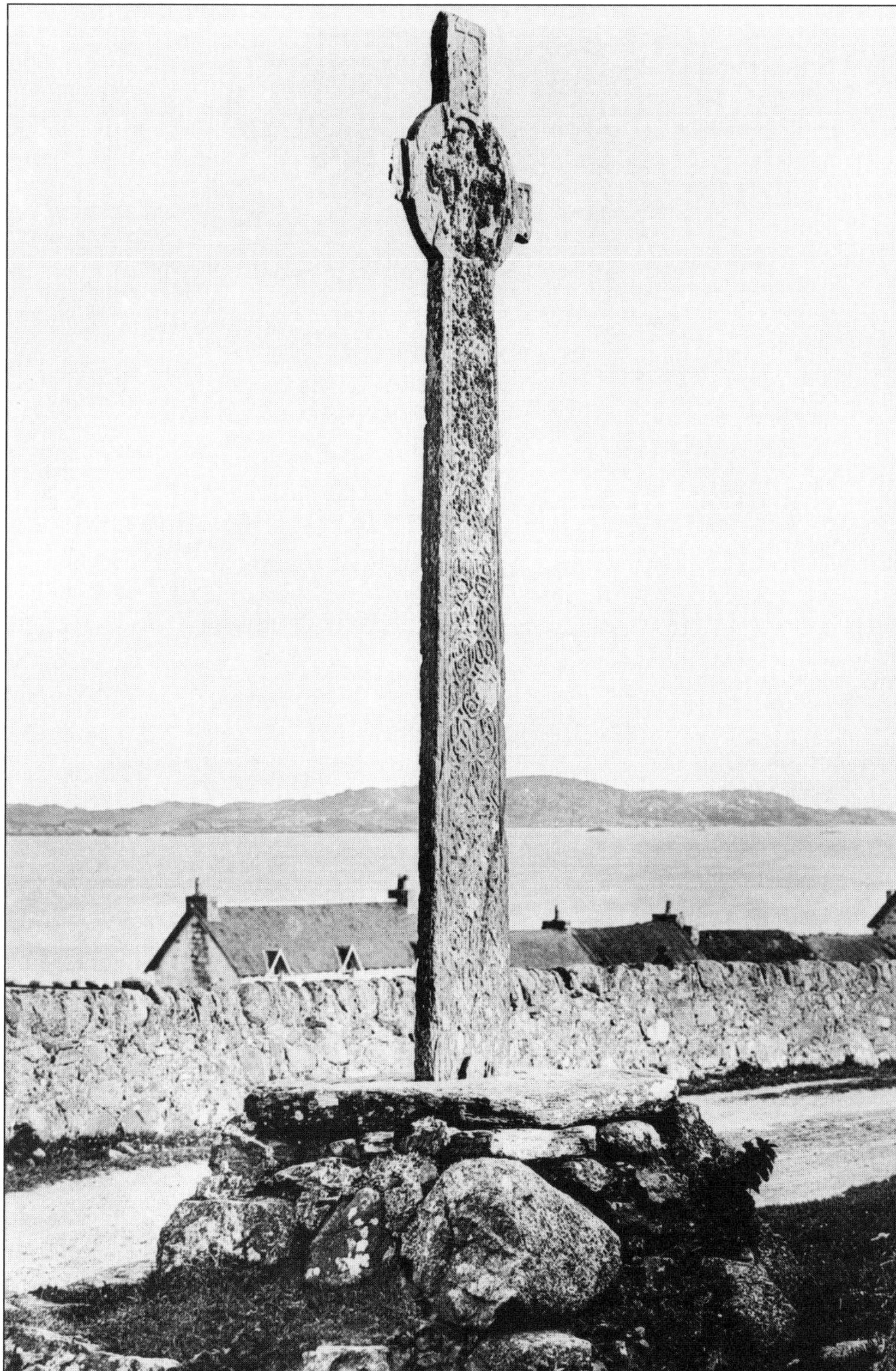

Iona, MacLean's Cross 1903 50894

Iona is of paramount importance as a Christian historical site, with an impressive legacy of Celtic and medieval buildings and monuments. The MacLean cross is the tallest on Iona; its shaft is a fine example of the Celtic interlacing pattern with a disc-headed crucifixion.

Celtic Crosses

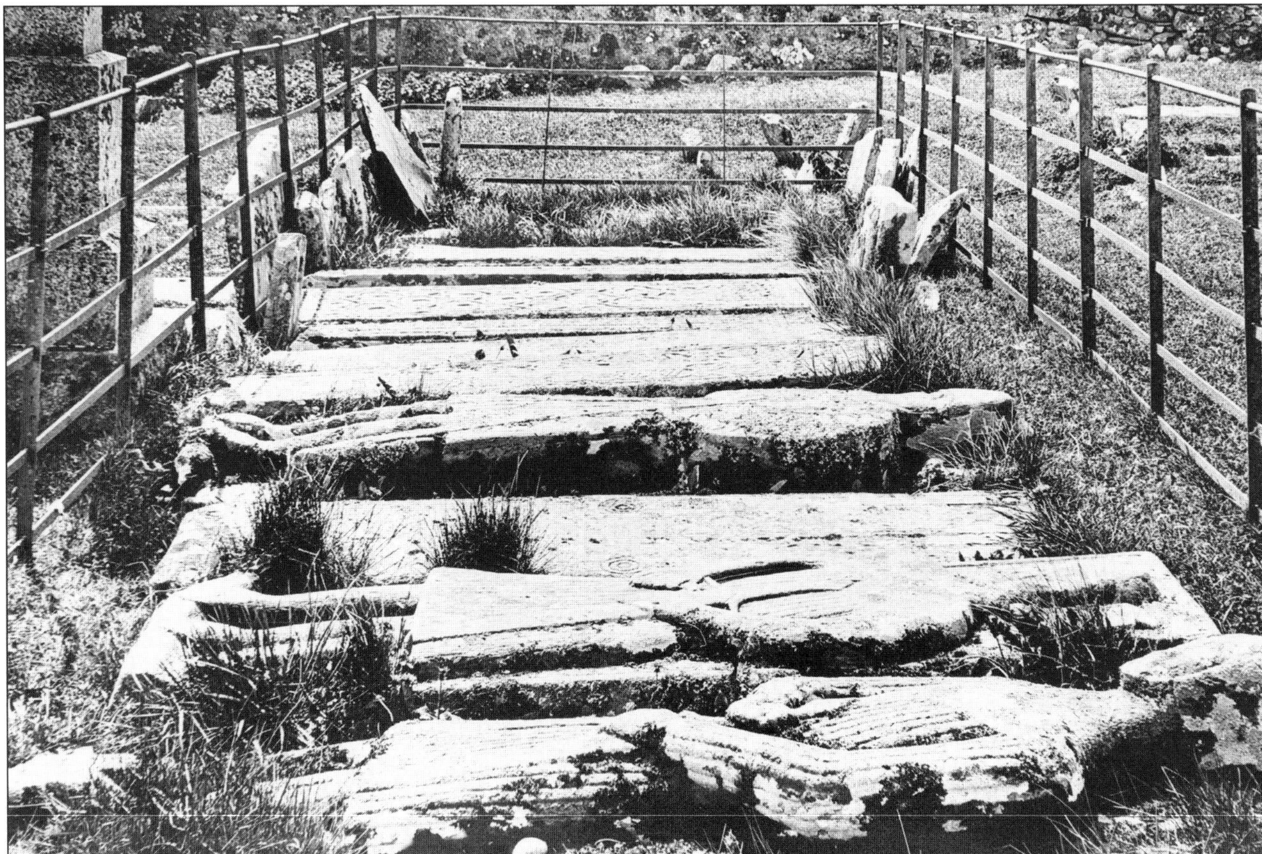

Above: Iona, The Tombs of the MacLeans 1903 50893

Such was Iona's importance in Scottish history that nearly 50 of the country's kings are buried here, along with many chieftains of the local clans. This plot, looking somewhat neglected at this time, is the final resting-place of many of the Clan MacLean.

Right: Iona, The Cathedral, West Front 1903 50891

The island of Iona, near Mull off the west coast of Scotland, is known as the cradle of Scottish Christianity or 'The Mecca of Gael'. St Columba built his monastery here in AD563. The medieval abbey church was rebuilt in the 1930s and became the home of the famous Iona community.

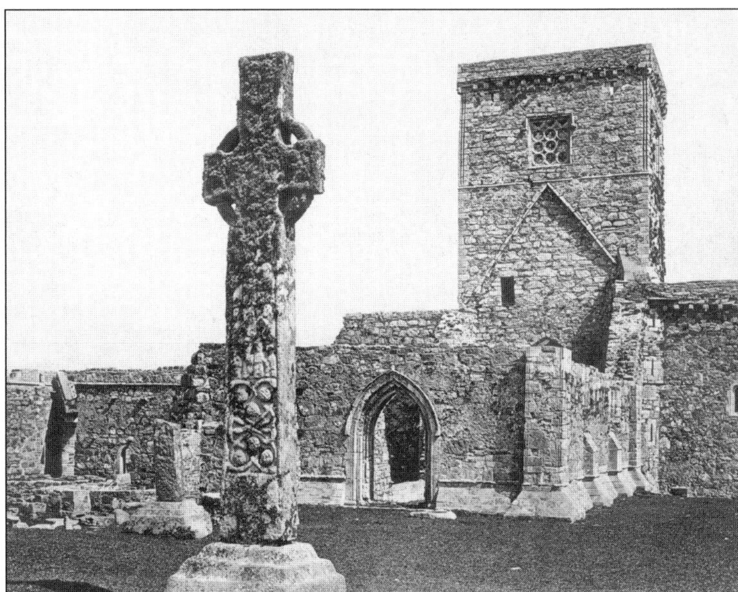

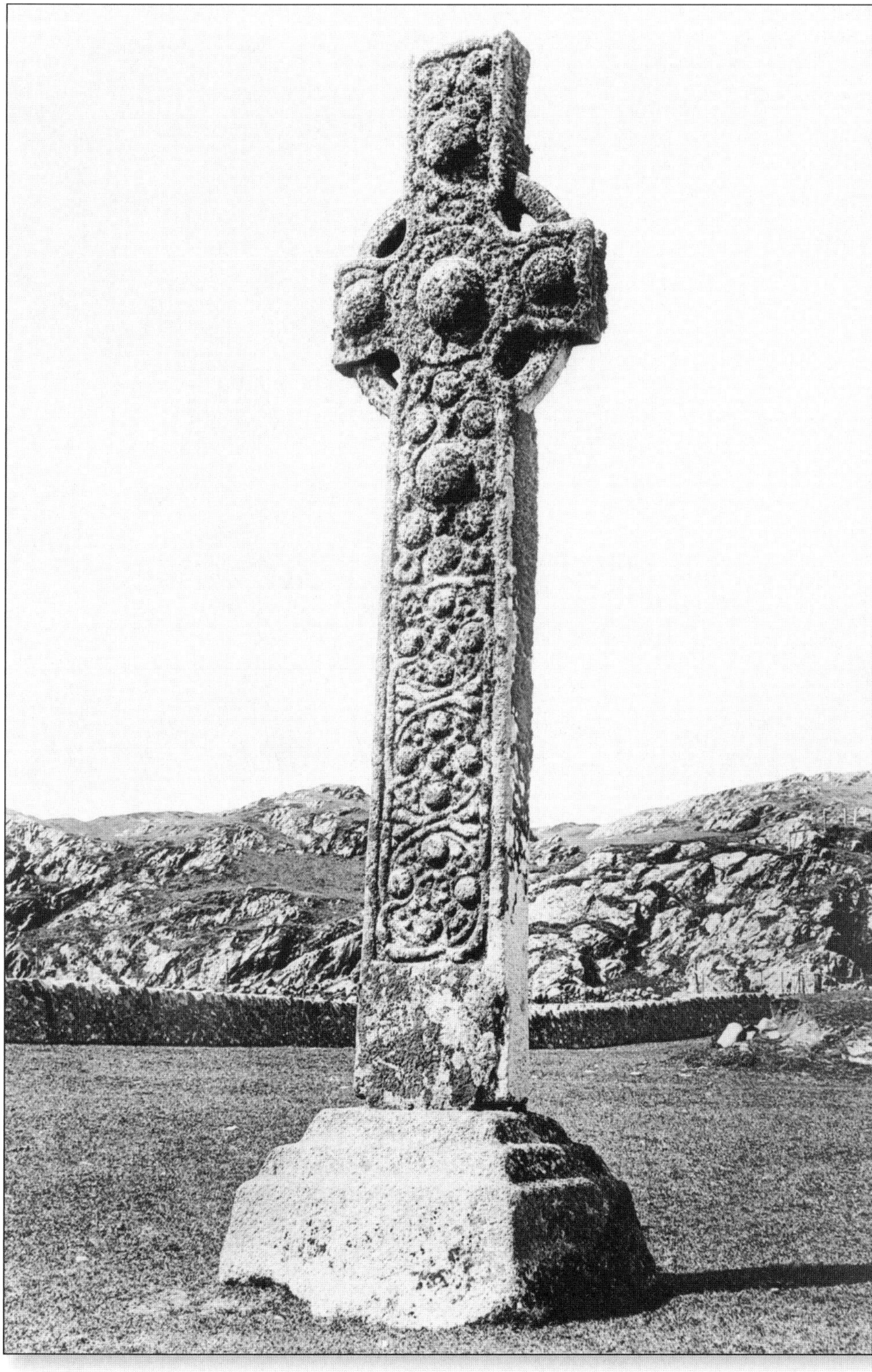

IONA, ST MARTIN'S CROSS 1903 50895

St Martin's cross is the best and most famous of the free-standing high Celtic crosses that survive on Iona. It dates from the 8th century. It is over 17 feet high, and is beautifully carved with biblical scenes on one side and on the other the 'boss and serpent' design associated with pre-Christian pagan worship.

Celtic Crosses

Redruth, Carn Brea 1906 56457

Most of England's Celtic legacy is to be found in Cornwall. Carn Brea, between Camborne and Redruth, has a very long archaeological record commencing with a large walled Neolithic settlement, one of the oldest in England. In this rather dramatic photograph, the remains of a medieval castle are on the left, whilst the stone monument on the right was erected in memory of a Victorian local landowner.

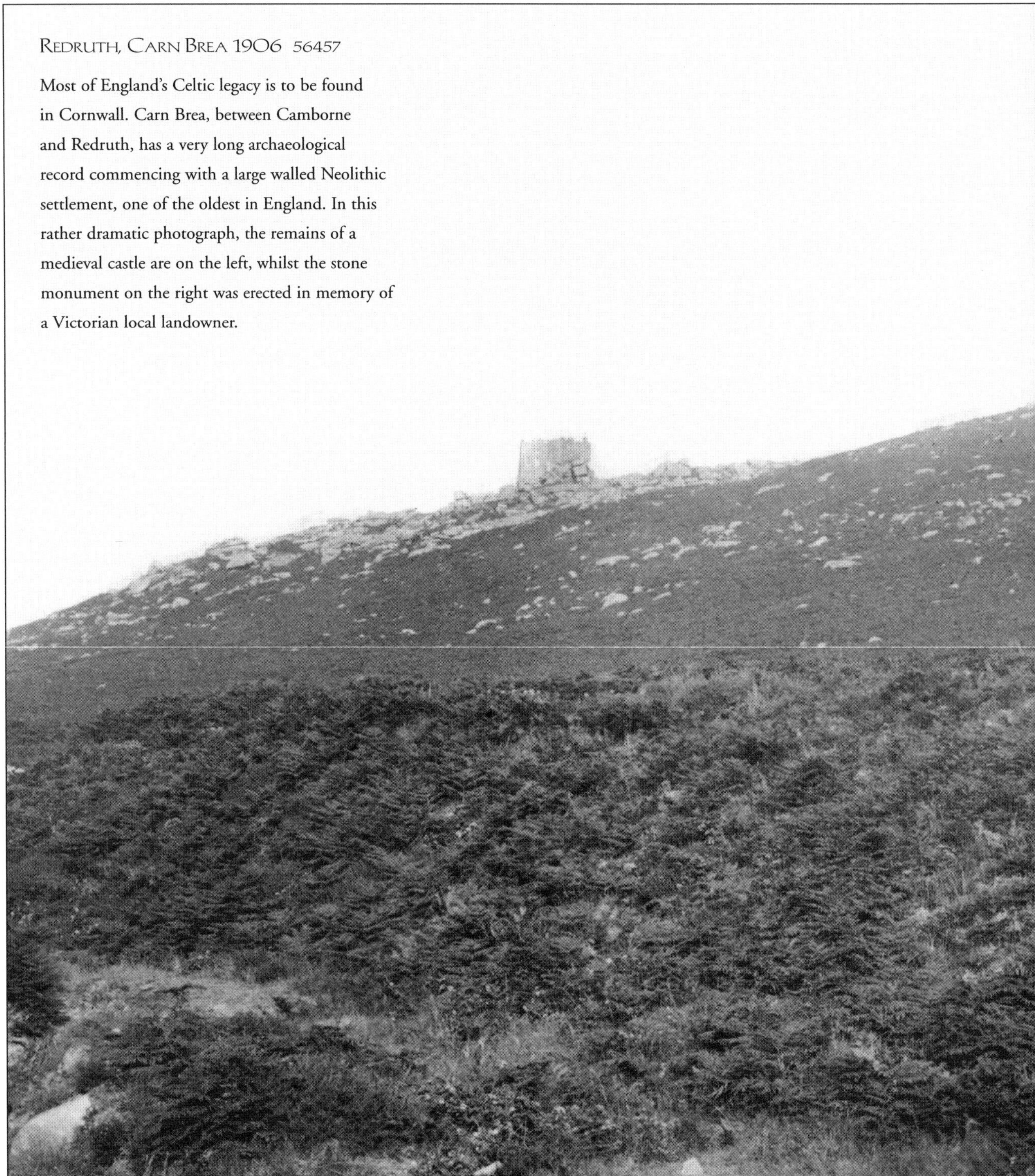

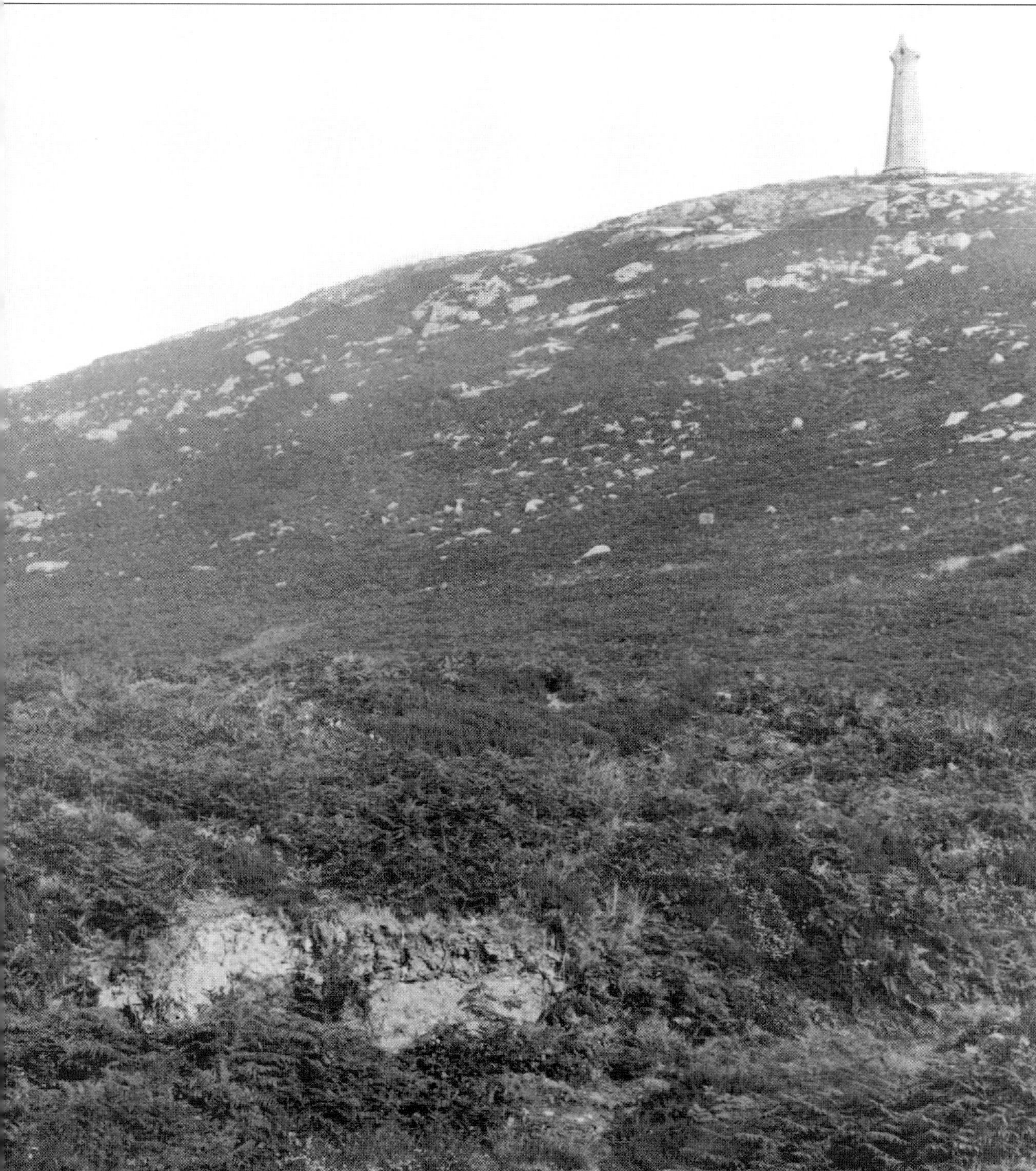

CELTIC CROSSES

BELOW: LISKEARD, ST CLEER'S WELL 1938 88595

On the edge of Bodmin Moor, near Liskeard, are several important archaeological sites with Celtic remains. This is St Cleer's Holy Well in the village named after him. The well is protected by the picturesque 15th-century chapel erected over it.

TOP RIGHT: LISKEARD, ST KEYNE'S WELL 1938 88596

Pilgrims seeking their curative powers have long venerated the healing properties of sacred wells. Early Christians would drink or even immerse themselves in 'holy' water. Votive offerings were often thrown into the water: today, tourists often do the same by throwing coins into fountains and wells.

BELOW RIGHT: LISKEARD, THE KING STONE C1955 L53051

A few miles away from St Cleer's Well is the King Stone (actually two stones), which is also known as King Doniert's stone. The granite stones date from the 9th century. The inscription is thought to commemorate, erroneously as it turns out, the last Cornish King, Doniert (formerly known as Durngarth) who died in AD870.

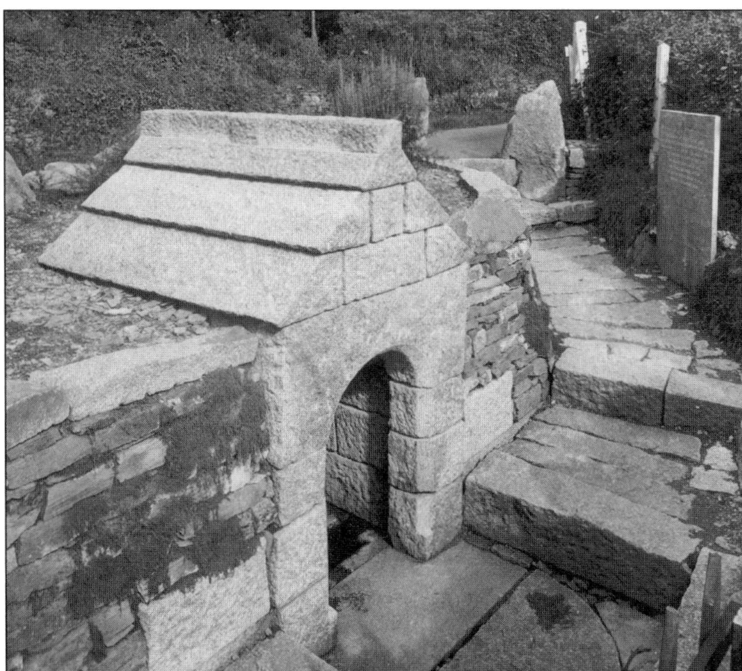

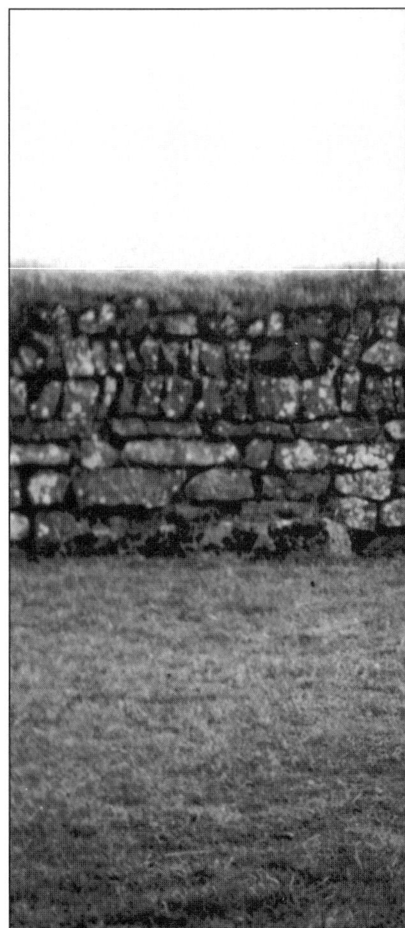

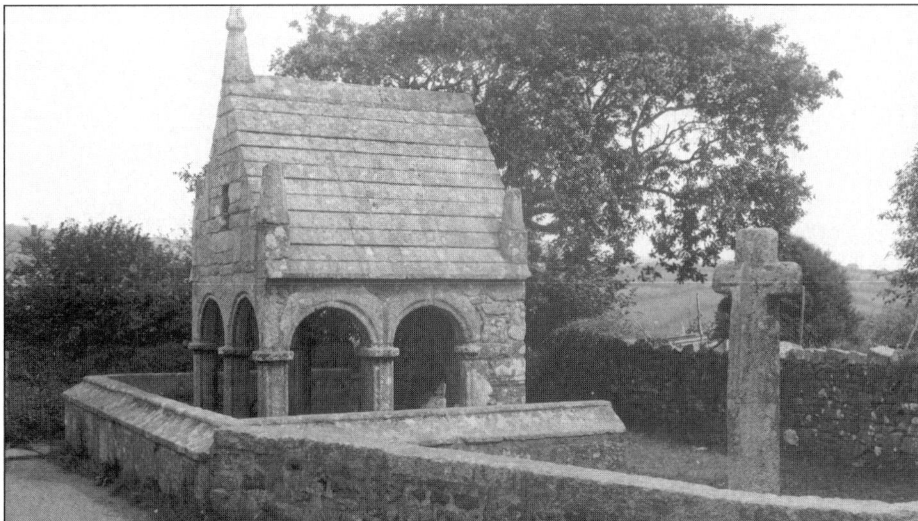

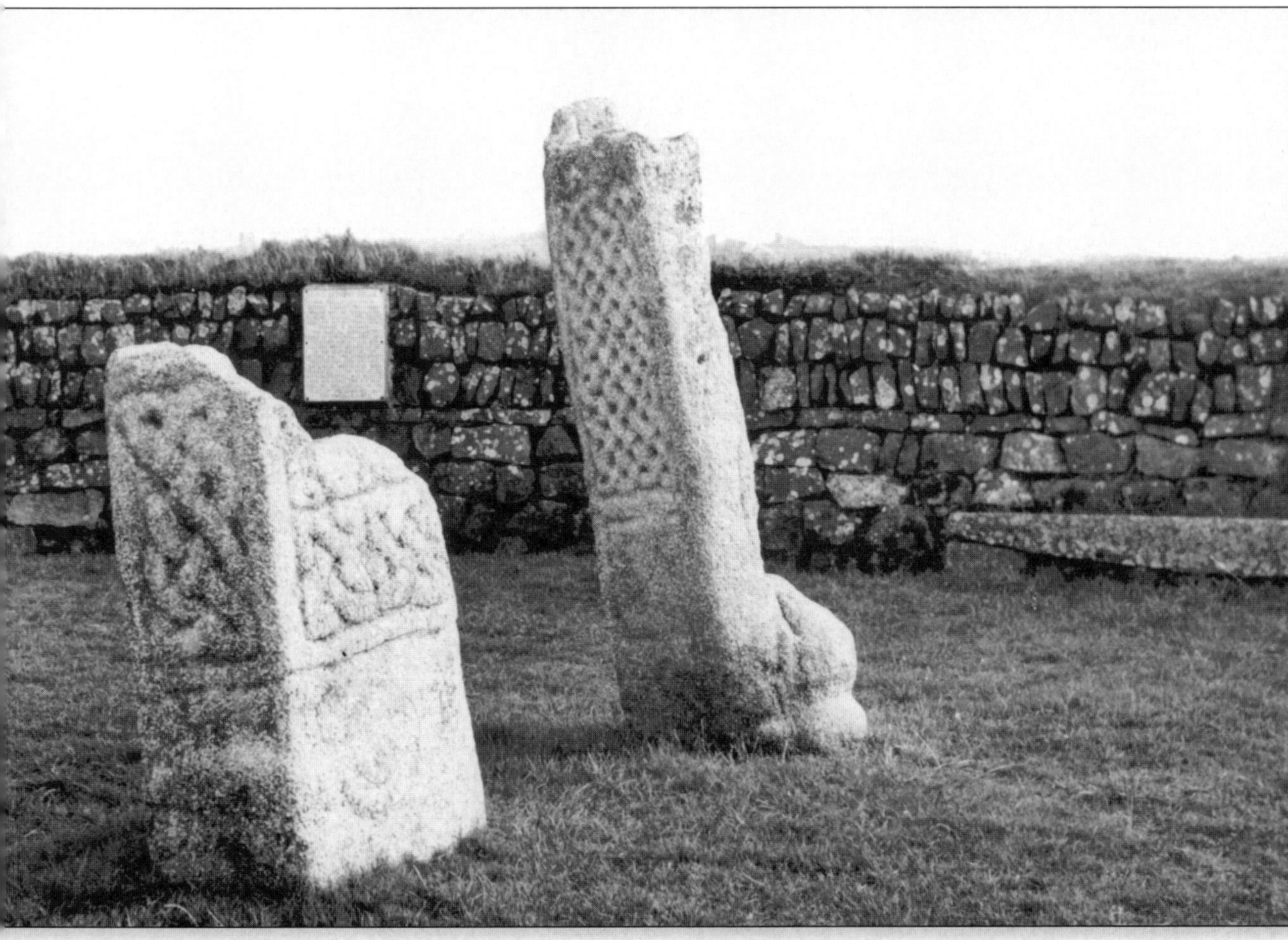

Celtic Crosses

LISKEARD, THE KING STONE 1938 88594

This view invokes mystery and isolation, sentiments strongly associated with Celtic history. The stones have a Latin inscription, which reads 'Doniert ordered this for the good of his soul'.

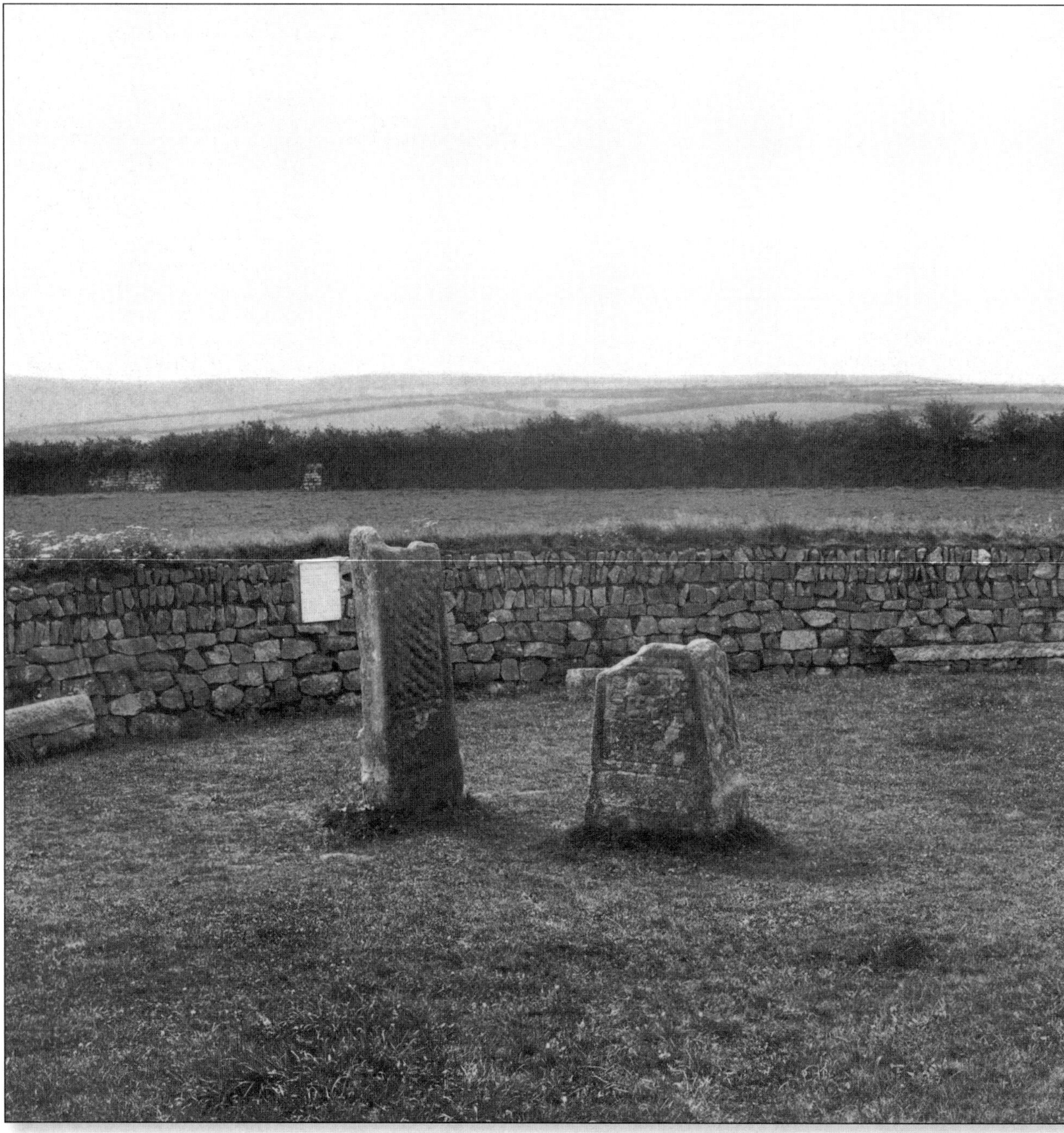

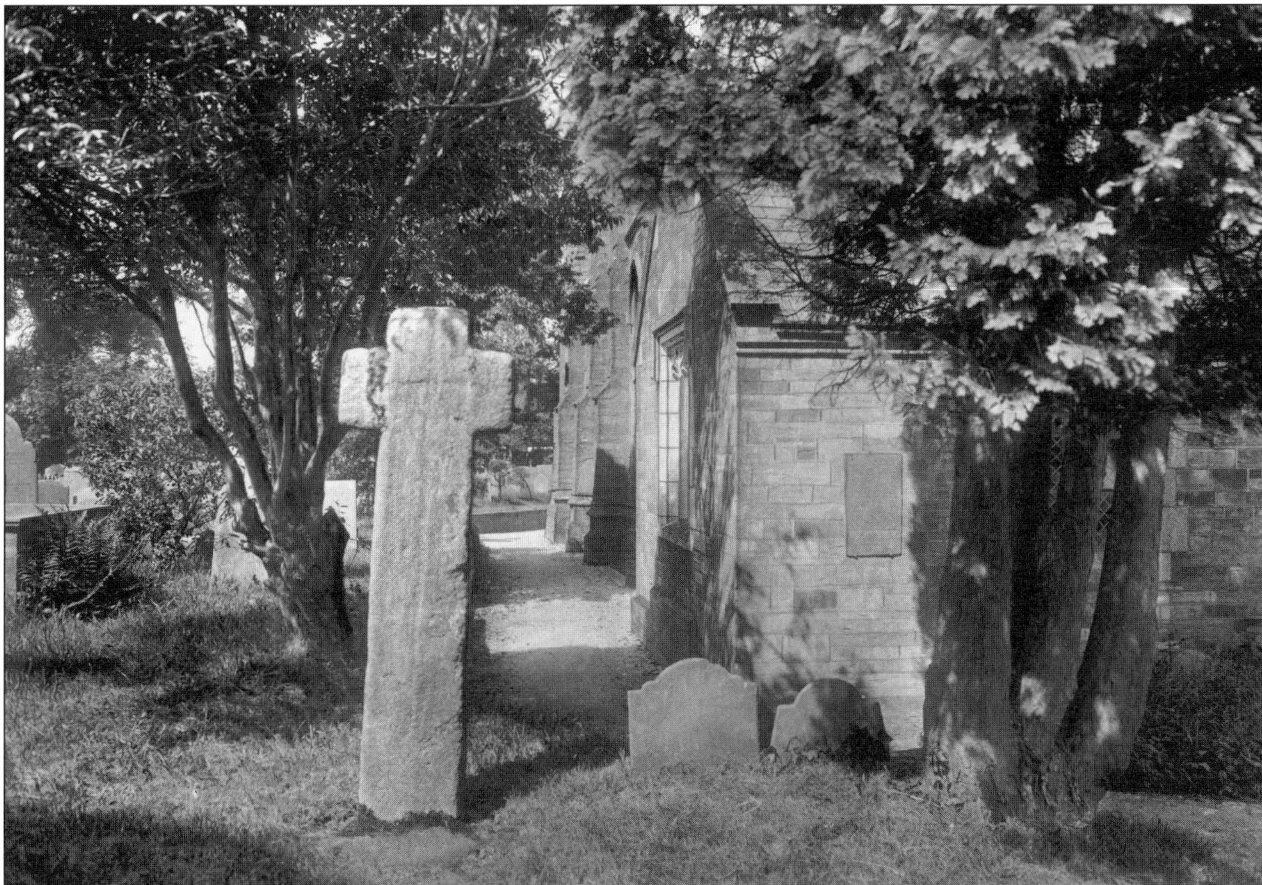

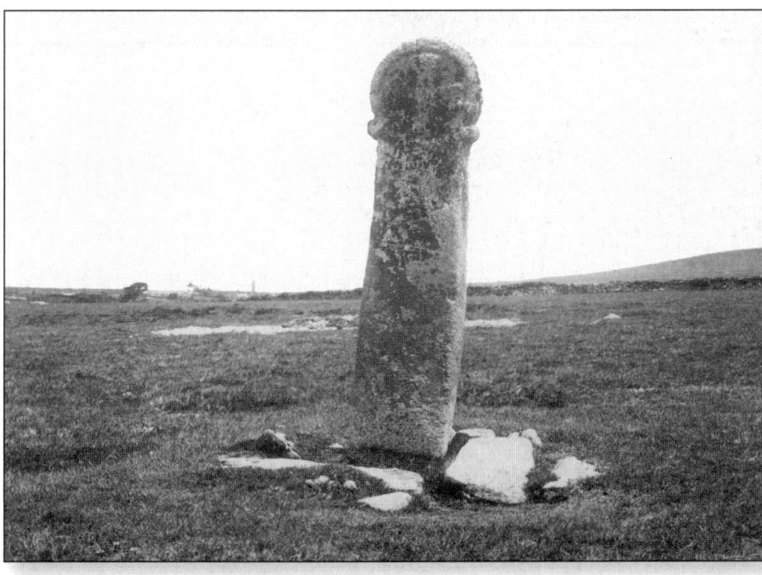

ABOVE: LISKEARD, OLD CORNISH CROSS 1928 81358

LEFT: LISKEARD, CHEESEWRING, LONG TOM 1908 59769

At Cheesewring, a mile or two from St Cleer, there are dozens of mysterious stone monuments on the moor. They include megalithic stone circles, standing stones and old Celtic carved crosses. This one is known as Long Tom.

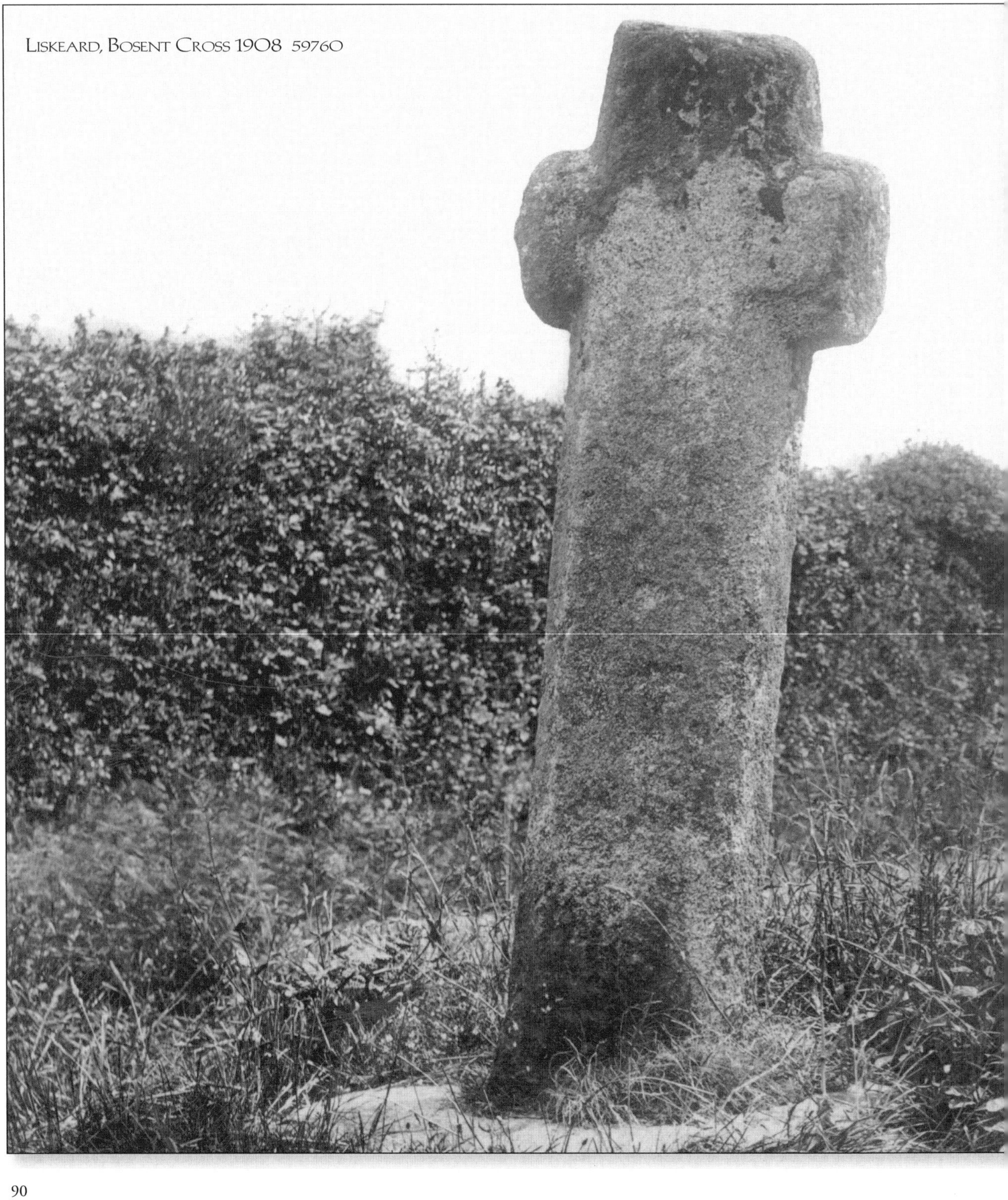

LISKEARD, BOSENT CROSS 1908 59760

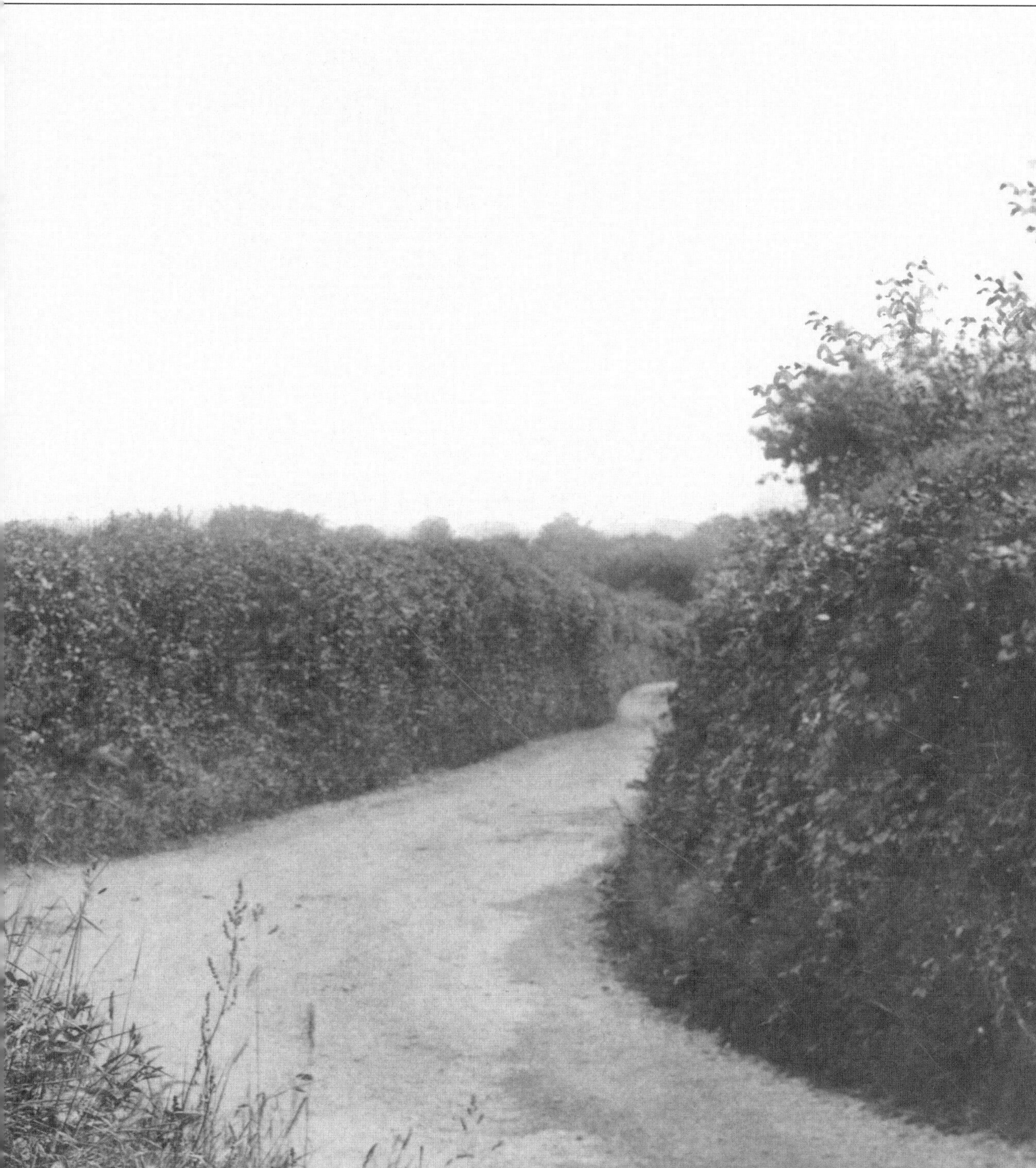

Celtic Crosses

QUETHIOCK,
THE CELTIC CROSS
1908 59763

The Quethiock cross is a fine and typical example of a tall freestanding Cornish Celtic cross with a plain shaft and a wheel-headed cross.

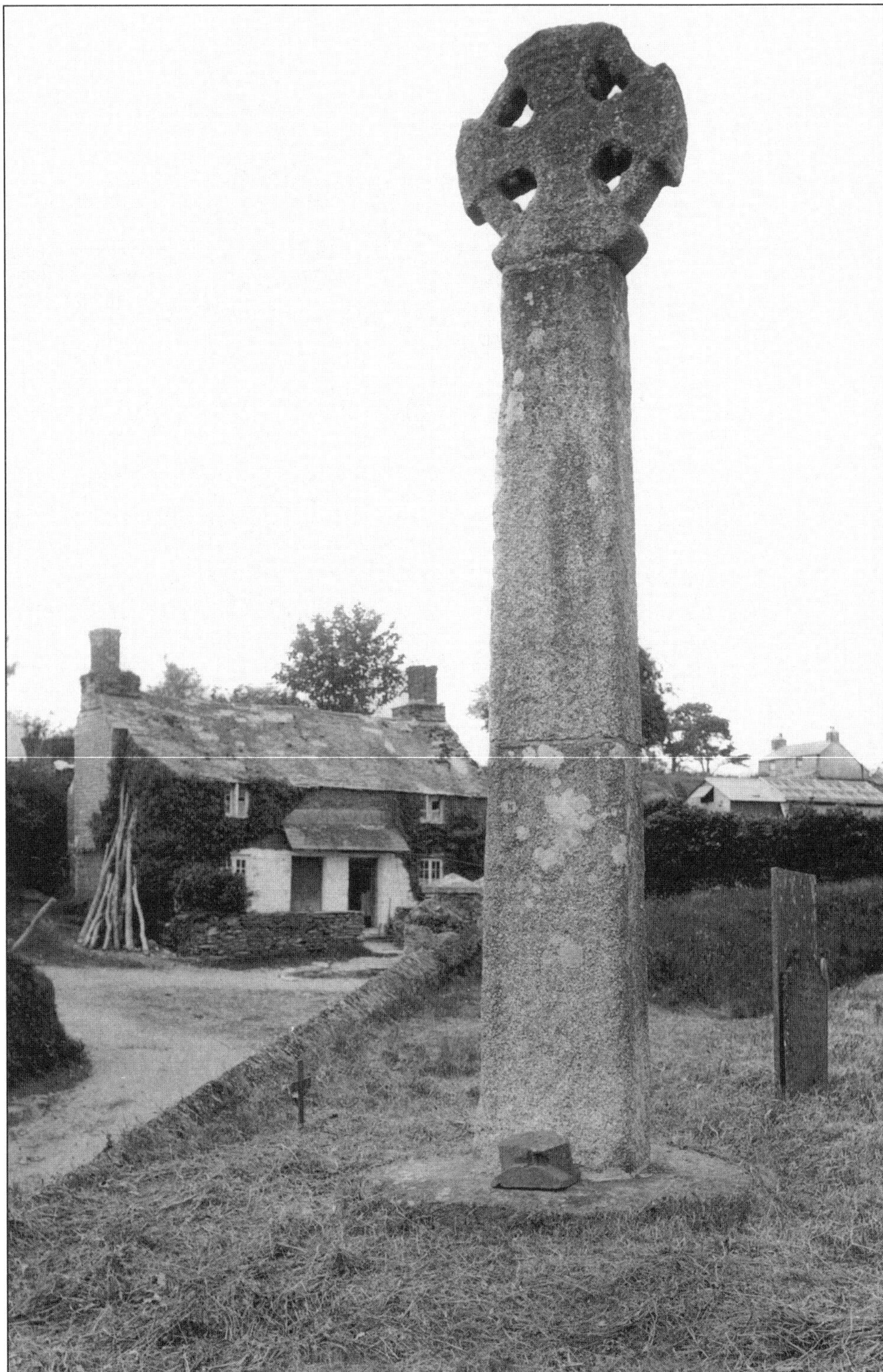

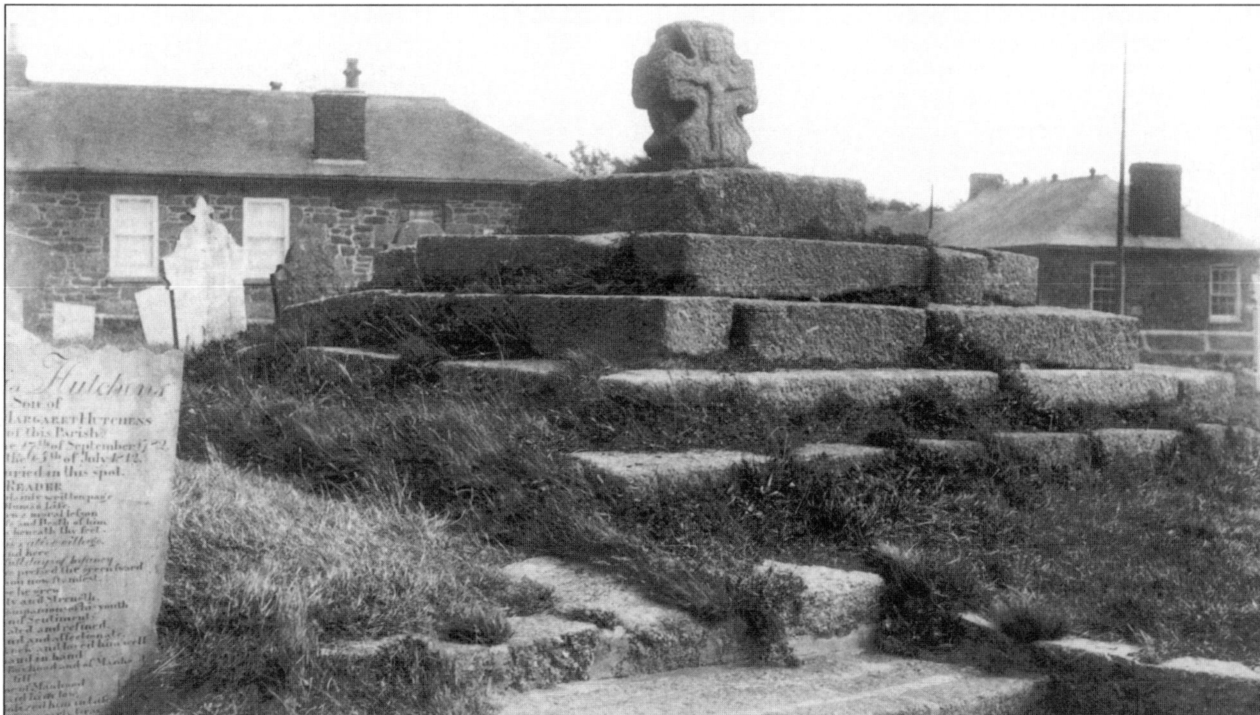

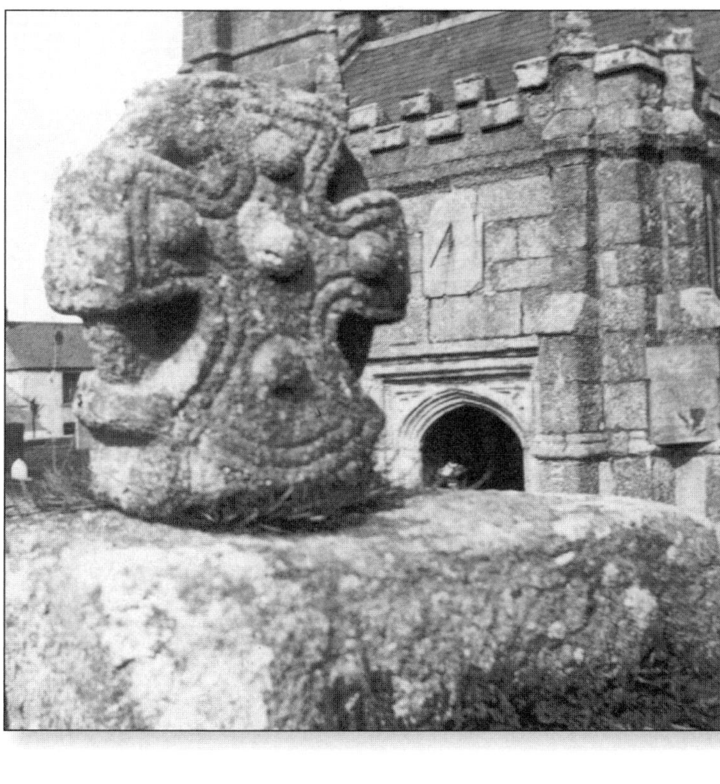

ST BURYAN, THE CROSS 1908 61267A (ABOVE)

St Buryan, near Penzance, is now thought to have been an important Celtic monastic site. The churchyard contains several strange, small carved crossheads (this is a typical example) with a crucifix figure dating from the 10th century.

ST BURYAN, THE CROSS 1903 50859

Celtic Crosses

St Buryan, The Cross
1890 27745

Another of the stunted carved crossheads in St Buryan's churchyard. The crucified Christ figure is robed; this indicates an eastern Byzantine style rather than western Roman influences.

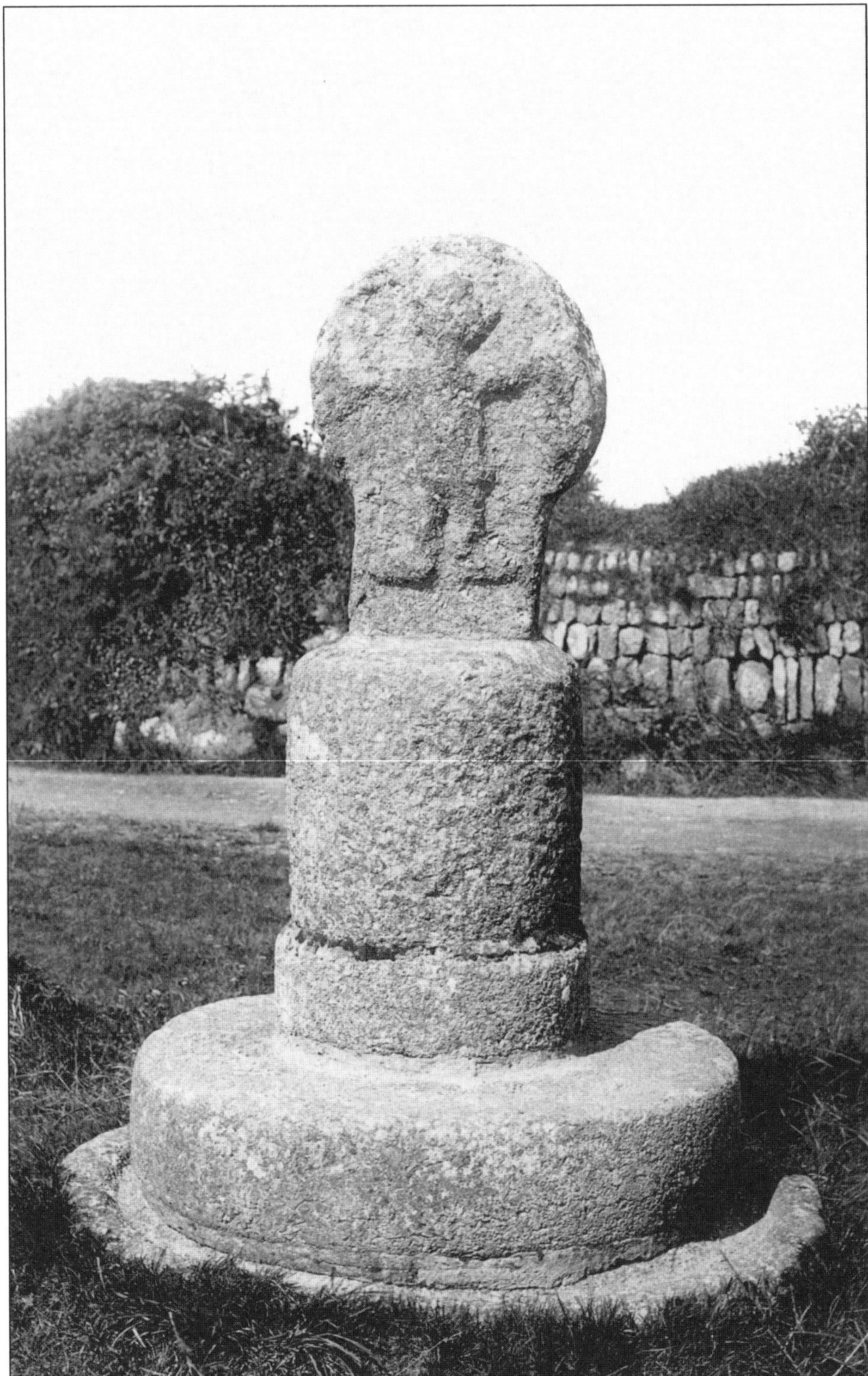

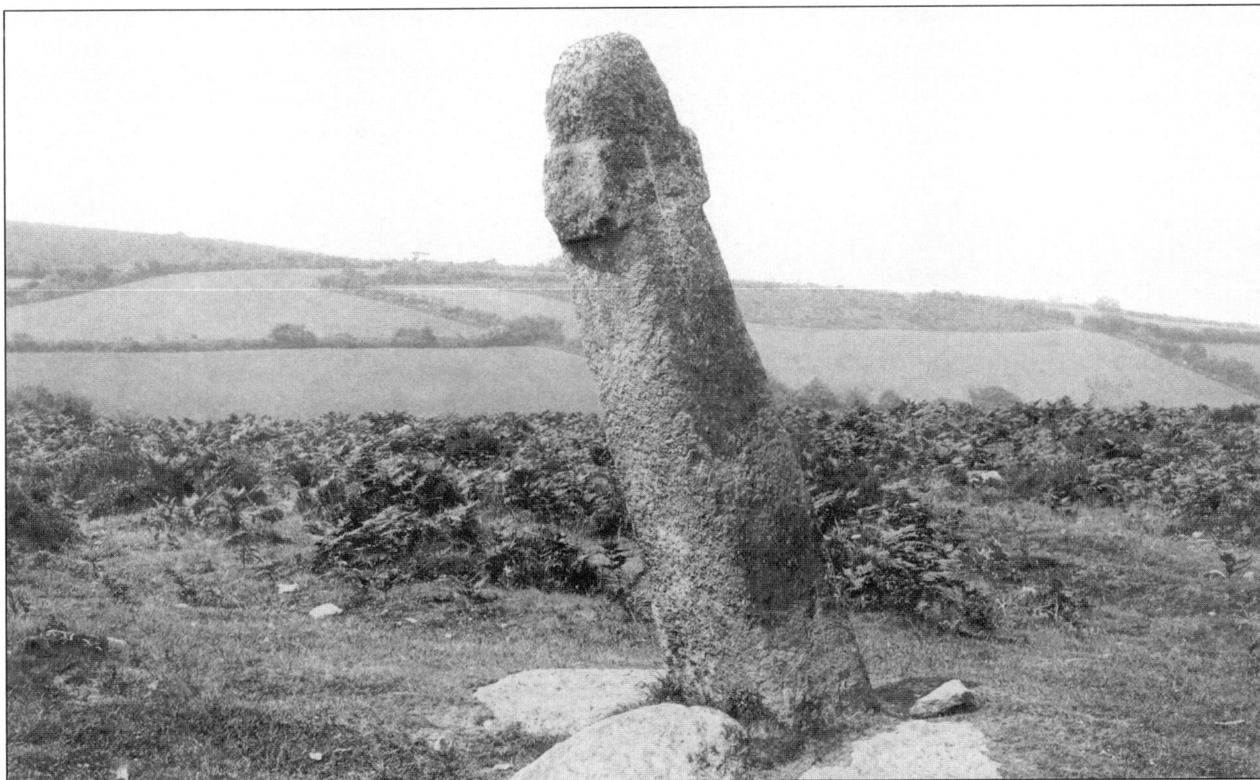

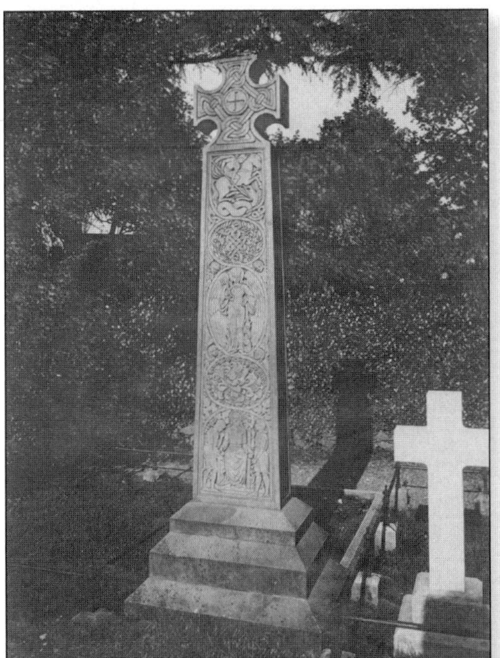

ABOVE: LISKEARD, OLD CORNISH CROSS 1928 81358

LEFT: CONISTON, RUSKIN'S MONUMENT 1912 64286

Celtic motifs became very popular with Victorian designers in the 19th century. This Celtic-style monument in the Lake District marks the grave of John Ruskin, the artist and philosopher, who helped to bring about the Gothic revival in Victorian architecture and a resurgance of interest in Celtic art.

Celtic Crosses

Penzance, Old Cross in Morrab Gardens 1906 56518

In Victorian times many old Celtic crosses and other monuments were 'recycled' as the designs became fashionable: this one is in the Victorian Morrab Gardens near the sea front in Penzance.

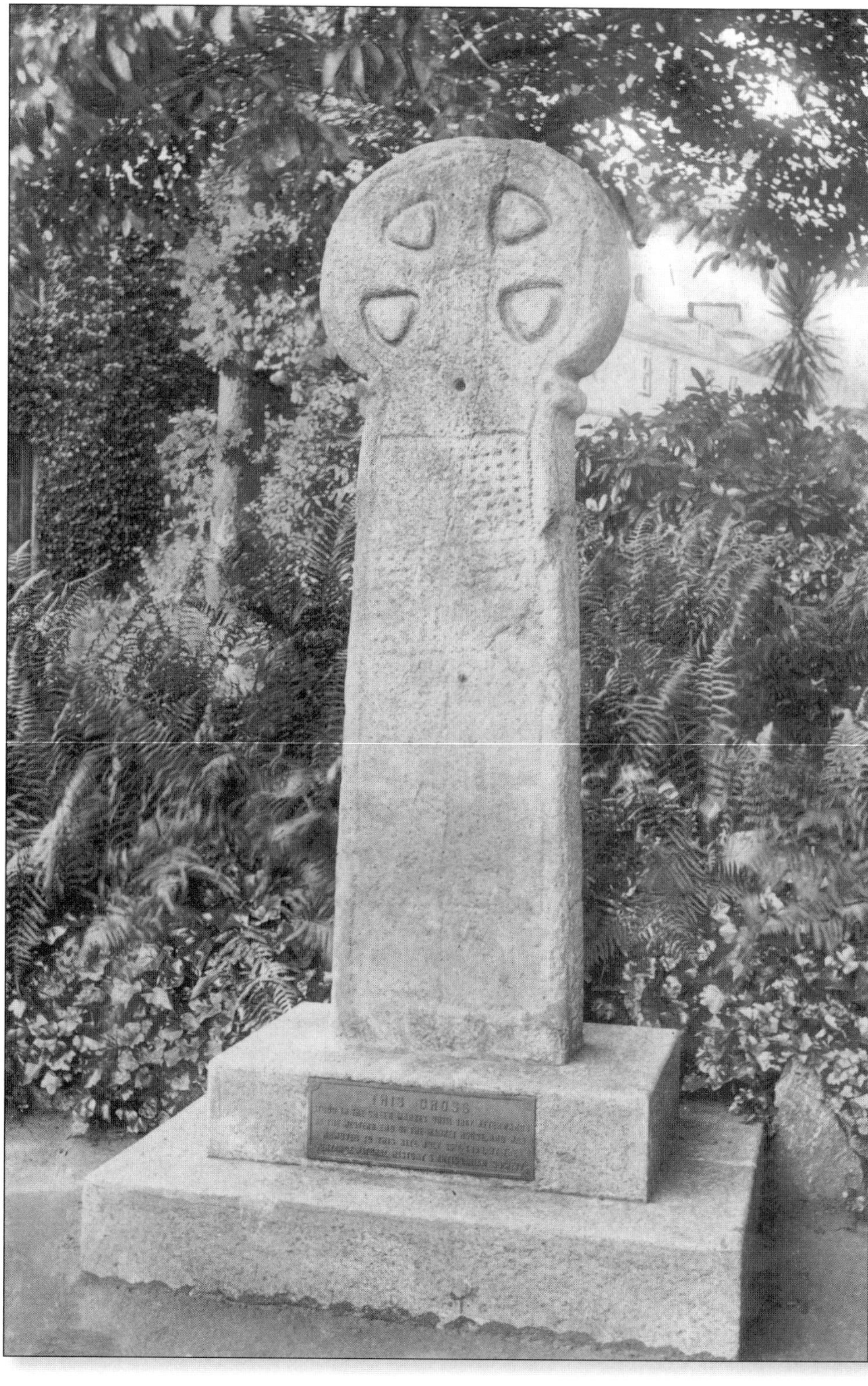

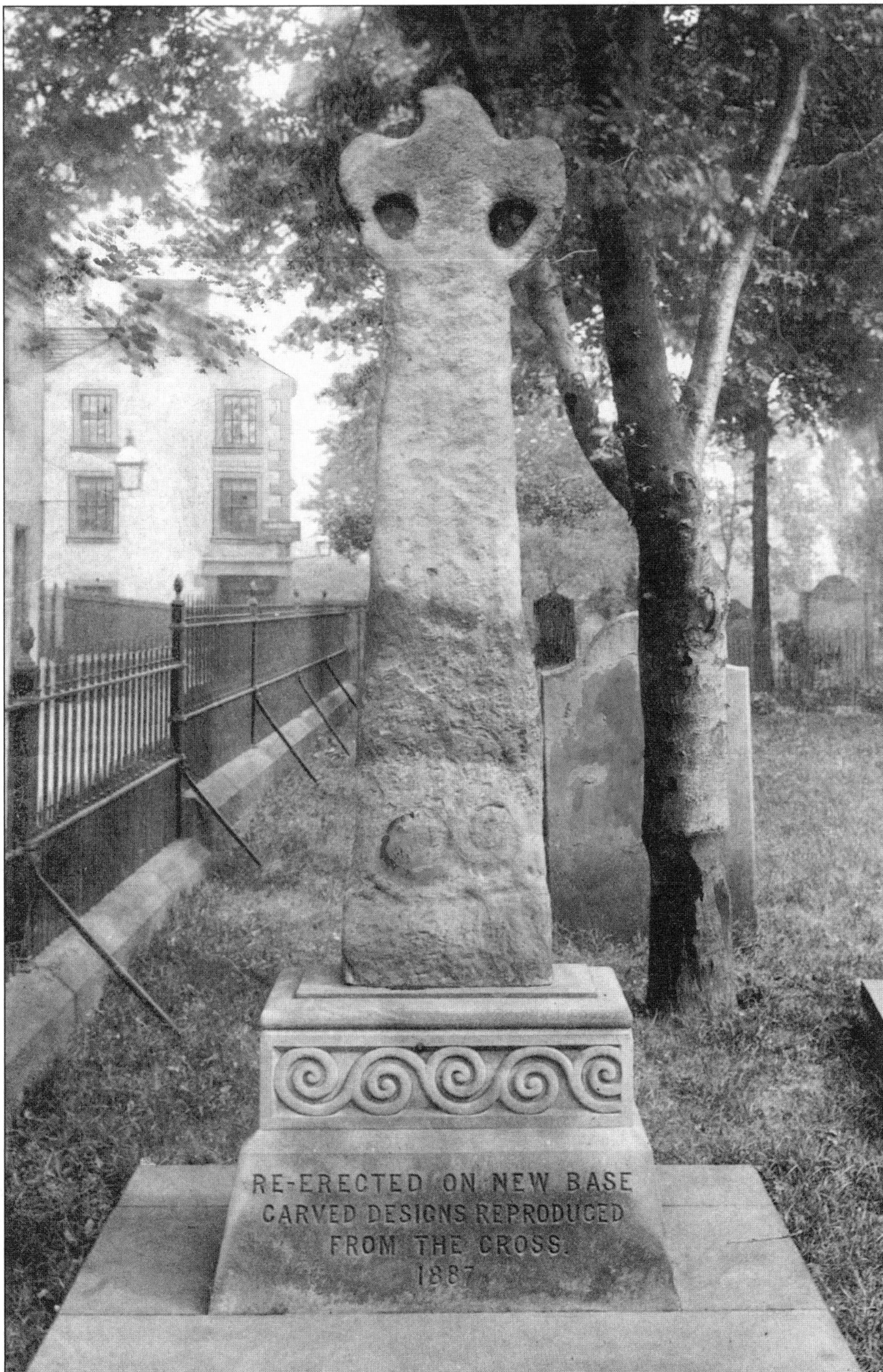

PENRITH, THE PARISH CHURCH, THE GIANT'S THUMB 1893 32927

A further example of the Victorians restoring and re-erecting an old Celtic cross, perhaps inventing a suitable fanciful nickname for it too!

CELTIC CROSSES

ILKLEY, THE SAXON CROSSES 1916 *67326*

These three fine and well-known Celtic crosses (now kept inside All Saints' Church) are marked with pre-Christian symbols and some later markings. The plaited design on their shafts is common in the Celtic era.

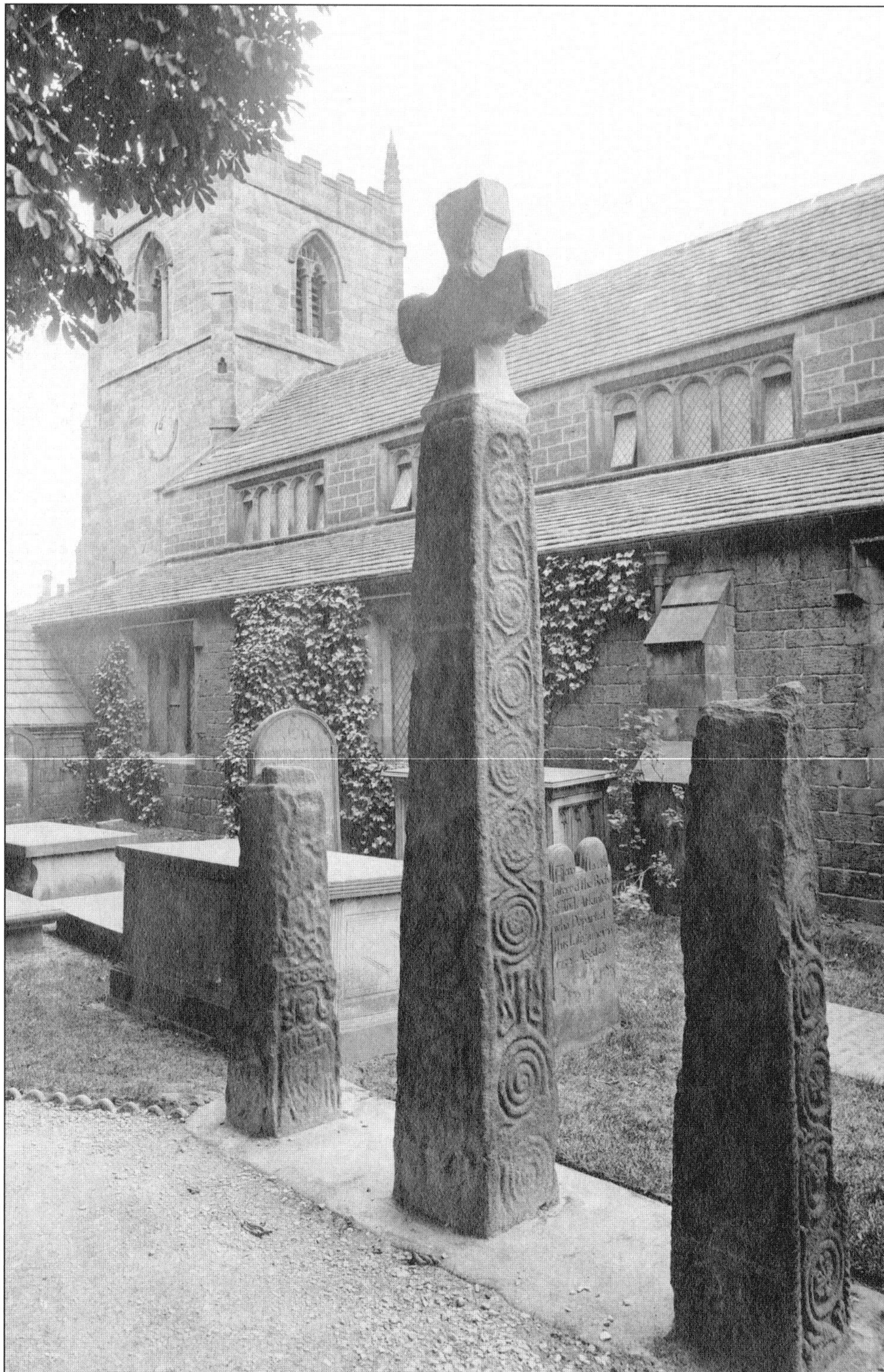

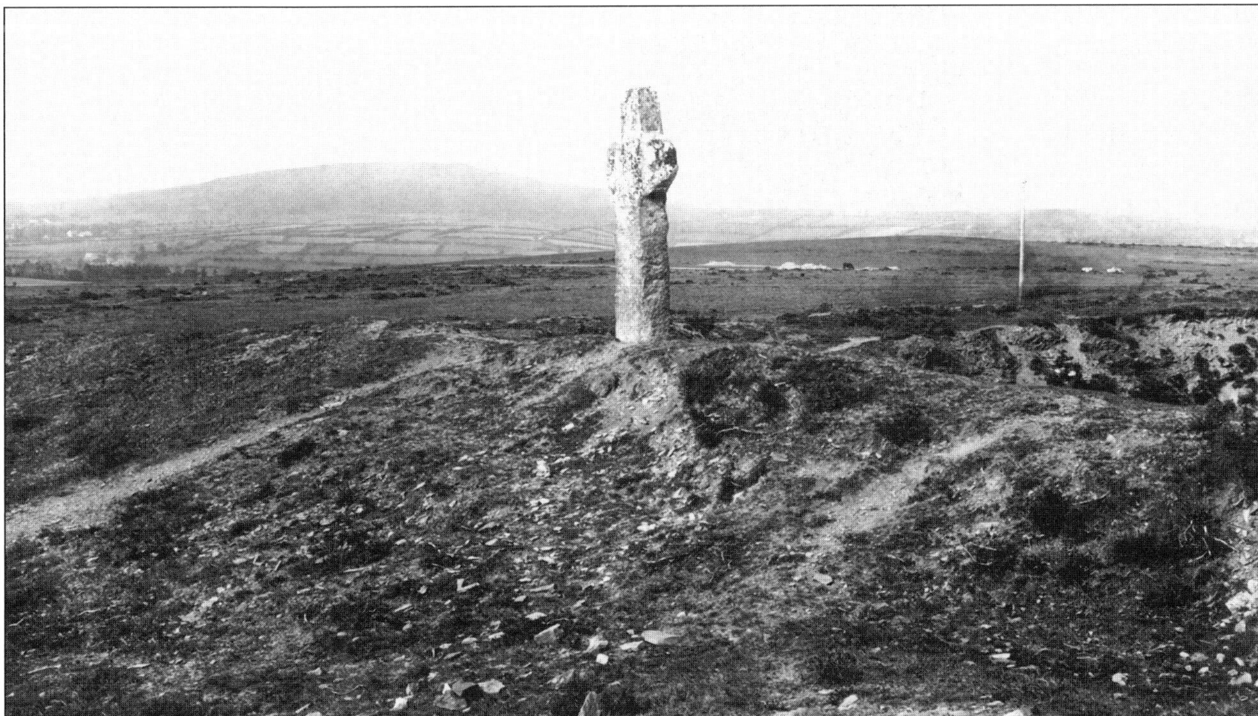

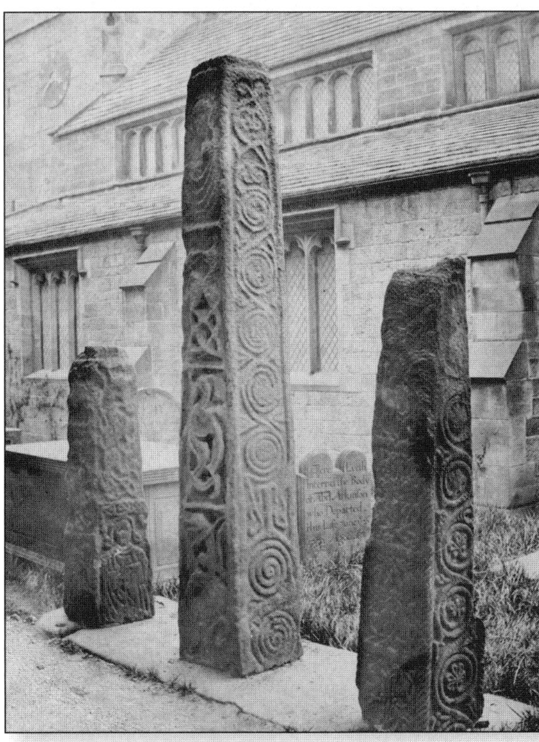

Above: Tavistock, Pixies' Cross and Whitchurch Down 1893 32143

Left: Ilkley, Saxon Crosses in the Churchyard c1874 7290

An early photograph of the crosses before restoration had taken place, as seen in 67326, page 98. It is believed that they were originally used as grave markers where the gospel would be preached before the church was built.

Celtic Crosses

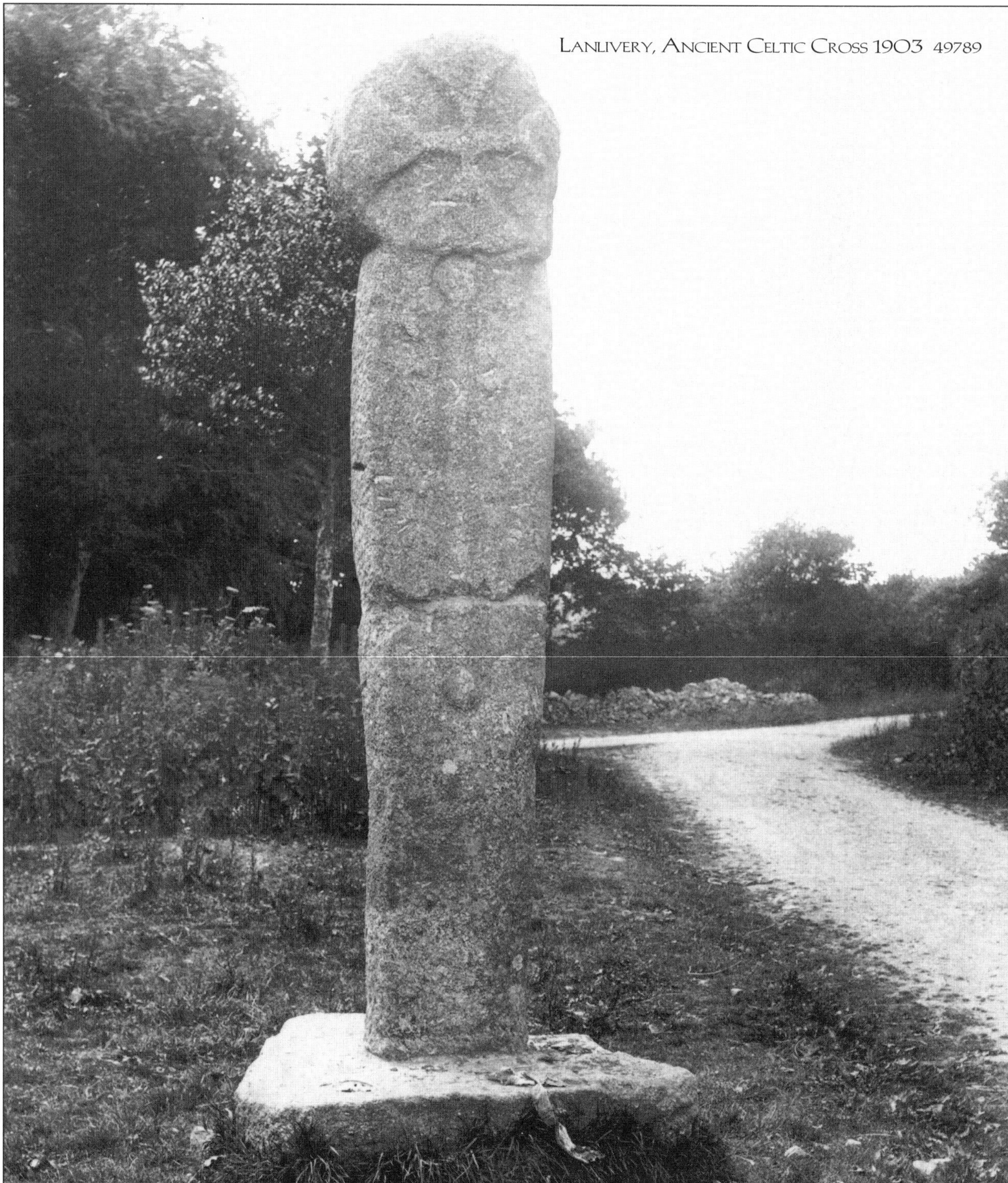

Lanlivery, Ancient Celtic Cross 1903 49789

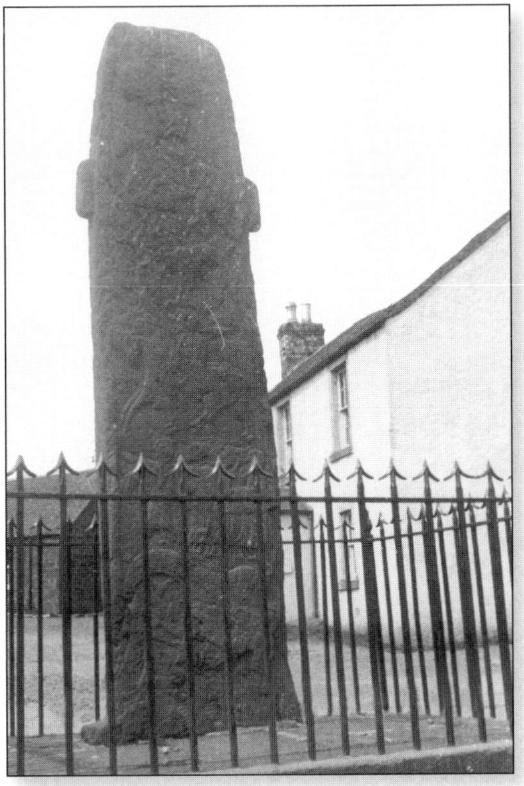

Left: Fowlis Wester, 8th-Century Cross c1950 F1183002

Below: Heysham, The Churchyard, Hogback Stone 1912 64232

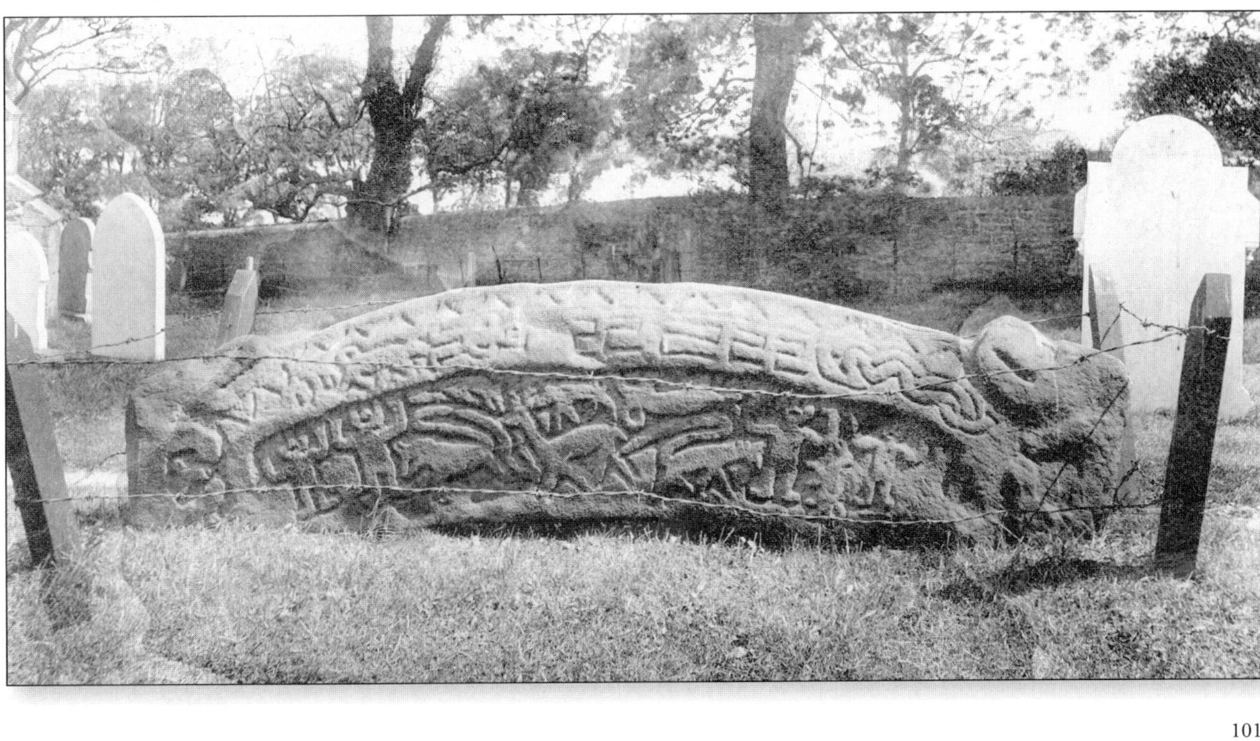

ROMANCE & MYTH

It is widely believed that King Arthur probably was a real person, but beyond that there is little agreement about who he was, what he did or even when he lived. None of the early sources refer to him as king. He appears to have been a British leader who opposed the Saxon invasions. It seems that every historic town with strong Celtic connections claims a stake in the life of Arthur. Where romance ends and myth begins seems unimportant, so ingrained has he become in our historic culture. He is traditionally associated with the victory at Mount Badon around the year AD500. It is Geoffrey of Monmouth, who published his 'History of the Kings of Britain' in about AD1136, who created the medieval legend of Arthur and his wizard, Merlin. The story of Arthur, his twelve knights of the Round Table and the return of his sword, Excalibur, to the Lady of the Lake, is exciting fable. That it cannot be accurately verified hardly seems to matter.

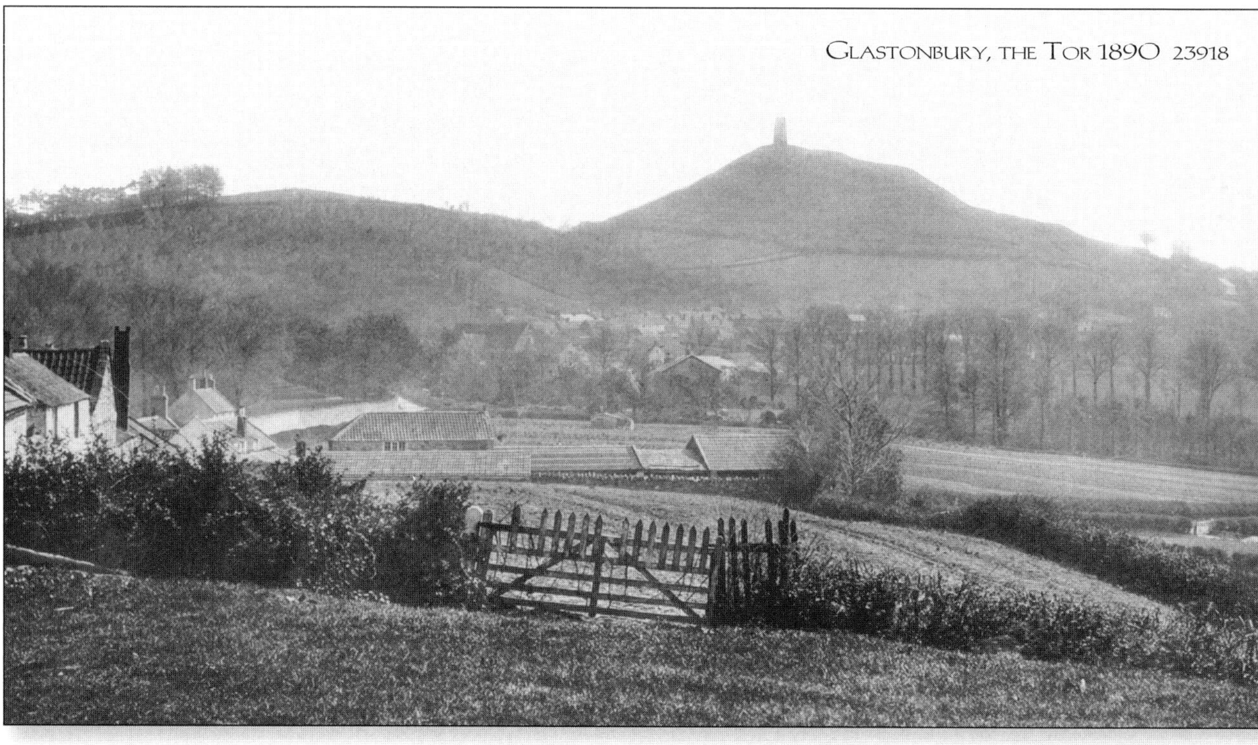

GLASTONBURY, THE TOR 1890 23918

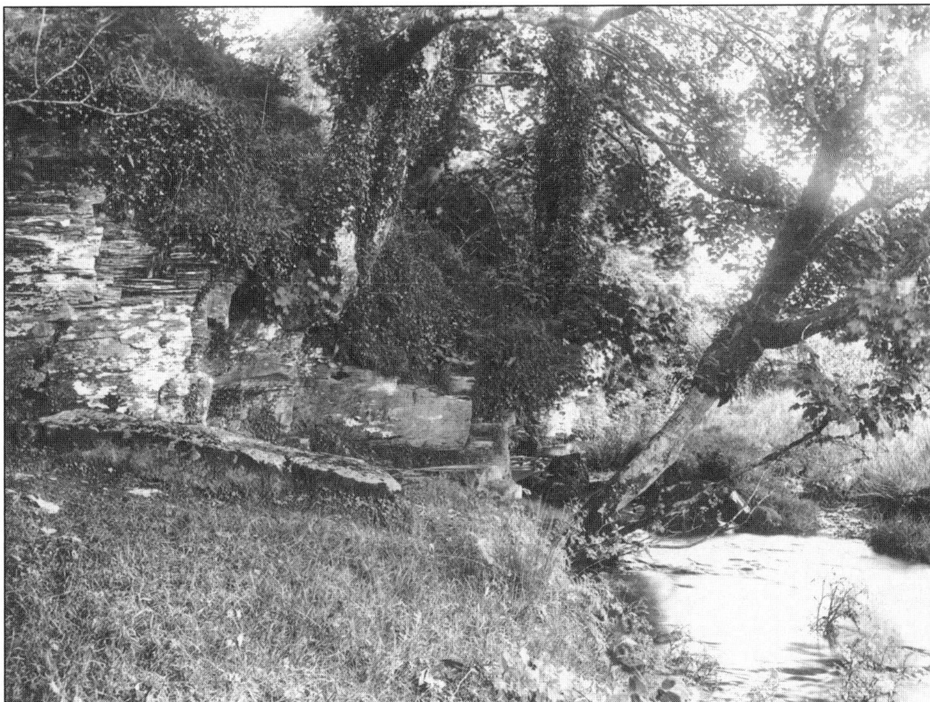

CAMELFORD, KING ARTHUR'S GRAVE 1906
56167

Many places stake a claim to be either the burial place of King Arthur or the site of his last battle. His last battle was at Camlann, whose name means crooked bank, or glen.

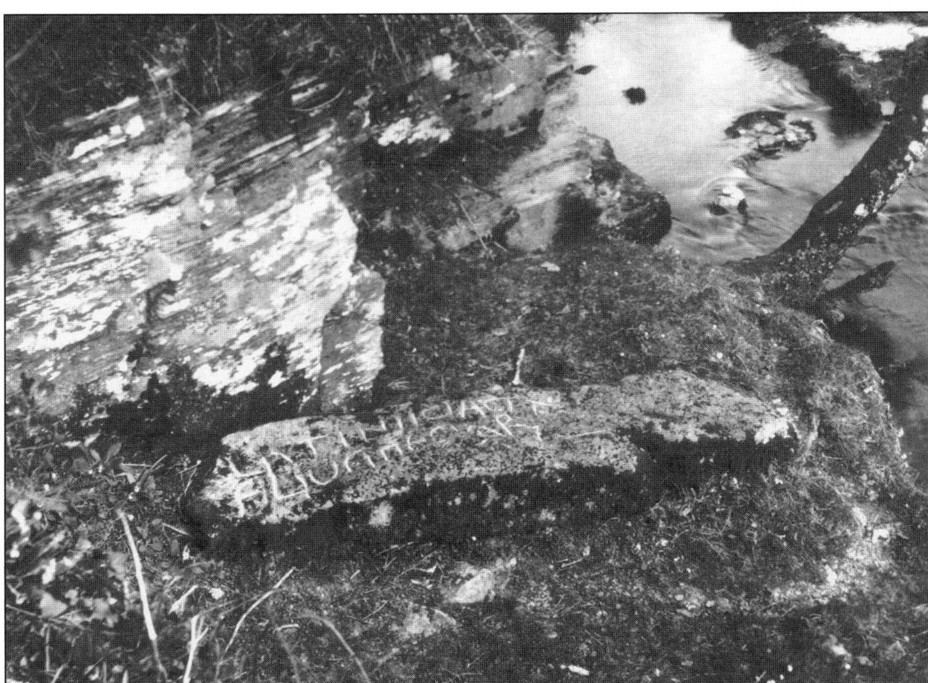

CAMELFORD, THE GRAVE OF KING ARTHUR C1960
C15009

Since there is no evidence of Arthur ever existing, the claim that this is his grave is academic, though it would be foolish to ignore the power of handed-down legend.

GLASTONBURY, THE TOR 1890 23918

According to legend, Glastonbury Tor is Avalon, an earthly Celtic paradise, rich in fruits and crops. Glastonbury certainly invokes strong feelings of sanctity, and it possesses a powerful aura of mystery. It is said that Joseph of Arimathaea brought to Glastonbury the Holy Grail, the vessel used by Christ at the Last Supper. Geoffrey of Monmouth wrote in the 12th century that King Arthur was taken here after his last battle. The monks of the abbey reputedly found his grave in Glastonbury. The building on top of the tor is St Michael's Church.

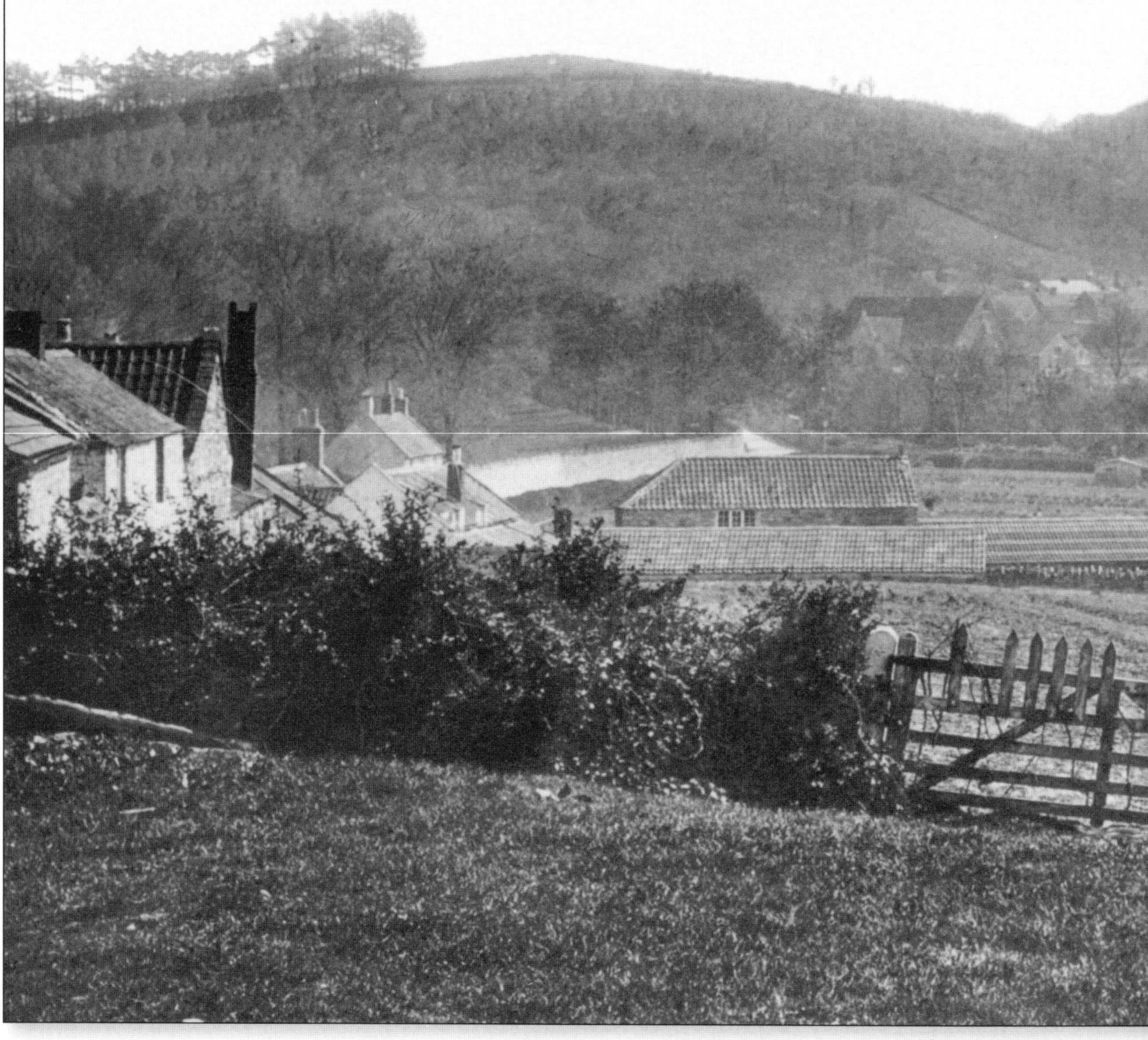

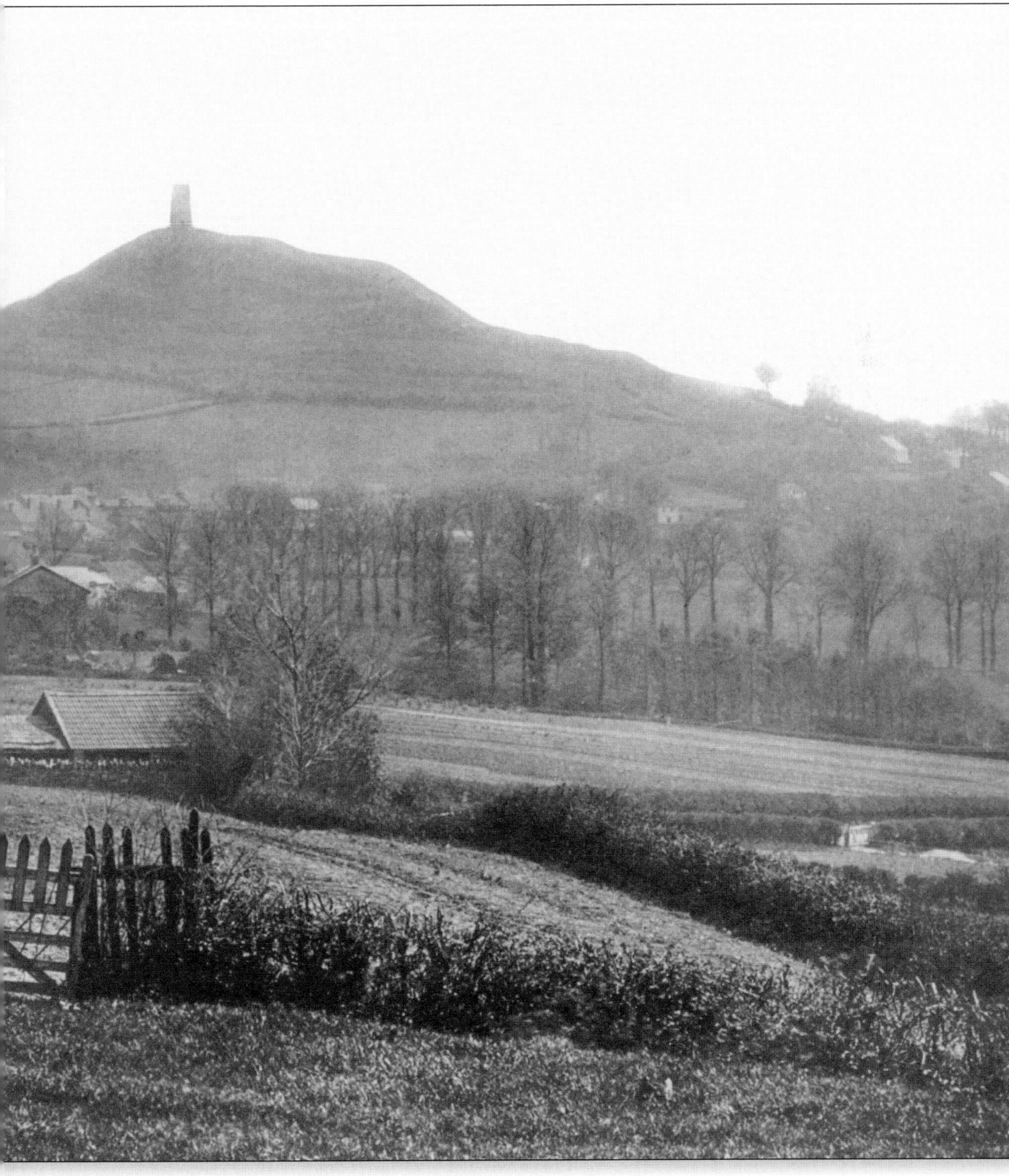

Hill Figures

The white horses of the chalk downland in Southern England are among the best-known features of the countryside. Other large-scale hillside figures cut into the turf (including giants, birds, crosses, badges and others) can be found all over Britain and abroad. This form of turf cutting is a very old and widespread art - albeit a rather obscure one - but it does seem to be a peculiarly English undertaking.

The Wessex region, with its abundance of chalk downlands, possesses most of the examples that have survived. Almost all of the horses were cut in the late 18th century, and a few in the 19th century. The reasons for such laborious work vary greatly, from the whim of the landowner to historical or religious significance, but the origins and purpose of the few examples from prehistoric times are still not known.

By far the most important and best-known of these lies on the Berkshire Downs at Uffington, close to several ancient earthworks and burial mounds, overlooking an area which has been known as the Vale of the White Horse for more than a thousand years. To many people it is the most beautiful of all the hill figures in this country: it is certainly very old and mysterious. It is larger than all the subsequent horses at 365 feet in length; it is also quite different in appearance, facing right and apparently galloping. Its body is thin - almost stylised - displaying a bird-like head. The same sort of design is associated with the ancient Iron Age tribe, the Atrebates people, who lived and occupied the hill-forts in the local area. Finds of their coinage have revealed a similar horse, which could have been their tribal emblem. Some archaeologist suggest that the symbol of the horse may even pre-date the Iron Age people.

The county of Wiltshire abounds in figures carved into the chalk downlands, of which the horse is the most prominent. The Westbury Horse, a few miles to the south-west, is a much later and more natural-looking horse, facing left and apparently standing still. When it was cut into the hillside in 1788 it was the second horse on that site. That it replaced an earlier one gives testimony to the long tradition of white horses in this area. The earlier horse probably resembled the one at Uffington; among the many different accounts of its origins is an enduring legend that it was cut out by King Alfred to commemorate his victory over the Danes in 878 at nearby Edington. Unfortunately, the old horse was considered too primitive and ugly; hence it was obliterated by a more contemporary design.

UFFINGTON, THE WHITE HORSE C1960 U24025

The most famous of all white horses, the Uffington horse lies on the Berkshire Downs near Wantage. Its primitive and stylised design link it, through coinage, with the ancient Iron Age tribe the Atrebates, who ruled the area before the Roman invasion. Scouring the white horse is described by Thomas Hughes (author of 'Tom Brown's Schooldays') in his book 'The Scouring of the White Horse' in 1853.

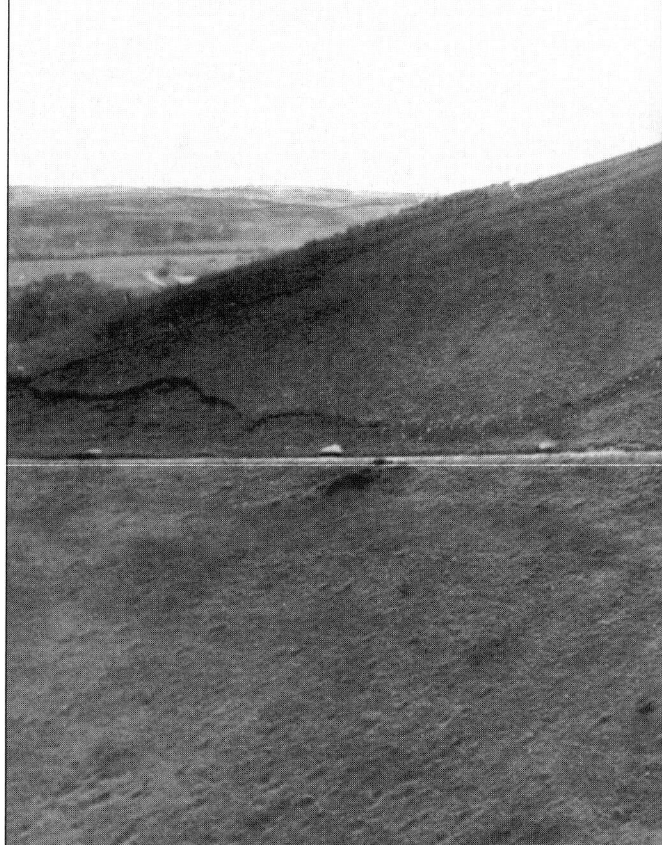

The cutting of the Westbury White Horse is significant, since it seems to have started a trend. Several others followed shortly afterwards, particularly on the downlands of Wiltshire. Probably the best of them is at Cherhill, near Calne, cut only two years later in 1780; it closely resembles the Westbury horse.

Apart from the horses, the most spectacular hill figures are the giants, such as those at Cerne Abbas in Dorset and Wilmington

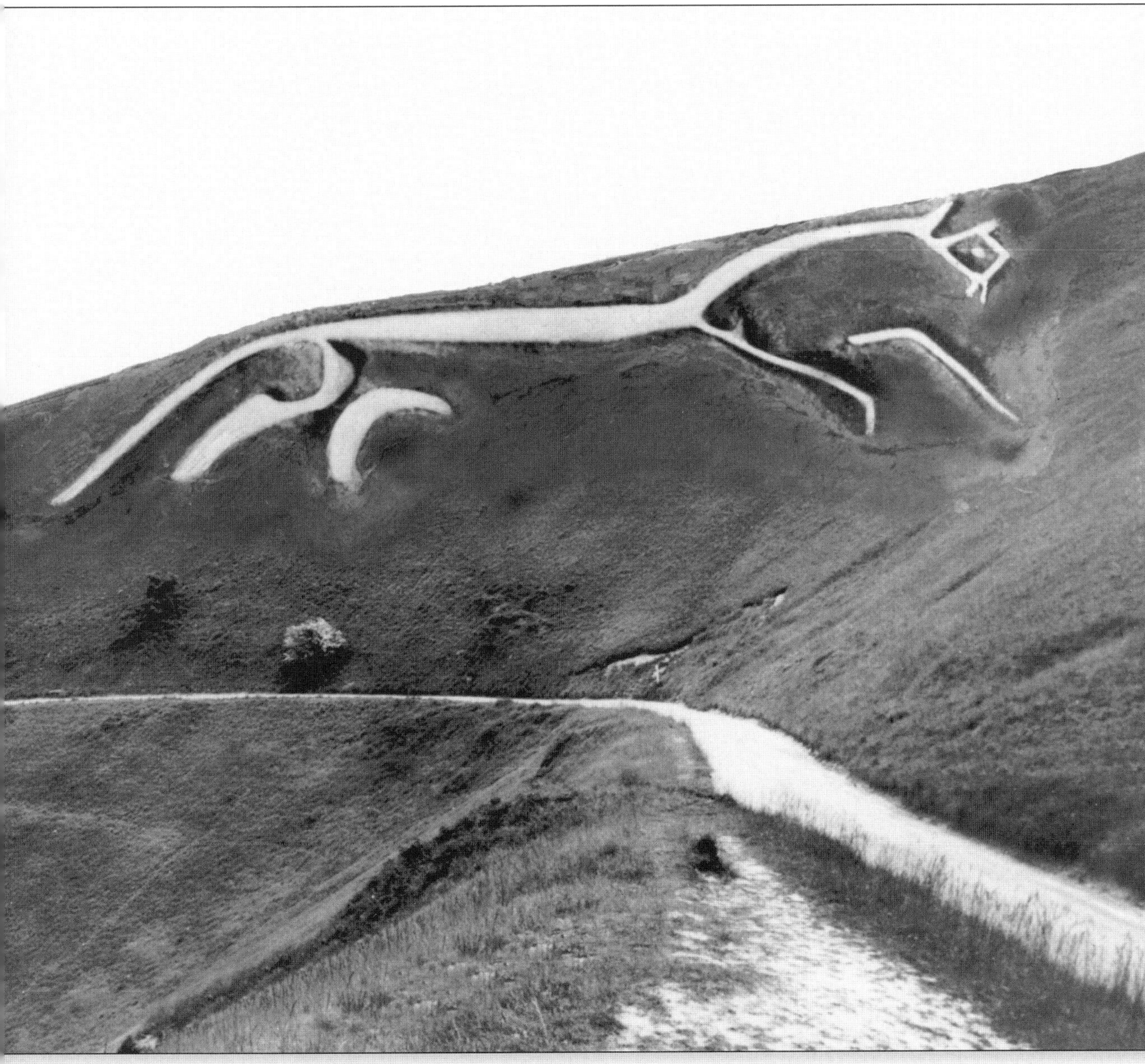

in Sussex. The latter is an enormous figure of a man (over 200 feet high) holding a staff in each hand, cut into the chalk hillside near Eastbourne. As with the Uffington Horse, the Long Man of Wilmington lies close to ancient earthworks as well as to the site of a medieval priory: it may have been cut by the monks as a landmark for pilgrims. It is surprising that it was not discovered until 1873; its style clearly indicates a much older date.

The fact that the Long Man of Wilmington was not found until 1873 is a reminder of the importance of 'scouring' - the process of repairing and cleaning the figure; otherwise it would gradually become overgrown and dilapidated (especially on the relatively soft chalk). It is still possible, given climatic changes, more sophisticated technology and a change in farming methods, that there are still other ancient monuments waiting to be discovered.

HILL FIGURES

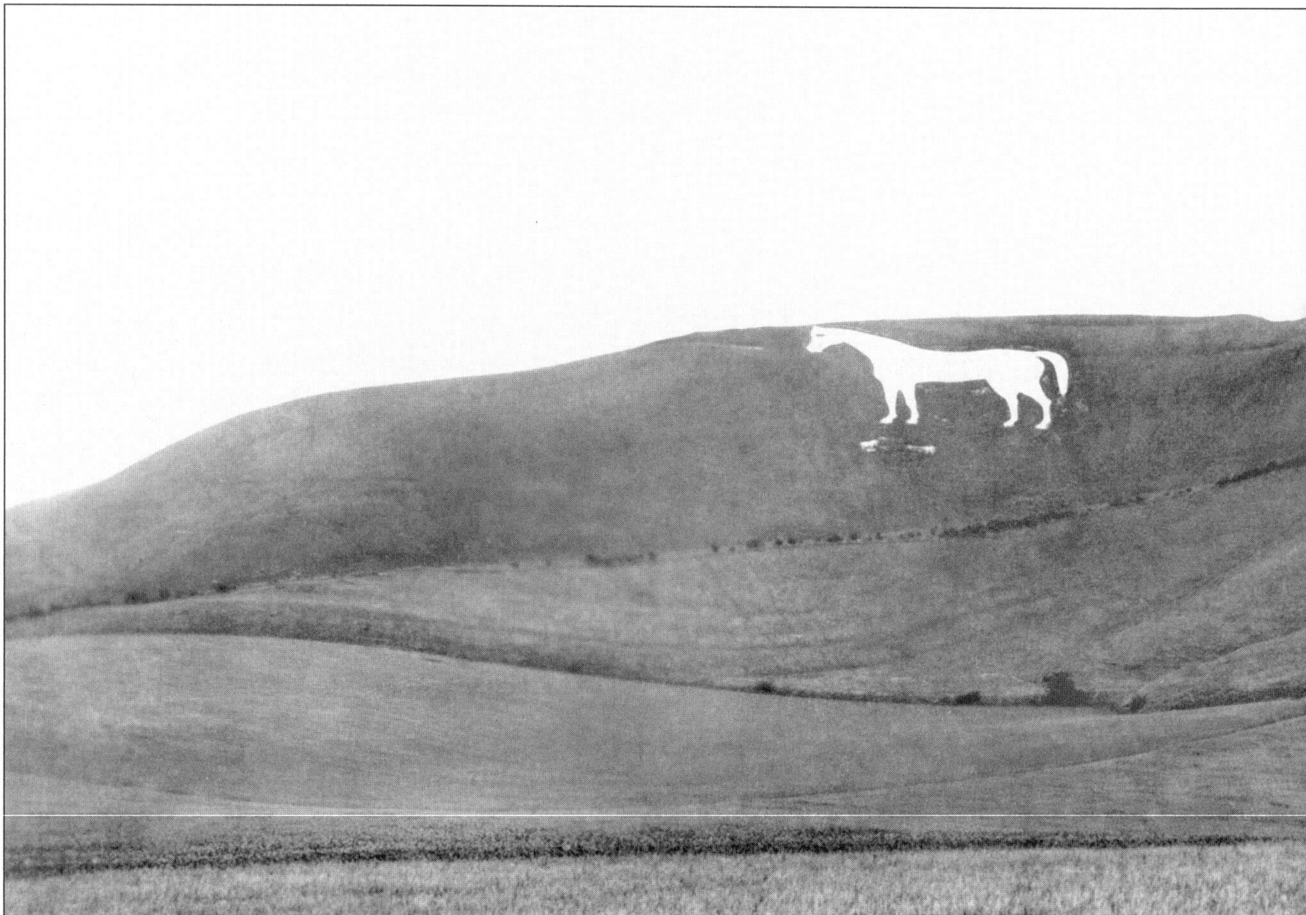

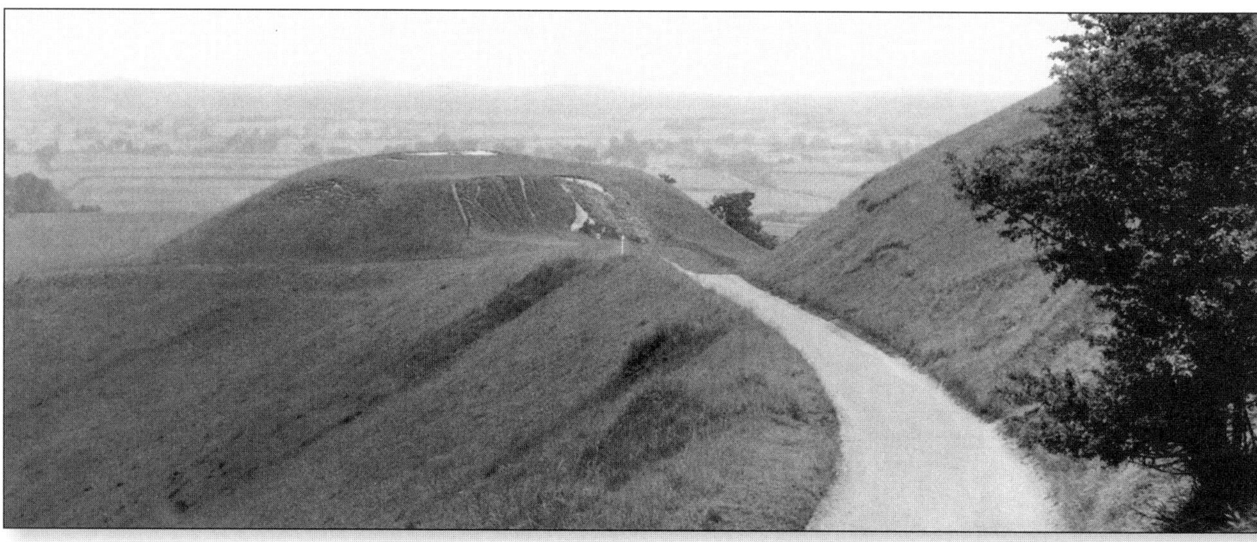

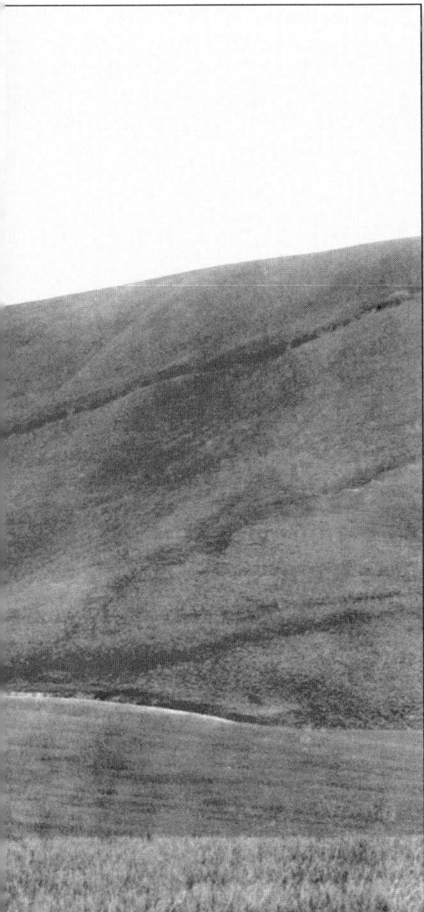

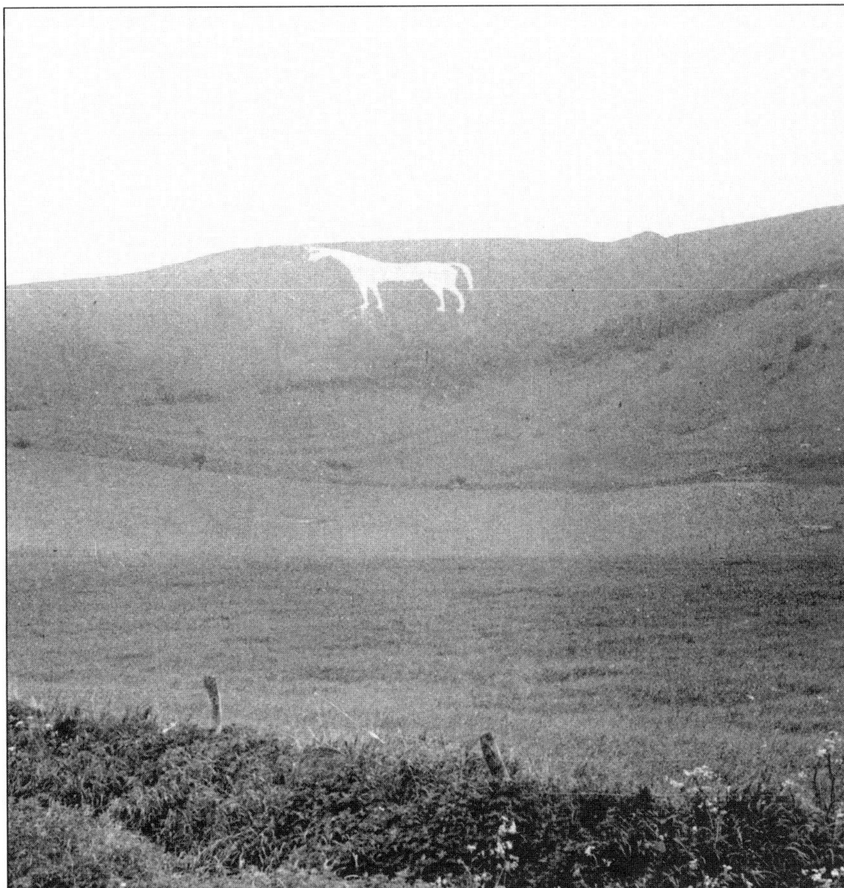

ABOVE LEFT: WESTBURY, THE WHITE HORSE 1900 45365

The present horse on this site dates from 1778 and was the first of several figures cut in the chalk downs of Wiltshire during the next half-century. Immediately above it is the outline of the ancient Bratton Camp, an Iron Age fortification.

ABOVE RIGHT: WESTBURY, THE WHITE HORSE C1955 W263001

The same view is virtually unchanged half a century after photograph No 45365 in the 1950s. However, the present horse replaced an even earlier one reputedly cut by King Arthur!

BOTTOM LEFT: UFFINGTON, DRAGON'S HILL C1960 U24004

Looking down from the White Horse can be seen the flat-topped Dragon's Hill where, legend has it, St George slew the Dragon; the white markings on the side are where the blood of the Dragon ran down in rivulets. The area beyond is the Vale of the White Horse.

HILL FIGURES

CHERHILL, THE WHITE HORSE c1955 C228076

This horse, dating from 1780, is very similar in size, shape and aspect to that at Westbury only a few miles away. The man responsible for cutting it (a local eccentric vicar) was a great admirer of the equestrian paintings of the 18th-century painter George Stubbs.

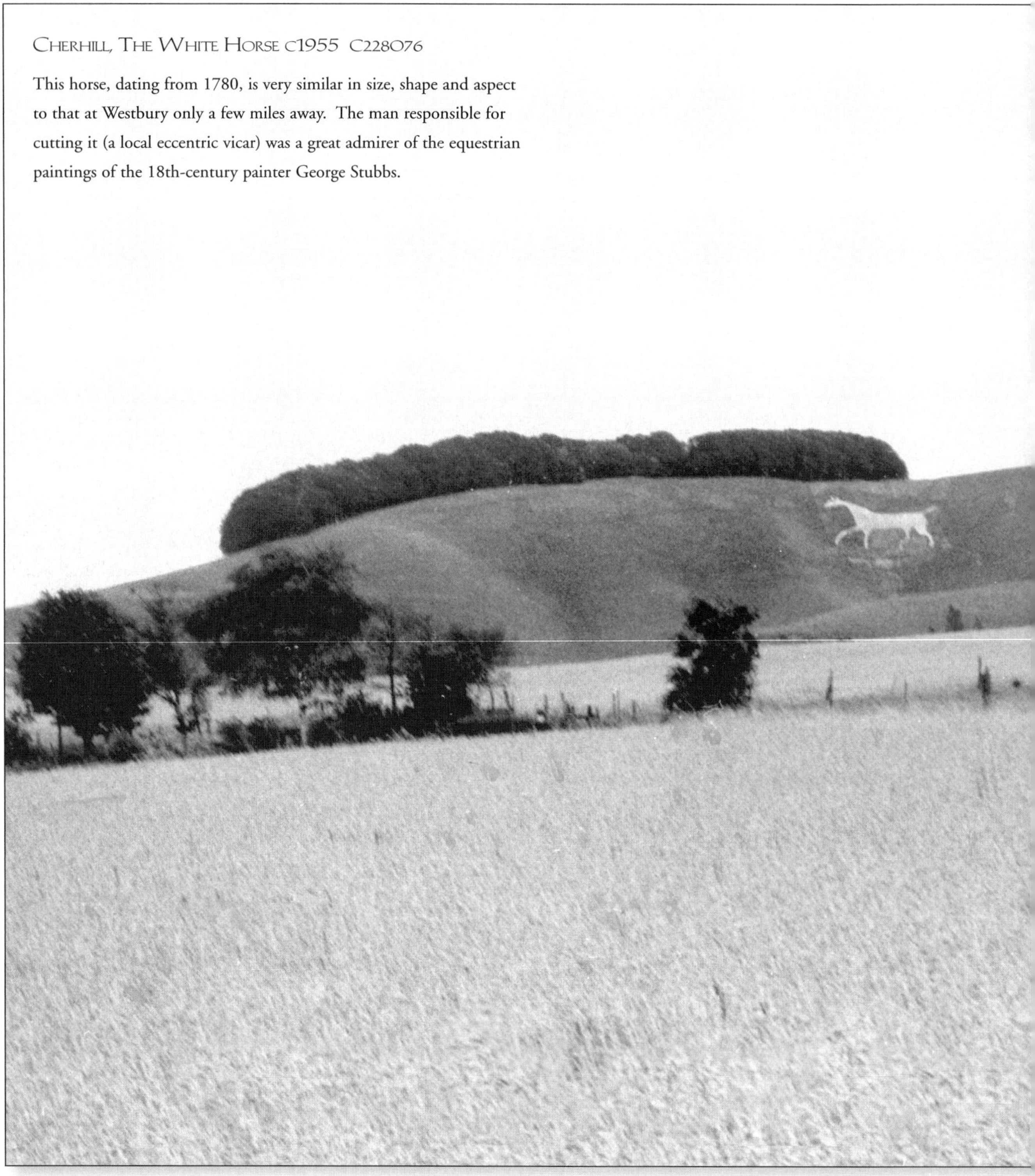

& STONE CIRCLES HILL FIGURES

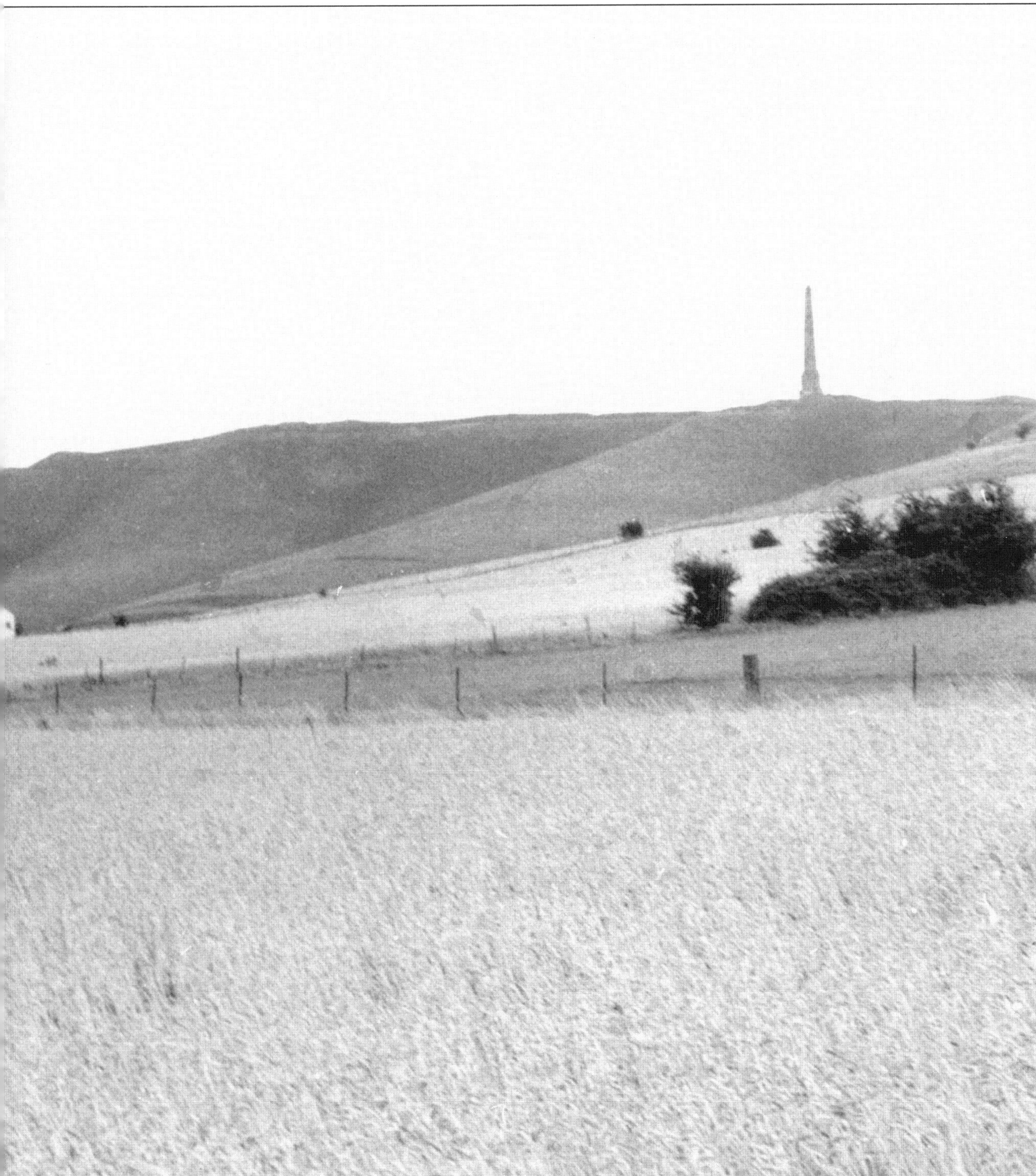

HILL FIGURES

CHERHILL, THE WHITE HORSE AND THE MONUMENT
c1955 C228050

On the top of the hill are the remains of Oldbury Castle (an Iron Age fort) and the striking Lansdowne Monument erected in 1845 to the memory of an ancestor of a local landowner.

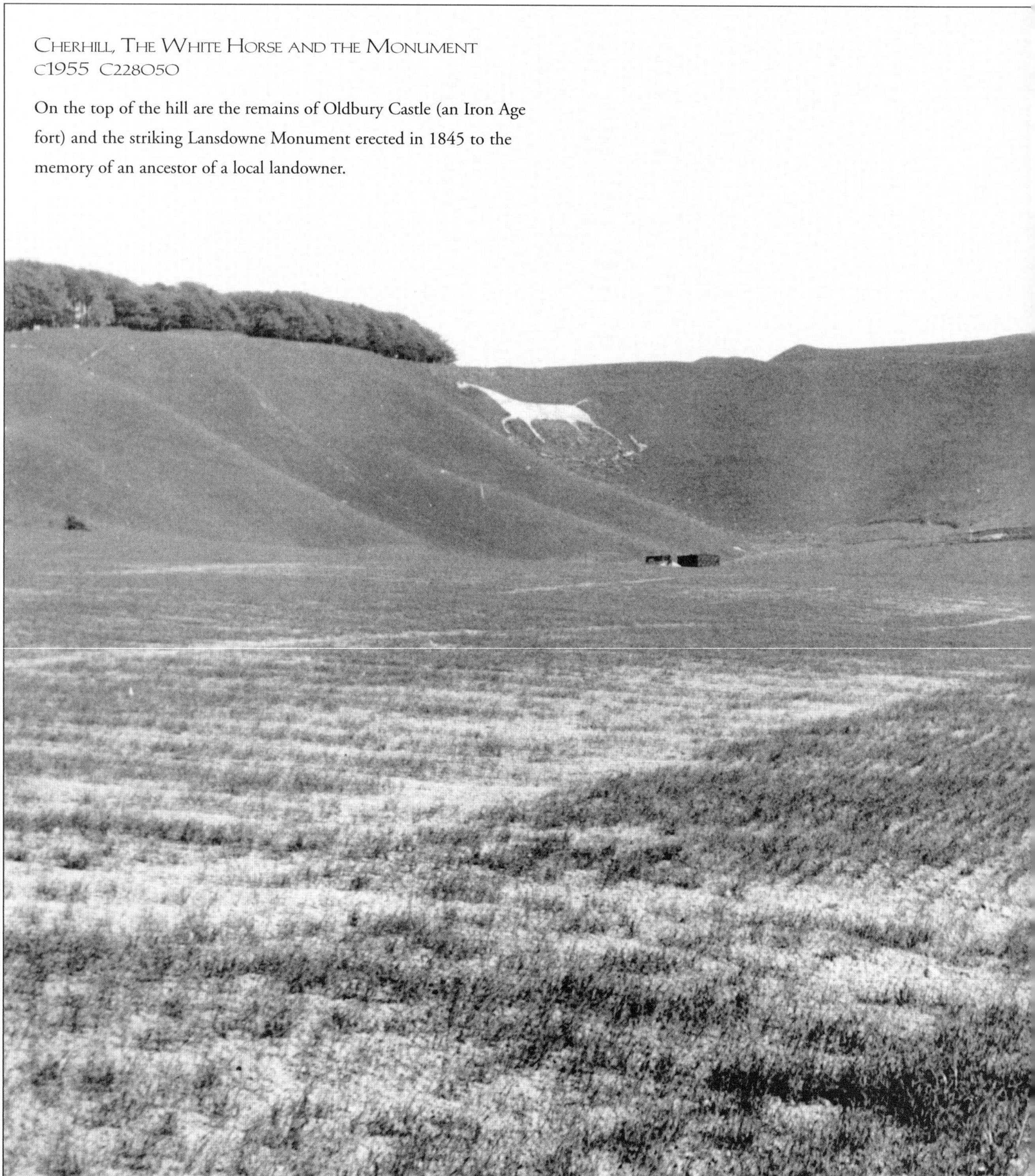

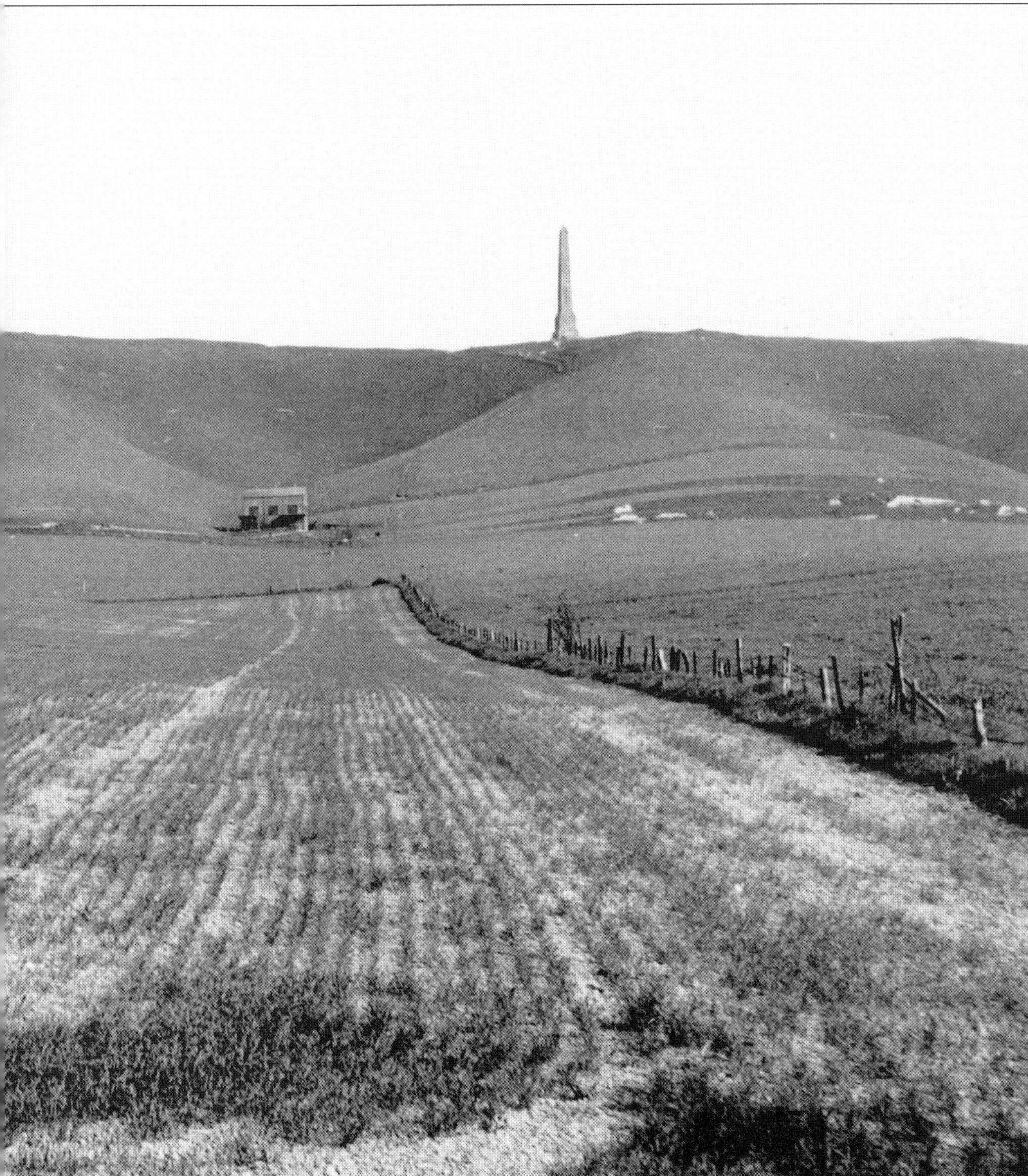

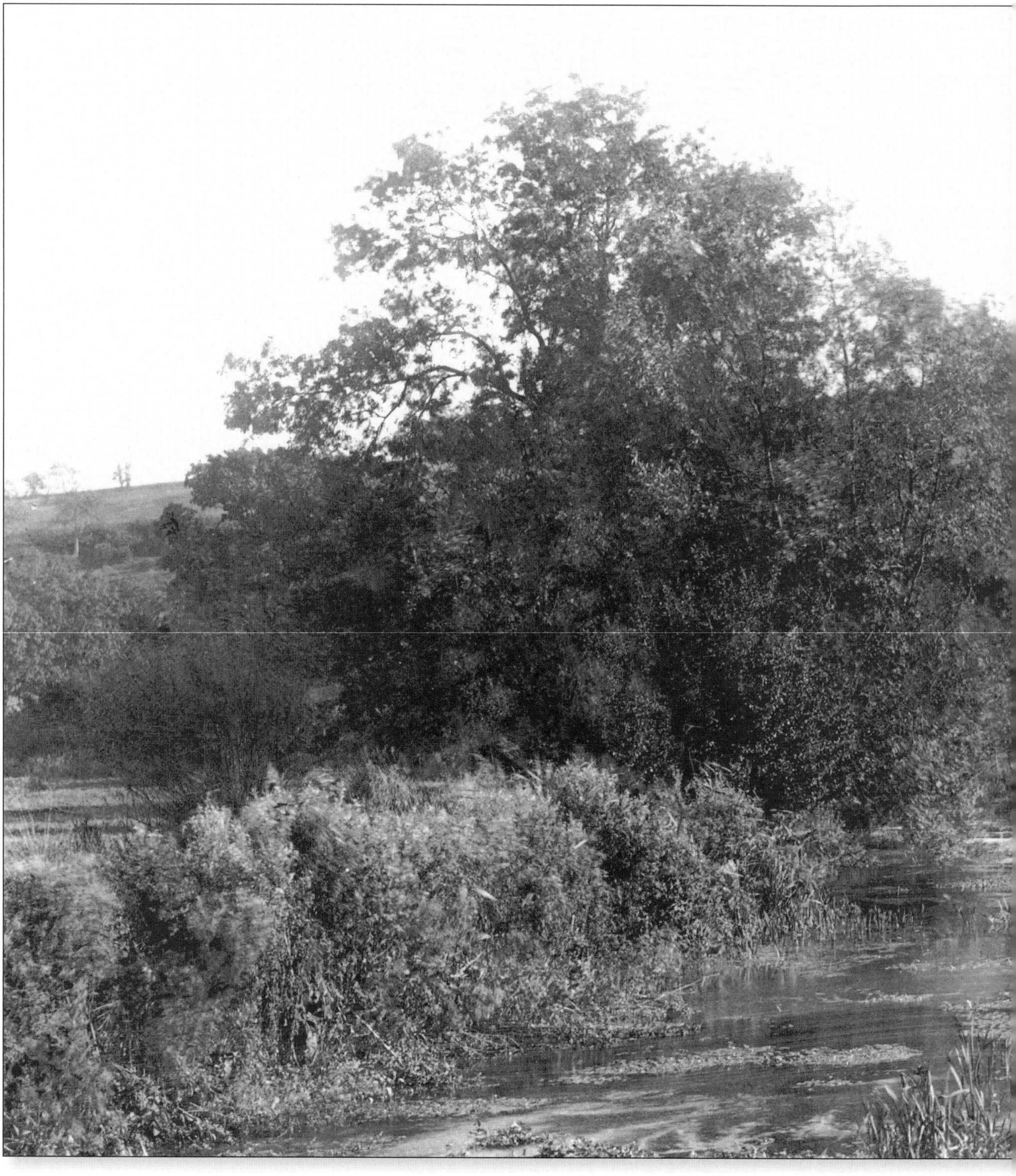

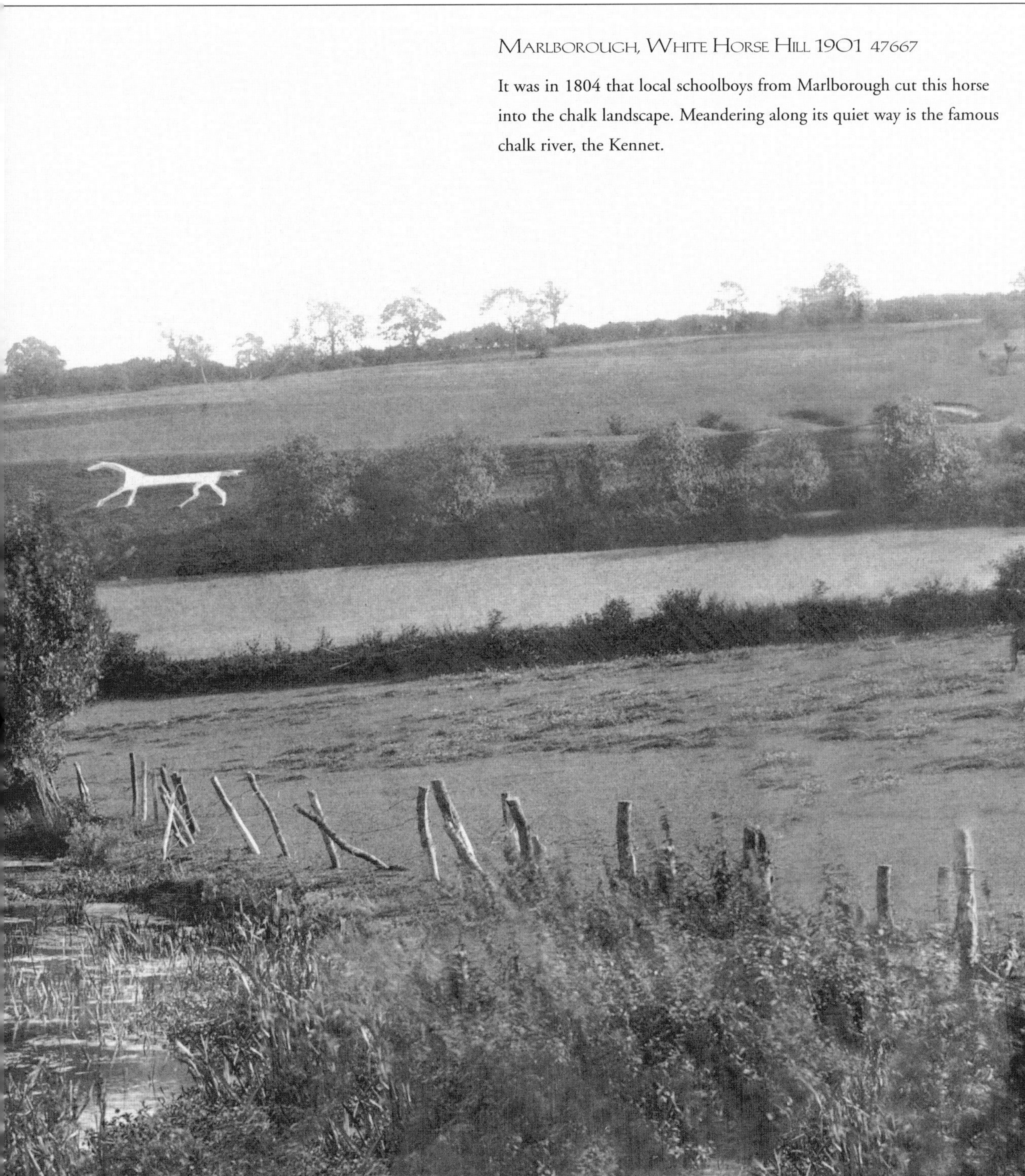

MARLBOROUGH, WHITE HORSE HILL 1901 47667

It was in 1804 that local schoolboys from Marlborough cut this horse into the chalk landscape. Meandering along its quiet way is the famous chalk river, the Kennet.

Hill Figures

RIGHT: WILMINGTON, THE LONG MAN c1960 W406004

The design of this huge, ancient giant, on the South Downs near Eastbourne, is cleverly elongated vertically to counteract the effect of foreshortening when viewed from below the hillside. It is one of the largest representations of the human figure in the world. 'Discovered' in 1873 and restored the following year, its origin is still unknown. It may represent a pilgrim, and this may link it to the medieval Wilmington Priory nearby.

BELOW LEFT: PEWSEY, THE WHITE HORSE c1960 P51079

Like Westbury, this is the second horse on this site just outside Pewsey. Volunteers from the local fire brigade cut it in 1937 to commemorate the coronation of King George VI. A small earlier horse dated from around 1785.

BELOW RIGHT: BROAD HINTON, THE WHITE HORSE c1955 B377003

The Broad Hinton (or Hackpen) white horse is on Hackpen Down between Avebury and Swindon on the Marlborough Downs. It is amateurish in design, and the least impressive of all the Wiltshire horses. It was cut in 1838 to commemorate Queen Victoria's coronation. When the photograph was taken it was clearly in need of scouring.

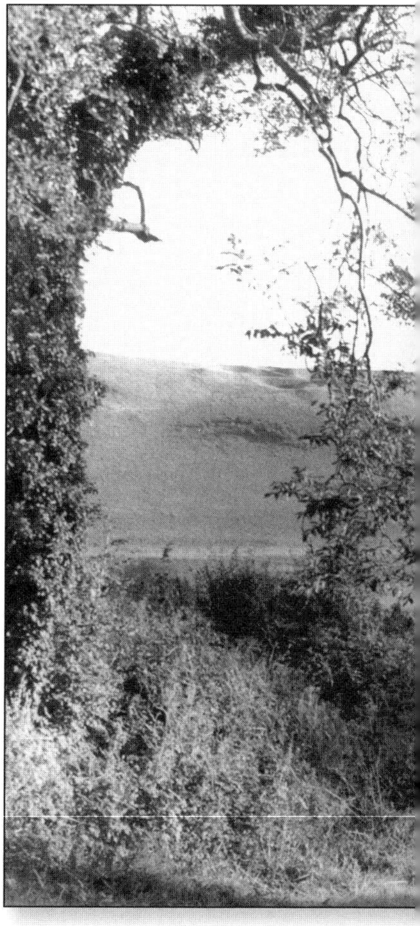

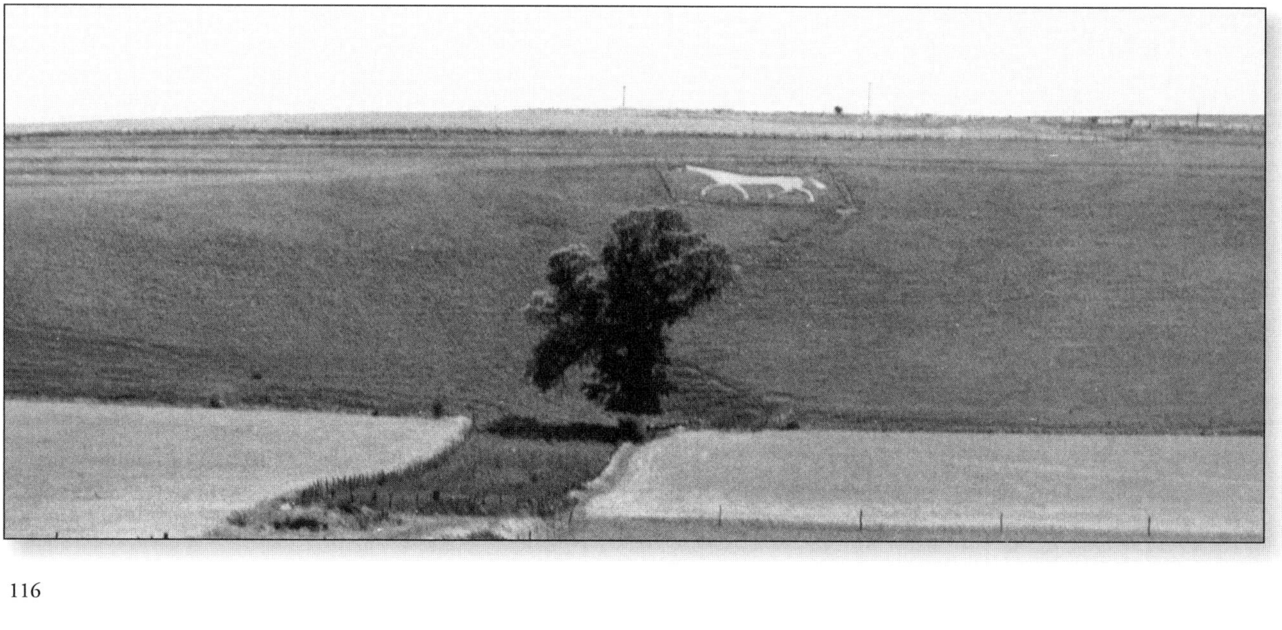

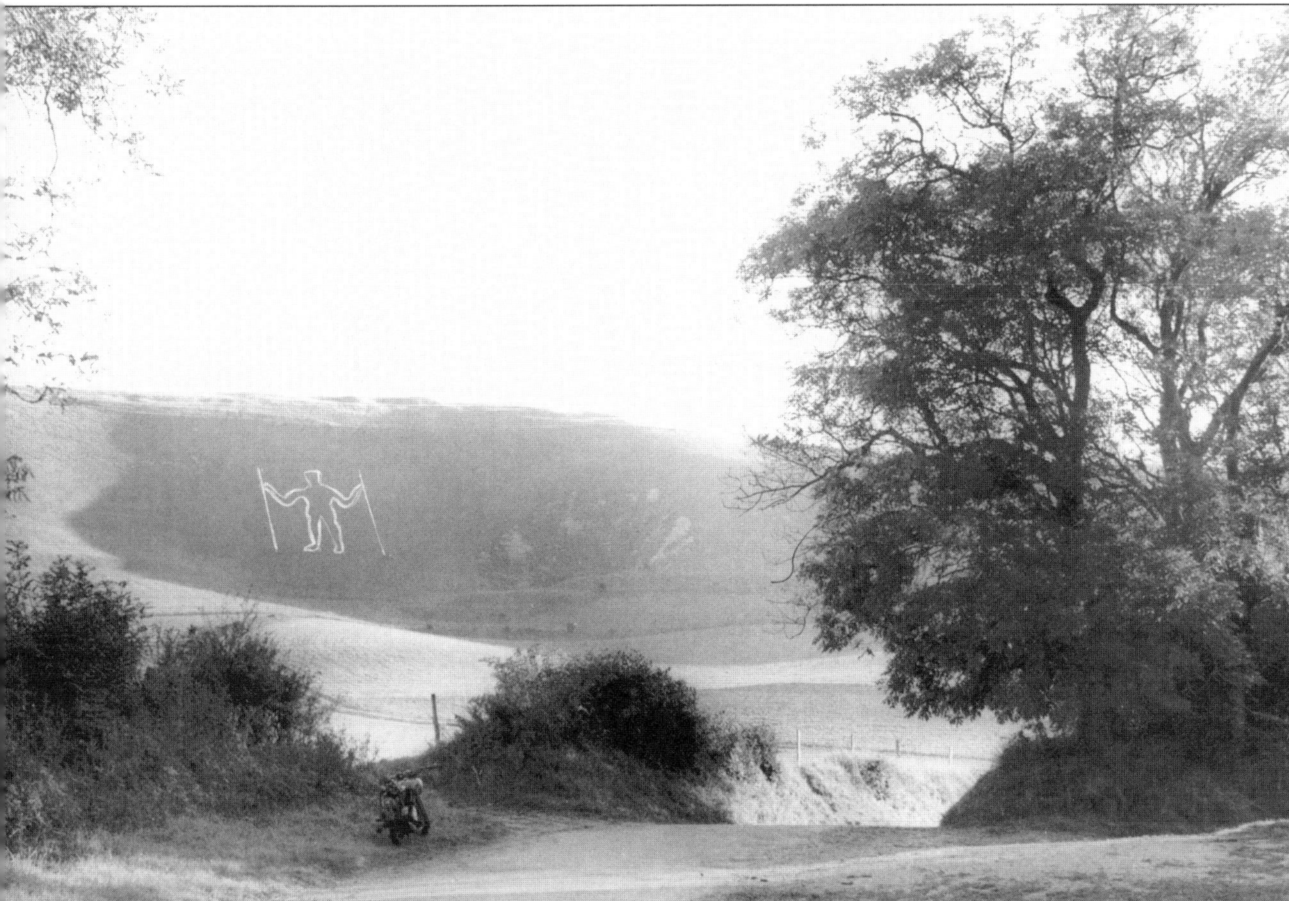

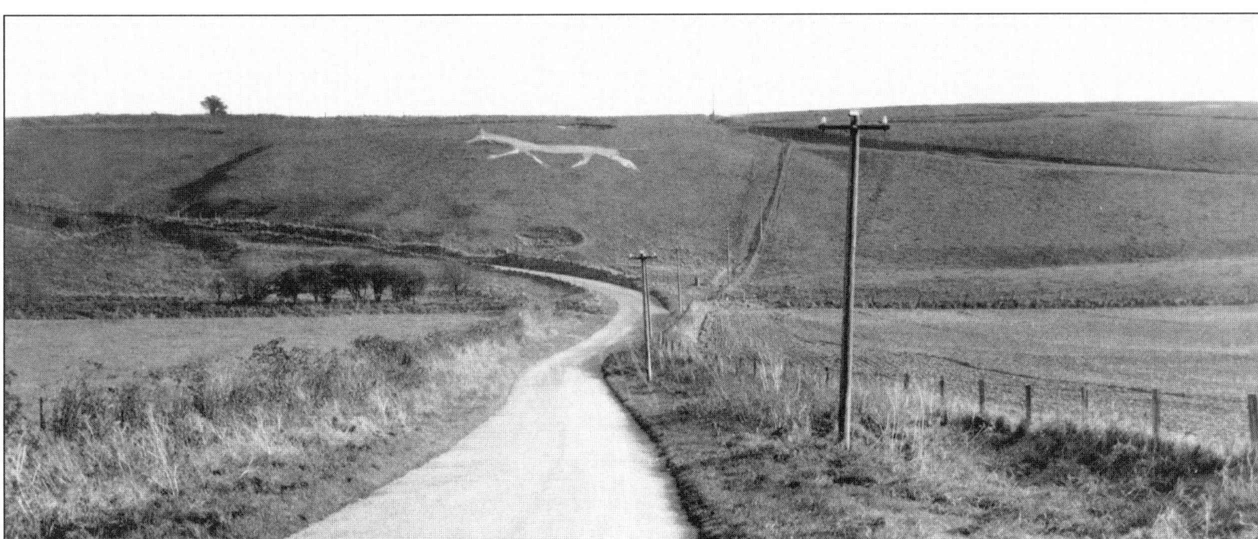

INDEX

The Francis Frith Collection Titles

www.francisfrith.co.uk

The Francis Frith Collection publishes over 100 new titles each year. A selection of those currently available is listed below. For latest catalogue please contact The Francis Frith Collection. ***Town Books*** 96 pages, approximately 75 photos. ***County and Themed Books*** 128 pages, approximately 135 photos (unless specified). All titles hardback with laminated case and jacket, except those indicated pb (paperback)

Accrington Old and New
Alderley Edge and Wilmslow
Amersham, Chesham and Rickmansworth
Andover
Around Abergavenny
Around Alton
Aylesbury
Barnstaple
Bedford
Bedfordshire
Berkshire Living Memories
Berkshire PA
Blackpool Pocket Album
Bognor Regis
Bournemouth
Bradford
Bridgend
Bridport
Brighton and Hove
Bristol
Buckinghamshire
Calne Living Memories
Camberley PA
Canterbury Cathedral
Cardiff Old and New
Chatham and the Medway Towns
Chelmsford
Chepstow Then and Now
Cheshire
Cheshire Living Memories
Chester
Chesterfield
Chigwell
Christchurch
Churches of East Cornwall
Clevedon
Clitheroe
Corby Living Memories
Cornish Coast
Cornwall Living Memories
Cotswold Living Memories
Cotswold Pocket Album
Coulsdon, Chipstead and Woodmanstern
County Durham
Cromer, Sheringham and Holt
Dartmoor Pocket Album
Derby
Derbyshire
Derbyshire Living Memories
Devon
Devon Churches
Dorchester
Dorset Coast PA
Dorset Living Memories
Dorset Villages
Down the Dart
Down the Severn
Down the Thames
Dunmow, Thaxted and Finchingfield
Durham
East Anglia PA
East Devon
East Grinstead
Edinburgh
Ely and The Fens
Essex PA
Essex Second Selection
Essex: The London Boroughs
Exeter
Exmoor
Falmouth
Farnborough, Fleet and Aldershot
Folkestone
Frome
Furness and Cartmel Peninsulas
Glamorgan
Glasgow
Glastonbury
Gloucester
Gloucestershire
Greater Manchester
Guildford
Hailsham
Hampshire
Harrogate
Hastings and Bexhill
Haywards Heath Living Memories
Heads of the Valleys
Heart of Lancashire PA
Helston
Herefordshire
Horsham
Humberside PA
Huntingdon, St Neots and St Ives
Hythe, Romney Marsh and Ashford
Ilfracombe
Ipswich PA
Isle of Wight
Isle of Wight Living Memories
King's Lynn
Kingston upon Thames
Lake District PA
Lancashire Living Memories
Lancashire Villages

Available from your local bookshop or from the publisher

The Francis Frith Collection Titles (continued)

Lancaster, Morecombe and Heysham Pocket Album
Leeds PA
Leicester
Leicestershire
Lincolnshire Living Memoires
Lincolnshire Pocket Album
Liverpool and Merseyside
London PA
Ludlow
Maidenhead
Maidstone
Malmesbury
Manchester PA
Marlborough
Matlock
Merseyside Living Memories
Nantwich and Crewe
New Forest
Newbury Living Memories
Newquay to St Ives
North Devon Living Memories
North London
North Wales
North Yorkshire
Northamptonshire
Northumberland
Northwich
Nottingham
Nottinghamshire PA
Oakham
Odiham Then and Now
Oxford Pocket Album
Oxfordshire
Padstow
Pembrokeshire
Penzance
Petersfield Then and Now
Plymouth
Poole and Sandbanks
Preston PA
Ramsgate Old and New
Reading Pocket Album
Redditch Living Memories
Redhill to Reigate
Rhondda Valley Living Mems
Richmond
Ringwood
Rochdale
Romford PA
Salisbury PA
Scotland
Scottish Castles
Sevenoaks and Tonbridge
Sheffield and South Yorkshire PA
Shropshire
Somerset
South Devon Coast
South Devon Living Memories
South East London
Southampton PA
Southend PA
Southport
Southwold to Aldeburgh
Stourbridge Living Memories
Stratford upon Avon
Stroud
Suffolk
Suffolk PA
Surrey Living Memories
Sussex
Sutton
Swanage and Purbeck
Swansea Pocket Album
Swindon Living Memories
Taunton
Teignmouth
Tenby and Saundersfoot
Tiverton
Torbay
Truro
Uppingham
Villages of Kent
Villages of Surrey
Villages of Sussex PA
Wakefield and the Five Towns Living Memories
Warrington
Warwick
Warwickshire PA
Wellingborough Living Memories
Wells
Welsh Castles
West Midlands PA
West Wiltshire Towns
West Yorkshire
Weston-super-Mare
Weymouth
Widnes and Runcorn
Wiltshire Churches
Wiltshire Living memories
Wiltshire PA
Wimborne
Winchester PA
Windermere
Windsor
Wirral
Wokingham and Bracknell
Woodbridge
Worcester
Worcestershire
Worcestershire Living Memories
Wyre Forest
York PA
Yorkshire
Yorkshire Coastal Memories
Yorkshire Dales
Yorkshire Revisited

Frith Products & Services

Francis Frith would doubtless be pleased to know that the pioneering publishing venture he started in 1860 still continues today. Over a hundred and forty years later, The Francis Frith Collection continues in the same innovative tradition and is now one of the foremost publishers of vintage photographs in the world. Some of the current activities include:

Interior Decoration

Today Frith's photographs can be seen framed and as giant wall murals in thousands of pubs, restaurants, hotels, banks, retail stores and other public buildings throughout the country. In every case they enhance the unique local atmosphere of the places they depict and provide reminders of gentler days in an increasingly busy and frenetic world.

Product Promotions

Frith products are used by many major companies to promote the sales of their own products or to reinforce their own history and heritage. Frith promotions have been used by Hovis bread, Courage beers, Scots Porage Oats, Colman's mustard, Cadbury's foods, Mellow Birds coffee, Dunhill pipe tobacco, Guinness, and Bulmer's Cider.

Genealogy and Family History

As the interest in family history and roots grows world-wide, more and more people are turning to Frith's photographs of Great Britain for images of the towns, villages and streets where their ancestors lived; and, of course, photographs of the churches and chapels where their ancestors were christened, married and buried are an essential part of every genealogy tree and family album.

Frith Products

All Frith photographs are available Framed or just as Mounted Prints and Posters (size 23 x 16 inches). These may be ordered from the address below. From time to time other products - Address Books, Calendars, Table Mats, etc - are available.

The Internet

Already ninety thousand Frith photographs can be viewed and purchased on the internet through the Frith websites and a myriad of partner sites.

For more detailed information on Frith companies and products, look at these sites:

www.francisfrith.co.uk
www.francisfrith.com
(for North American visitors)

See the complete list of Frith Books at:

www.francisfrith.co.uk

This web site is regularly updated with the latest list of publications from The Francis Frith Collection. If you wish to buy books relating to another part of the country that your local bookshop does not stock, you may purchase on-line.

For further information, trade, or author enquiries please contact us at the address below:

The Francis Frith Collection, Frith's Barn, Teffont, Salisbury, Wiltshire, England SP3 5QP.
Tel: +44 (0)1722 716 376 Fax: +44 (0)1722 716 881 Email: sales@francisfrith.co.uk

See Frith books on the internet at www.francisfrith.co.uk

FREE PRINT OF YOUR CHOICE

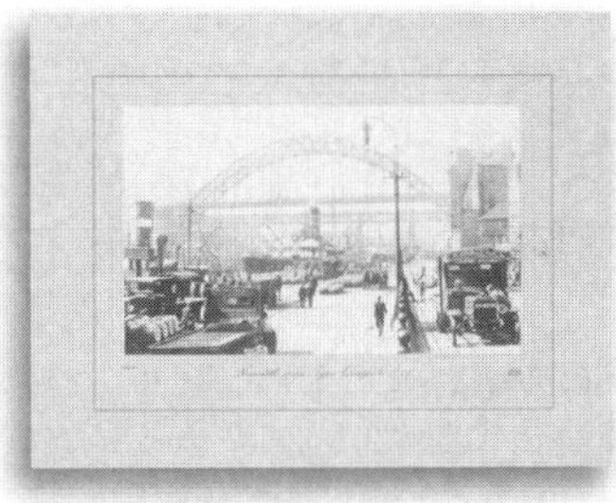

Mounted Print
Overall size 14 x 11 inches (355 x 280mm)

Choose any Frith photograph in this book.
Simply complete the Voucher opposite and return it with your remittance for £2.25 (to cover postage and handling) and we will print the photograph of your choice in SEPIA (size 11 x 8 inches) and supply it in a cream mount with a burgundy rule line (overall size 14 x 11 inches).
Please note: photographs with a reference number starting with a "Z" are not Frith photographs and cannot be supplied under this offer.
Offer valid for delivery to one UK address only.

***PLUS:* Order additional Mounted Prints at HALF PRICE - £7.49 each** (normally £14.99)
If you would like to order more Frith prints from this book, possibly as gifts for friends and family, you can buy them at half price (with no additional postage and handling costs).

***PLUS:* Have your Mounted Prints framed**
For an extra £14.95 per print you can have your mounted print(s) framed in an elegant polished wood and gilt moulding, overall size 16 x 13 inches (no additional postage and handling required).

IMPORTANT!

These special prices are only available if you use this form to order . You must use the ORIGINAL VOUCHER on this page (no copies permitted). We can only despatch to one UK address. This offer cannot be combined with any other offer.

Send completed Voucher form to:
The Francis Frith Collection, Frith's Barn, Teffont, Salisbury, Wiltshire SP3 5QP

CHOOSE A PHOTOGRAPH FROM THIS BOOK

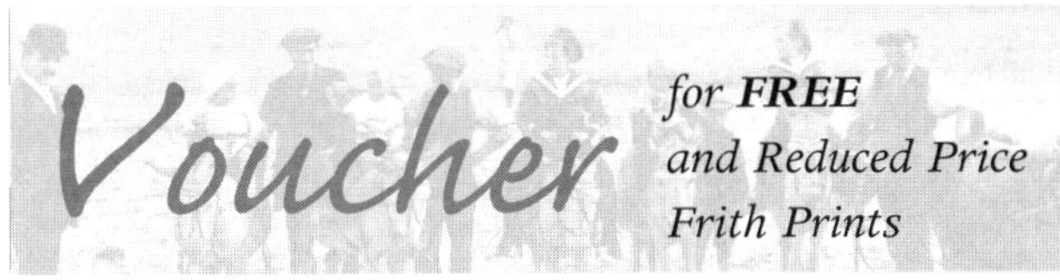

Please do not photocopy this voucher. Only the original is valid, so please fill it in, cut it out and return it to us with your order.

Picture ref no	Page no	Qty	Mounted @ £7.49	Framed + £14.95	Total Cost £
		1	Free of charge*	£	£
			£7.49	£	£
			£7.49	£	£
			£7.49	£	£
			£7.49	£	£
			£7.49	£	£
			* Post & handling		£2.25
			Total Order Cost		£

Please allow 28 days for delivery.
Offer available to one UK address only

Title of this book . . . .
I enclose a cheque/postal order for £ . . . .
made payable to 'The Francis Frith Collection'

OR please debit my Mastercard / Visa / Maestro / Amex card, details below

Card Number

Issue No (Maestro only)		Valid from (Maestro)

Expires		Signature

Name Mr/Mrs/Ms ....
Address ....
....
....
.... Postcode ....
Daytime Tel No ....
Email ....

ISBN 1-85937-864-1		Valid to 31/12/08

Free Print - see overleaf

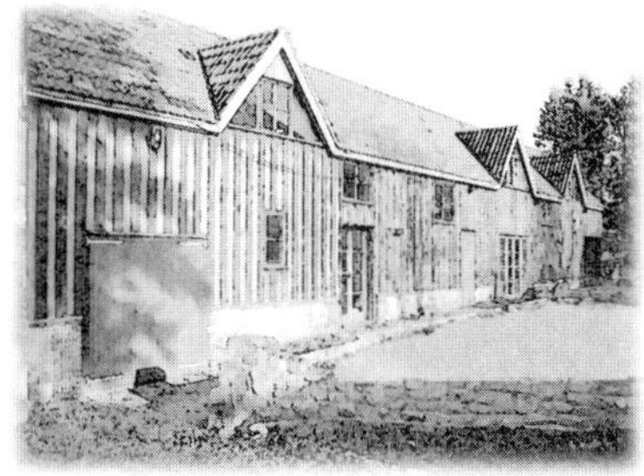

Can you help us with information about any of the Frith photographs in this book?

We are gradually compiling an historical record for each of the photographs in the Frith archive. It is always fascinating to find out the names of the people shown in the pictures, as well as insights into the shops, buildings and other features depicted.

If you recognize anyone in the photographs in this book, or if you have information not already included in the author's caption, do let us know. We would love to hear from you, and will try to publish it in future books or articles.

Our production team

Frith books are produced by a small dedicated team at offices in the converted Grade II listed 18th-century barn at Teffont near Salisbury, illustrated above. Most have worked with the Frith Collection for many years. All have in common one quality: they have a passion for the Frith Collection. The team is constantly expanding, but currently includes:

Paul Baron, Jason Buck, John Buck, Heather Crisp, David Davies, Louis du Mont, Isobel Hall, Lucy Hart, Julian Hight, Peter Horne, James Kinnear, Karen Kinnear, Tina Leary, Stuart Login, Sue Molloy, Sarah Roberts, Kate Rotondetto, Dean Scource, Eliza Sackett, Terence Sackett, Sandra Sampson, Adrian Sanders, Sandra Sanger, Julia Skinner, Miles Smith, Lewis Taylor, Shelley Tolcher, Lorraine Tuck, Miranda Tunnicliffe, David Turner and Ricky Williams.